**STUDIES IN ENGLISH LITERATURES**

Edited by Koray Melikoğlu

Paul Fox and Koray Melikoğlu (eds.)

# Formal Investigations

## Aesthetic Style in Late-Victorian and Edwardian Detective Fiction

## STUDIES IN ENGLISH LITERATURES

Edited by Koray Melikoğlu

ISSN 1614-4651

1 *Özden Sözalan*
The Staged Encounter
Contemporary Feminism and Women's Drama
2nd, revised edition
ISBN 3-89821-367-6

2 *Paul Fox (ed.)*
Decadences
Morality and Aesthetics in British Literature
2nd, revised and expanded edition
ISBN 3-89821-573-3

3 *Daniel M. Shea*
James Joyce and the Mythology of Modernism
ISBN 3-89821-574-1

4 *Paul Fox and Koray Melikoğlu (eds.)*
Formal Investigations
Aesthetic Style in Late-Victorian and Edwardian Detective Fiction
2nd, revised and expanded edition
ISBN 978-3-89821-593-0

5 *David Ellis*
Writing Home
Black Writing in Britain Since the War
ISBN 978-3-89821-591-6

6 *Wei H. Kao*
The Formation of an Irish Literary Canon in the Mid-Twentieth Century
ISBN 978-3-89821-545-9

7 *Bianca Del Villano*
Ghostly Alterities
Spectrality and Contemporary Literatures in English
2nd, revised editon
ISBN 978-3-89821-714-9

8 *Melanie Ann Hanson*
Decapitation and Disgorgement
The Female Body's Text in Early Modern English Drama and Poetry
ISBN 978-3-89821-605-5

9 *Shafquat Towheed (ed.)*
New Readings in the Literature of British India, c.1780-1947
ISBN 978-3-89821-673-9

10 *Paola Baseotto*
"Disdeining life, desiring leaue to die"
Spenser and the Psychology of Despair
ISBN 978-3-89821-567-1

Paul Fox and Koray Melikoğlu (eds.)

# FORMAL INVESTIGATIONS

## Aesthetic Style in Late-Victorian and Edwardian Detective Fiction

*ibidem*-Verlag
Stuttgart

**Bibliografische Information der Deutschen Nationalbibliothek**
Die Deutsche Nationalbibliothek verzeichnet diese Publikation in der Deutschen Nationalbibliografie; detaillierte bibliografische Daten sind im Internet über http://dnb.d-nb.de abrufbar.

**Bibliographic information published by the Deutsche Nationalbibliothek**
Die Deutsche Nationalbibliothek lists this publication in the Deutsche Nationalbibliografie; detailed bibliographic data are available in the Internet at http://dnb.d-nb.de.

Cover illustration:
*Horrible London: Or, The Pandemonium of Posters.*
*Punch, or the London Charivari* 95 (1888): 170-71.

Second, Revised and Expanded Edition

∞

Gedruckt auf alterungsbeständigem, säurefreien Papier
Printed on acid-free paper

ISSN: 1614-4651

ISBN-13: 978-3-89821-593-0



Printed in Germany

## CONTENTS

## No Respecter of Class: The Ubiquitous Appeal of Late-Victorian Crime Fiction

The cover illustration of this volume appears alongside a verse description of the same cartoon in the October $13^{th}$, 1888 edition of *Punch* magazine under the title of *Horrible London: Or, The Pandemonium of Posters*. The illustration portrays a bill-sticker pasting up posters that gaudily proclaim the thrills to be had reading stories of murder. The verse description predicts the delinquent social effect of such tales upon the lowest classes in society. Depicting this demonic figure advertising gory murder, alongside the written suggestion that crime narratives held a dangerous appeal for the urban working-classes, was particularly topical. The Ripper murders in London's East End had been headline news for several weeks. Many of the capital's lower classes were packed into the districts through which the Ripper prowled and avidly followed the newspapers' reports of the murders. *Punch* was simply bringing to the forefront of public debate the question of collusion between literature, crime and class.

The "penny dreadfuls" that the figure advertises in *Punch*'s illustration were cheap, lurid serial fictions aimed at the lower classes. By the last decades of the nineteenth century, the popularity and availability of these pulp serials in London made them a publishing phenomenon. If the verse alongside the cartoon suggests that this fiction "A sympathy morbid and monstrous must win / From the groveling victims of gloom and bad gin" (171), the illustration itself depicts a subject-matter that is no respecter of class: on the right-hand poster is the standard, bestial depiction of the disheveled, working-class man, in his hand a dripping, bloody knife; but on the left-hand poster a gentleman crouches astride a lady in her death throes, a knife protruding from her chest while his face and fist are contorted in, presumably, a murderous rage. The demon's paste-brush hides the initial letters of this second poster's legend, only leaving on display the word "EAT." Consumer appetites for these sensational crime stories were evidently worthy of serious interest to critics of the genre and its social influence. They certainly were to advertisers, authors, and to the publishing industry.

In the demon's hat is a long feather, and the obvious association of this adornment with a writer's quill marks the figure as not just the advertiser but the producer of crime fiction. The verse description of the demon's craft underscores an interpretation of the figure as author by emphasizing just this indulgence in craft. The demon is in "a novel disguise" (170), marking the literary form of his enterprise; his productions have "fiendish designs," "sinister lines," and display "the style of the vilest sensational prints / Or the vulgarest penny romances." Of course, if the demon-artist reproduces only "in the style" of these cheap forms then his own productions must presumably be something somewhat different. The initial suggestion of his being in a "novel" disguise reveals the genre in which middle-class readers of *Punch* would be more likely to find him.

*Punch*'s concern then is not simply with the penny dreadfuls but with sensational crime fiction marketed also to the higher classes. The demon walks London "with wallet at waist" (170) and money could be made from all readers in the city, irrespective of their social station. The lurid appeal of a genre was not confined to the eastern slums of the city, and certainly reports of the Ripper's murders were closely followed by Whitechapel and West End readers equally. The first Sherlock Holmes mystery, *A Study in Scarlet*, had been serialized the year before in 1887 and had found an audience that transcended traditional class distinctions and literary tastes; the *Punch* demon, ubiquitously fashionable, appears wearing a type of deerstalker hat, the style of headwear worn by Conan Doyle's famous detective. The cartoon's associations have a target clearly higher than those readers of only pulp fiction and the magazine's own middle- and upper-class subscribers are cases in point. Murder sold, then as now, and the more ambitious the story in terms of shocking detail and mystery, the more popular it was. The seeming ubiquity of the "pan-demon" of sensation fiction in urban markets becomes the targeted concern of *Punch*'s illustration and verse.

The irony of *Punch*'s depiction is, of course, that it indulges equally in attention-grabbing sensationalism. It is true that the demon's "sanguine paint-splashes" (170) are not reproduced in the black and white illustration, but the "horrible subject" portrayed with "flamboyant flare" certainly is. The magazine becomes another addition to the pandemoniac appeal of the genre. In presenting a critique employing the very sensationalist forms it criticizes, *Punch* both undercuts its own argument against the dangerously low appeal of sensation fiction, and demonstrates its popularity by presenting it appealingly to a higher class of reader. The attraction of this type of literature is linked explicitly by *Punch* to the manner of its presentation: the bold strokes of its depictions; the grotesque structure of its subject matter; the ordering of criminal transgression by aesthetic form. Whether through *Punch*'s own depiction with pen and ink or in the rhythms of its verse description, the penny dreadfuls or the serial adventures of Holmes, art orders sensation, making it amenable to the intellect if still titillating the lower instincts of readers. Aesthetic form as a vehicle for the depiction of transgression is simultaneously the means of structuring that disorder in a way which affords the possibility of comprehending criminal motive, method and manner.

The detective's craft is the personification of aesthetic ordering within crime fiction. The various methods pursued to solve crime are expected to allow the reformation of society after its being disrupted by criminal acts. Like *Punch*'s cartoon and verse, the genre sows disorder in the presentation of crime, but limits the effects of social fragmentation in the very structure of that presentation. But methods do vary: if Holmes could transmute the sensationalism of crime fiction into a rationally explained series of events, his fellow detectives were very often not so successful, or employed entirely different means to solving crimes. Scientific method is as frequently critiqued as followed in the texts of the period. The variety of approaches the detectives pursued can only be designated as similar in the attempts made to assign a meaning to the events under investigation. It is not unusual to discover in the solution to the crimes a sensationalist method that surpasses the depiction of the crimes themselves.

The essays in this volume explore a variety of structuring taxonomies, the relationships between the aesthetic forms, styles and methodologies of detective and crime fiction in the late-Victorian and Edwardian periods. The influences on the artists in the genre are as varied as the interests of the period in scientific method, forensics, archaeology, aesthetics, medicine, and the paranormal. But the formalizing tendencies of investigative process remain, and it is this adherence, in artist and detective alike, to seeing crime and its resolution as a stylistic imposition of structure on disorder that is under examination. If the *Punch* cartoon and verse ultimately suggest that the genre of crime fiction had a broad appeal that could not be restricted to traditional expectations of class reading appetites, so the texts themselves cross literary, taxonomic boundaries. The formal strategies deployed by author and detective proliferate and intersect with the manifold interests of the late-Victorian and Edwardian periods, and their variety is examined in the following pages.

Rudolph Glitz begins the collection by investigating Conan Doyle's depiction of the relationship between narrative and literary realism. George M. Johnson continues this investigation of realism in Algernon Blackwood's stories, seeing the author as one of the first Modernists in his depiction of the imaginative potential of the new psychology. Paul Fox examines Arthur Machen as a proponent of the aesthetic of the 1890s, and Nick Freeman explores the aesthetic influence of Oscar Wilde upon the detective fiction of the same and following decade. Aaron Parrett interprets the stories of Robert Eustace and L. T. Meade as evidence of the aesthetic relationship between new scientific theories of degeneration and literature. Helen Sutherland continues this interest in literary concerns with the nineteenth-century advances in science by exploring Conan Doyle's and G. K. Chesterton's attitudes to geology in their fiction.

Elizabeth Anderman examines the use of Pater and Ruskin by Wilkie Collins as influences on how to read detective fiction. Lucy Sussex explores the connection between Anna Katherine Green's detective fiction and her husband Charles Rohlfs' furniture-making as redolent of an Arts and Crafts aesthetic. Alison Jaquet interprets Ellen Wood's Johnny Ludlow series as evidence of a relationship between domesticity and power structures. Therie Hendrey-Seabrook argues for an appreciation of a gendered fracture between female detective characters and their male counterparts in the fiction of the 1890s. Linda Schlossberg examines the work of E. C. Bentley as a modern detective novel that shows the flaws in a reliance on logic and deduction within the genre.

Paul Fox

## Works Cited

Conan Doyle, Arthur. *A Study in Scarlet. The New Annotated Sherlock Holmes*. Ed. Leslie S. Klinger. Vol. 3. New York: Norton, 2006. 3-208.

*Horrible London: Or, The Pandemonium of Posters. Punch, or the London Charivari* 95 (1888): 170-71.

# Horrifying Ho(l)mes: Conan Doyle's Bachelor Detective and the Aesthetics of Domestic Realism

Rudolph Glitz
University of Amsterdam

**Abstract:** This chapter investigates the various Sherlock Holmes stories that are concerned with domestic crimes or misdemeanours. With reference to these as well as various programmatic statements by Balzac and Zola, it highlights the striking but as yet barely explored connection between Holmes' professional outlook as a provider of narrative solutions and the aesthetics of French literary realism as opposed to realism in the broader sense of the term. This connection is not only well worth noting in its own right, but can also help illuminate several meta-fictional strategies and intertextual allusions in Conan Doyle's detective fiction.

## I

On the way to a crime scene in "The Adventure of the Copper Beeches" (1892), Sherlock Holmes surprises Watson with a chilling observation:

> You look at these scattered houses, and you are impressed by their beauty. I look at them, and the only thought which comes to me is a feeling of their isolation and of the impunity with which crime may be committed there. [. . .] They always fill me with a certain horror. (363)[1]

[1] Unless otherwise indicated, all page references are to the relevant volumes of Klinger, which I choose here over the in some respects more scholarly Oxford edition of 1993 because of the more detailed background information provided and Klinger's sometimes useful inclusion of so-called Sherlockian or Sherlockological debates (i.e. usually tongue-in-cheek debates by amateur scholars about Holmes

"Who would associate crime with those dear old homesteads," Watson asks in response, but the houses' peaceful appearance is not the only reason why the declaration seems unusual. As we know since Holmes' cold-blooded shooting of the hound of the Baskervilles (589), "horror" is not one of his most frequently expressed emotions, and it might be worth asking what exactly that feeling consists of here. The houses in question are situated in the spacious Hampshire countryside – as opposed to any densely populated city where, as Holmes further explains, there is "no lane so vile that the scream of a tortured child, or the thud of a drunkard's blow, does not beget sympathy and indignation among the neighbours" (363). This dead-pan explanation is revealing. Even though, at first sight, the contrast seems to be simply between town and country, the detective's suggestive reference to children and drunkards adds to his comments a more far-reaching socio-political thrust. It invokes two stereotypes of Victorian family life gone bad, two of the more notorious by-products of that self-enclosed and patriarchally governed privacy which, while perhaps most strikingly embodied by the isolated country house, had long been generally accepted as the ideal of middle-class domesticity. According to the governmental census report of 1851, the Englishman's own free-standing domicile throws "a sharp, well-defined circle round his family and hearth," and it is simply "in the order of nature that a family should live in a separate house" (xxxv-xxxvi).[2]

---

"the man" as opposed to fictional character). Original publication dates will be given upon first mention in the main text.

2 Regarding the commonplace nature of marital abuse in the Victorian period, cf., for instance, Watson's remarks on the subject in "A Case of Identity" (75) and the various primary documents – including the sketch from *Punch* – that Klinger adduces in the corresponding footnote. That the maltreatment of children was similarly familiar to the Victorian public is amply illustrated by, and in fact largely due to, contempo-

The English are, of course, not the only nineteenth-century society for whom the self-enclosed family unit constitutes the social norm. As I will show throughout this chapter, Holmes' prosaic horror of its latent cruelties can be seen as part of a literary development that spread throughout Europe and was largely centred in France. This is not to say that I am in any way challenging the story-internal psychological reasons for the bachelor detective's aversion to family life. According to both Watson and Holmes, in "A Scandal in Bohemia" (1891) and *The Sign of Four* (1890), it is clearly the latter's professionalism, his fear of being emotionally incapacitated in his profession of a "reasoning and observing machine" that forms the primary motive for his marital abstinence ("Scandal" 5; see also *Sign* 378). Over and above this reason, however, (as well as several others) one can explain Holmes' in Watson's eyes rather peculiar horror at the more abstract level of literary genre. By analysing, for the most part, those stories of the Holmes canon in which the detective encounters, and occasionally shows himself unsettled by, what can broadly be classed as domestic crimes, I will highlight a literary allegiance of his that has so far been neglected by scholars.

The figure of Holmes has been compared to many social, ideological, and literary types. Reading Watson as a Boswellian biographer, for example, Richard D. Altick likens the detective to Dr Johnson. Ian Ousby points out Holmes' resemblance to Darwinian scientists of the type of Huxley (154-55) as well as, in the early novels, contemporary decadents (156-57). Rosemary Hennessy and Rajeswari Mohan see him as embodying "the interests of the middle-class, western, white male" (338). Dennis Porter compares him, together with the literary detective in general, to "a well-

rary novelists such as Dickens and Gaskell. For a detailed overview of recent studies of Victorian domesticity, see Chase and Levinson.

trained critic" (226). Without taking issue with these varied – and variedly plausible – characterisations of Holmes' outlook, I would add to them by arguing that his perspective on traditional domesticity, and thus part of the Holmes *corpus* as a whole, is quite manifestly rooted in the nineteenth-century aesthetics of French literary realism. By doing so, I aim to go beyond the standard and usually pejorative characterisation of the Holmes stories as typical examples of "realism" in a broader and often misleading sense of the term. Working within a more clearly defined and historically circumscribed framework, I hope to bring out the complex generic tensions in the stories, which regularly juxtapose recognisably realist themes and plot lines with elements from competing traditions such as Gothic or sensation fiction.

## II

A rather typical association of the Holmes stories with the concept of realism can be found in Catherine Belsey's influential textbook classic *Critical Practice*. In order to demonstrate the interpretive methods of Pierre Macherey and Roland Barthes, Belsey subjects some of Conan Doyle's detective fiction to a reading against the grain that, although briskly persuasive overall, is not quite conceptually consistent. For while Belsey initially describes the Holmes stories as among "other forms besides realist fiction" (100-01), this generic distinction of hers gradually breaks down in the heat of interpretation: "The project of the stories themselves," she claims, "enigma followed by disclosure, echoes precisely the structure of the classic realist text. The narrator himself draws attention to the parallels between them" (103). After quoting a passage from "The Adventure of the Crooked Man" (1893), which demonstrates this precise echoing, Belsey continues to blur her initial distinction:

> The project also requires the maximum degree of "realism" – verisimilitude, plausibility. In the interest of science no hint of the fantastic or the implausible is permitted to remain once the disclosure is complete. This is why even their own existence as writing is so frequently discussed within the texts. The stories are alluded to as Watson's "little sketches," his "memoirs." They resemble fictions because of Watson's unscientific weakness for story-telling. [. . .] In other words, the fiction itself accounts even for its own fictionality, and the text thus appears wholly transparent. (103-04)

Belsey's insights into Conan Doyle's narrative strategies are relevant in their own right, and I will return to them later. At this point, however, note more generally her increasing identification of the Holmes stories with not only "the classic realist text" but also "realism" in the broader sense of "verisimilitude, plausibility." These dominant realist allegiances are subverted, according to her, by the recurrent surfacing of female sexuality as a suppressed because rationally inexplicable factor in many of Holmes' adventures (see 101-02 and 104-07). Yet despite this "implicit critique of their limited nature," Belsey still concludes her discussion by labelling the stories as "characteristic examples of classic realism" (107) and thus conflates what she initially described as similar but separate.

For the most part, the conceptual contradictions in Belsey's account can be ascribed to her wavering use of the term "realism" (even where she qualifies it with "classic"). On the one hand, and in fact predominantly, she uses the term to refer to an epistemologically defined mode of writing. This mode of writing is by no means ahistorical: in her first chapter Belsey links it "roughly to the last two centuries" and "the period of industrial capitalism" (7). Yet within these broad parameters, it can appear almost anywhere in fiction, drama, or even poetry, and is certainly not limited to a specific group of works.[3] On the other hand, and although she never actually defines it as such, Belsey occasionally seems to relapse into an alternative use of the term as designating a more or less clearly defined literary canon. When she initially locates the Holmes *corpus* outside "classic realism," she presumably means by the latter a body of texts regarded as more serious in their mimetic pursuits than the popular crime and adventure story, a body of texts which would include the works of Honoré de Balzac, for instance, or later in England, say, George Eliot's and Thomas Hardy's.[4] However theoretically useful Belsey's broader understanding of the term may be, and although, in the last analysis, the two might not be entirely separable, it is primarily this second, more narrow and historically established use of "realism" that I will adopt in my discussion.

This methodological preference conforms largely with that of another scholarly account of the Holmes stories. In his Bourdieu-informed study *British Literary Culture and Publishing Practice, 1880-1914*, Peter D. McDonald maps out the early Conan Doyle's complex aesthetic allegiances within the contemporary literary field. Locating the author's professional role between the two extremes of "purist" and "profiteer," McDonald describes him as "a populist with high aspirations who became increasingly anxious about his own literary standing" (121). In this context, he refers to

[3] Immediately after the Holmes stories, Belsey discusses Matthew Arnold's ode "The Scholar-Gypsy." In fact, as shown by her references to Ruskin's theory of painting (cf. 7-9), the "expressive realism" she defines in her first chapter is not even specific to literature.

[4] Cf. 96 and also footnote 2 on 101, where Belsey invokes the question of canonicity (though not that of the "realist" canon in particular) and refers readers to Eagleton.

a historically very specific (if still many-sided) tradition of literary realism:

> The characteristic precariousness of [Conan Doyle's] position can initially be seen in his attitude to the various styles of literary Realism prevalent in the 1890s. Believing that issues of literary taste were best considered in a "broad and catholic spirit," he welcomed and, at times, vigorously supported, avant-garde experimentation despite his own less radical aesthetic and generic preferences. If he considered controversial New Women novelists like Hardy and "Lucas Malet" "extreme men" [. . .] he granted them their "mission," which was to "pave the way," and hoped they would help break the "spell of Puritanism" that had, in his view, prevailed in England for too long. Similarly – albeit even more prudently – in late 1889, when the controversy surrounding Henry Vizetelly's publication of Zola was still very much in the air, he described Zola's naturalist novels as "careful and candid" and noted their influence on George Moore's *A Mummer's Wife* (1885). (121-22)[5]

In view of, especially, "the Holmes saga with its celebrated male friendship," McDonald later links Conan Doyle with Stevensonian Romance rather than realism, classes him as a "manly Romantic" in contrast to the "manly Realists" grouped around the *New Review* and its influential editor W. E. Henley (123). Yet this overall assessment of the Holmes *corpus* does not necessarily apply to

[5] McDonald's quotations are from, in that order, the anonymous "A Dinner to Dr. Doyle" (1896), Blathwayt's interview with "Doyle" (1893), and the latter's own "Mr. Stevenson's Methods in Fiction" (1890).

each story or aspect of the stories in detail. It is precisely the tradition of realist writing in Britain as presented in McDonald's study whose presence in the Holmes stories I will trace in the following – a tradition, that is to say, which consists to a large extent of imported French fiction and, especially in its naturalist manifestations, was regarded as both "experimental" and "avant-garde" during the late nineteenth century.

## III

That Conan Doyle's detective fiction actively engages with the aesthetics of nineteenth-century realism is, first of all, reflected in a number of striking analogies between Holmes' professional outlook and that of the realist writer. The aesthetic principles of nineteenth-century realism were, one can assume, much more present to contemporary readers than they are to us – especially when they caused controversy. Yet even today, the connection seems rather an obvious one to draw. After all, scholars such as Belsey regularly describe Holmes' unshakeable epistemological confidence as an example of scientific positivism (103), of the same school of thought, in other words, that famously provided with a philosophical basis the most notoriously radical form of literary realism: I am referring to the circle around the French novelist Emile Zola, of course, some of whose programmatic pronouncements might very well constitute a direct source of the detective's aesthetic ideals.

The affinities between the naturalist variant of realism and Sherlock Holmes' criminological outlook are already visible in their publicised origins. As Conan Doyle gratefully acknowledged, much of the figure, methods, and even appearance of the detective was modelled on the Edinburgh diagnostician and dedicatee of *The Adventures of Sherlock Holmes* (1892): "my old teacher Joseph Bell, MD, &c."[6] Conan Doyle wrote to Bell that Holmes was built "round the centre of deduction and inference and observation which I have heard you inculcate," and in his autobiography he says of his teacher that "if he were a detective, he would surely reduce this fascinating but unorganized business to something nearer an exact science."[7] All this is closely analogous not just to Holmes', but also Zola's view of his profession, and for the French novelist, similarly, it was the work of an eminent physician that best exemplified the aesthetics of his movement. Basing his polemic defense of the "experimental novel" on Claude Bernard's *Introduction à l'étude de la médecine expérimentale* (1865), Zola, too, invokes the authority of science and stresses the importance of observation:

> The naturalistic novelists observe and experiment, and [. . .] all their work is the offspring of the doubt which seizes them in the presence of truths little known and phenomena unexplained, until an experimental idea rudely awakens their genius some day, and urges them to make an experiment, to analyze facts, and to master them. (309)

Zola's description of the naturalist writer (see also 306), bears obvious resemblances to Conan Doyle's methodical detective. It recalls both his famous powers of observation and his at least initially "experimental" reconstructions of the crimes he uncovers – even if, unlike the novelist, Holmes is usually "reasoning backwards," as he puts it in *A Study in Scarlet* of 1887 (198).

---

[6] This dedication is reproduced in Green's Oxford edition, 3.

[7] Conan Doyle's writings are not always readily accessible – in this case his autobiographical *Memories and Adventures*. My quotations are from Klinger's introductory essay "The World of Sherlock Holmes," xvii-lxvii (xxiv), and double-checked against Stashower 28.

Conan Doyle's Bohemian detective, then, shares with Zola's naturalist novelist his claim to scientific practices and the epistemological authority provided by them. Though the radical emphasis put on this claim might be a distinctive feature of naturalism in particular, as a basic aesthetic tendency it also characterises the realist genre as a whole. Gustave Flaubert's quasi-scientific ideal of authorial impartiality famously led to the court proceedings against *Madame Bovary* (1857), and in an even earlier text by Balzac, the "Preface to *The Human Comedy*" (1842), accurate observation, systematic classification, and the search for causes had already become crucial elements of the aesthetics of the novel:

> A writer could, if he adopted this method of rigorous literal reproduction, become a [. . .] painter of human types, narrator of the dramas of private life, archaeologist of social furniture, classifier of professions, and recorder of good and evil; but if I was to deserve the praises which any artist must aspire to, I must needs study the *causes or central cause* of these social facts. (144)

Holmes' extensive criminalistic filing system, his "great book" (1278) as invoked for instance in "The Adventure of the Red Circle" (1911) suggests at least some of these writerly qualities. And so does his voracious yet methodical interest in material signs. When the detective draws attention to the tell-tale outward traces of other people's professions, milieux, and states of mind, he resembles the realist novelist capturing the different "habits, clothing, words and dwellings of a prince, banker, artist, bourgeois, priest, or poor man" (Balzac 142). One could further point to Holmes' didactic bent, which, too, has a counterpart in Balzac's preface (see 144); or, at a more abstract level, to the rigid ideology the detective is held to promote for instance in Rosemary Jann's

"Sherlock Holmes Codes the Social Body," and which also underpins Balzac's project of fixing in writing "the panorama of society" (145). These and similar correspondences between Holmes' professional outlook and that of the realist writer all strongly reinforce, and add special significance to, more direct invocations of literary realism in the stories.

## IV

The most striking invocations of realism in the actual text of Conan Doyle's crime fiction can usually be found in Holmes and Watson's meta-fictional dialogues. It may be true that, as Belsey points out, the detective's comments on his friend's "little sketches" add verisimilitude by accounting for the latter's fictionality (in the sense of "craftedness"). Yet this is by no means their only function. Additionally loaded, I would argue, with more specific generic and aesthetic implications, they enact within many of the Holmes texts the very clash of values that preoccupied Conan Doyle throughout his career, namely that between serious art and popular entertainment or – which at the time practically amounted to the same – between realism and fantasy. The "realism of the late century," in the words of George Levine, "defines itself against the excesses, both stylistic and narrative, of various kinds of romantic, exotic, or sensational literatures" (5). And as one might expect after the above, the Bohemian detective regularly makes the case for realism, whereas Watson speaks in favour of fantasy and "imaginative" writing – supported, presumably, at least to some extent by the general reading public.[8]

---

[8] Watson's initial claim, in *A Study in Scarlet*, about his friend's remarkable "ignorance [. . .] of contemporary literature" (32) is of course thoroughly invalidated in many of the subsequent additions to the saga, for which Conan Doyle deliberately modified his character.

Several of the meta-fictional encounters between Holmes and Watson occur in the novels and in the two adventures narrated by Holmes himself. In *The Sign of Four*, for example, the detective deplores Watson's "romanticism" (217) and in "The Adventure of the Blanched Soldier" he remembers criticising Watson for his "pandering to popular taste" (1485). Yet by far the highest proportion of such dialogue takes place in a particular group of stories, whose composition, I would suggest, is far from coincidental. "The Adventure of the Speckled Band" (1892), that of the "Copper Beeches" (1892), of the "Abbey Grange" (1904), of the "Creeping Man" (1923), of the "Sussex Vampire" (1924), and, most revealingly as well as earliest, "A Case of Identity" (1891) – these stories are united by the fact that, while published at vastly different stages of Conan Doyle's career, they all share a common kind of setting that is itself broadly evocative of nineteenth-century realism. I am referring to the distinctive social domain that forms the more narrowly thematic concern of my discussion, i.e. familial domesticity. Its frequent concurrence with meta-fictional dialogue that deals with questions of genre and aesthetics is the first point to be noted about this setting to whose specific realist implications I will return later.

The one aspect of Watson's writing of which Holmes consistently expresses his approval – albeit still with some reservations – is his selection of interesting cases. This "atones for much," according to Holmes, who, in "The Abbey Grange," goes on to criticise his friend for dwelling "upon sensational details which may excite, but cannot possibly instruct, the reader" and thereby ruining "what might have been an instructive and even classical series of demonstrations" (1159). When, in "The Adventure of the Copper Beeches," the detective expands a little more on the positive qualities of Watson's writing, he reveals two particularly notable elements of his aesthetics:

> "To the man who loves art for its own sake," remarked Sherlock Holmes, tossing aside the advertisement sheet of *The Daily Telegraph*, "it is frequently in its least important and lowliest manifestations that the keenest pleasure is to be derived. It is pleasant to me to observe, Watson, that you have so far grasped this truth that in these little records of our cases which you have been good enough to draw up, and, I am bound to say, occasionally to embellish, you have given prominence not so much to the many *causes célèbres* and sensational trials in which I have figured, but rather to those incidents which may have been trivial in themselves, but which have given room for those faculties of deduction and of logical synthesis which I have made my special province." (351)

In addition to what has already been said about the differing ideals of the two friends, this passages reveals Holmes' aesthetic position as one that precariously straddles, on the one hand, disinterested artistic purity ("art for art's sake") and, on the other, an unflagging interest in the "least important and lowliest" to be found in, for instance, *The Daily Telegraph* – commonplace everyday mass culture in other words. Thus caught between two aesthetic poles, the detective lives out a contradiction notoriously prominent in the careers of many realist writers.

In Paul Barolsky's article "The Case of the Domesticated Aesthete," Holmes is compared with, among other artistic figures, Flaubert, who "once remarked that in writing Madame Bovary he steered a precarious course between the vulgar and the lyrical" (440). Given Flaubert's reputation as a pioneering realist, this comparison is no less apt in the context of my present argument. As is already indicated by his title, Barolsky is mainly concerned with the "lyrical" side of the detective. He reads Holmes as primarily an aesthete, an artistic "connoisseur" (447) who is constantly seeking to "escape from the 'commonplace'" (439). Yet just like in the case of the realist writer (another example would be the brothers Goncourt), this is only part of the story. Holmes might share Watson's disapproval of "the trivial" as such – later on in "The Copper Beeches" he suspects Watson of having succumbed to it and deplores the seeming triviality of his client's introductory note (353). At the same time, however, he wholeheartedly embraces it in typical realist fashion, namely when it can serve as raw material for his art. And judging by what is arguably the most explicit statement of his realist sympathies, it does so far more often than not.

The statement I am referring to is the opening paragraph of "A Case of Identity." Not only does it reveal Holmes' professional interest in the commonplace as opposed to the "queer [. . .] strange [. . .] wonderful," and "*outré*" (74), but in fact – and wholly in the spirit of contemporary realist writers such as, for instance, Arnold Bennett – collapses the distinction altogether:[9]

> "My dear fellow," said Sherlock Holmes as we sat on either side of the fire in his lodgings at Baker Street, "life is infinitely stranger than anything which the mind of man could invent. We would not dare to conceive the things which are really mere commonplaces of existence. If we could fly out of that window hand in hand, hover over this

[9] See, for example, Bennett's preface to *The Old Wives' Tale* (1908), where he elevates the general aging process to the status of "a tragedy" of "extreme pathos" (31-32).

> great city, gently remove the roofs, and peep in at the queer things which are going on, the strange coincidences, the plannings, the crosspurposes, the wonderful chains of events, working through generations, and leading to the most *outré* results, it would make all fiction with its conventionalities and foreseen conclusions most stale and unprofitable." (74)

Holmes' rapture in view of everyday reality is reinforced here by his Dickensian vision of himself and Watson practically removing what, in the realist theatre of their time, was becoming known as the "fourth wall" (although, in this case, it is strictly speaking the roof, of course). In another, and rather sophisticated intertextual twist, Conan Doyle also has Holmes invert Hamlet's famous disgust for "this world," "stale and unprofitable" (1.2), by substituting for the latter the conventions of popular fiction. Given his narrative reliance on these very conventions in his chronicling of Holmes' exploits, Watson naturally disagrees with his friend's assessment, and in the process explicitly identifies his own aesthetic anathema: "I am not convinced of it. [. . .] We have in our police reports *realism pushed to its extreme limits*, and yet the result is, it must be confessed, neither fascinating nor artistic" (74; my emphasis).

Predictably, the realist Holmes in turn rejects Watson's generic categorisation of police reports. In the following, invoking the argument of selectivity, he contrasts the "platitudes of the magistrate" (74) with the detailed observations of what Zola calls the "examining magistrates of men and their passion" (308), with realism proper, in other words. Another notable feature of Holmes' reply here is his defensive endorsement of the "realistic effect," a literary term whose technical sophistication alone would remind at least some early readers of the contemporary critical debates on the subject:

> "A certain selection and discretion must be used in producing a realistic effect," remarked Holmes. "This is wanting in the police report, where more stress is laid, perhaps, upon the platitudes of the magistrate than upon the details, which to an observer contain the vital essence of the whole matter. Depend upon it, there is nothing so unnatural as the commonplace." (74)

Evidently, terms such as "commonplace" can easily shift their meanings in the literary squabbles between Holmes and Watson, which might cause some confusion if one compares them across several different texts.[10] Nonetheless, there should be little doubt by now about Conan Doyle's clearly marked oppositional treatment of, on the one hand, Holmes, the criminological purist committed more or less exclusively to the key aesthetic principles of contemporary avant-garde realism, and, on the other hand, Watson, the populariser of Holmes' detections who regards his work primarily as entertainment and respects at least some of the conventions of fantastic, sensational, and romantic fiction. Needless to say, the dialectic combination of their two stances reflects quite closely the author's own position within the contemporary literary field, a position that hovered, as we know from McDonald (121), between the two extremes of "purist" and "profiteer."

---

[10] When, for example, at the beginning of "The Adventure of the Speckled Band," Watson speaks of Holmes' exclusive interest in "the unusual, or even the fantastic" (227), this could well be explained by the doctor's more easily excitable eye for these qualities.

## V

If, among other things, Sherlock Holmes is presented as a realist, to what extent and in what forms do his aesthetics manifest themselves in the main body of the stories themselves – outside Holmes and Watson's meta-fictional dialogues, that is, which are, after all, generally regarded as structurally extraneous supplements to the cases they introduce?[11] In the last section, I have already highlighted the detective's characteristic obsession with material detail, his cataloguing habits, and scientific methods. Furthermore, I mentioned the domestic familial settings that characterise my selection of stories. Apart from a vast body of European and English fiction – including *Le père Goriot* (1835), *Madame Bovary* (1857), *Germinie Lacerteux* (1864), *War and Peace* (1865-1869), *A Mummer's Wife* (1885), *Effi Briest* (1894), *The Old Wives' Tale* (1908), and many others – the strong historical link between nineteenth-century realism and the social dynamics of the family is also easily traceable in the two programmatic manifestos by Balzac and Zola. "I regard the Family and not the Individual as the true social unit," proclaims Balzac in the political section of his preface (146), and Zola echoes this thematic bias when, at one point in "The Experimental Novel," he equates the naturalist's task with "the study of a family" (313). That Holmes and Watson, too, see a special connection between the commonplace themes of realist writing and the family household is already indicated by one of my earlier quotations. The roofs Holmes imagines himself removing in order to reveal "the plannings, the crosspurposes, the wonderful chains of events, working through generations" ("Case" 74) clearly belong to family homes rather than, say, public buildings. In "The Adventure of the Copper

[11] At least I have not found a single critic who reads them differently.

Beeches," to give another example, it is a governess' query about the respectability of the household she is about to enter that prompts the detective to speak of a "zero-point" with regard to the "originality" of his cases (353).

Important as these thematic correspondences are, I would argue that there is something else to the central investigation of each story that reflects even more compellingly Holmes' realist aesthetics. This has to do with the sort of explanation Holmes regularly arrives at, and which usually constitutes the solution of the case at hand. It should be remembered that the detective's solutions to his cases basically describe sequences of events, i.e. those which lead to the states of affairs he is called on to explain. From a literary point of view, therefore, every one of Holmes' criminological hypotheses can always also be regarded simply as a narrative, or perhaps, more precisely, as a micro-narrative within the larger frame of the detective story as a whole. If one looks at the solutions to his domestic cases in this light, one quickly realises, moreover, that, as micro-narratives, they stand in direct competition with others. Watson, the police, Holmes' clients, the criminals themselves, the reader – one or more of these parties invariably produce alternative accounts of the events under investigation. These alternatives are usually far less clearly spelled out than Holmes' theories, and, in terms of their relative truth value, regularly invalidated by the latter. As stories, however, or at least patchy and speculative hints of stories, they perform the crucial function of providing a generic foil to Holmes' accounts of events.

Before looking at the detective's own storytelling in the texts, it will be useful to identify with what exactly Conan Doyle contrasts it there, and hence arguably defines it against. As in most other texts of the Holmes *corpus*, in my selected stories, too, it is mainly Watson who organises the narrated material – up to, and around, that is, the point of Holmes' final authoritative account, which is usually rendered *verbatim* and thus relatively unaffected by the doctor's interference. Together with what we have learnt of Watson's aesthetics from the meta-fictional debate discussed earlier, his central role as authorial narrator and editor would lead one to expect that the narratives in competition with Holmes' contain strong elements of the fantastic, romantic, or at least – less specifically – the sensational. And indeed, this expectation is fully confirmed by the texts. They all resemble one another in that they regularly juxtapose Holmes' account of the domestic events under investigation with narratives that quite conspicuously draw on the conventions of sensational literature. The particular sensations invoked might vary slightly and there are one or two exceptions, but most of these micro-narratives can in fact be easily accommodated within the popular sensationalist subgenre of the horror story.

A brief glance at the titles of the "Adventures" in question already provides some evidence for this affiliation. Whereas the somewhat exceptional "A Case of Identity" might still appear neutral, and trees and old buildings such as the eponymous "Copper Beeches" and "Abbey Grange" only mildly suggestive of untold horrors, the "Speckled Band," "Creeping Man," and "Sussex Vampire" openly invoke the sort of secret criminal societies, misshapen creatures, and children of the night that formed well-known stock ingredients of the horror genre at the various times in which they were written. The expectations of horrifying scenarios awakened by these titles are further heightened in the body of each text. Thus, in "The Adventure of the Speckled Band," the description of Helen Stoner's endangered situation abounds with suggestive details that evoke, and tenuously link together, horrors familiar from Gothic fiction. There are the "wandering gypsies"

(234) whom Holmes initially regards as prime suspects (257). There is a "very old" manor house with only one inhabited wing (235). There are mysterious whistling noises (236), the unexplained bond between twins (237), "horror-stricken" stares at slowly opening doors (237), etc. "We shall have horrors enough," Holmes predicts gloomily (253), and the appearance, in the story, of "the last survivor of one of the oldest Saxon Families in England" (232) combined with Helen Stoner's theory of her sister dying "from some sudden fright" (251) are directly reminiscent of "The Fall of the House of Usher," first of Edgar Allan Poe's aptly titled *Tales of the Grotesque and Arabesque* (1840). Similarly notable intertextual allusions appear in "The Copper Beeches" – this time especially to the Gothic elements of Charlotte Brontë's *Jane Eyre* (1847). If the fads and overpowering paternalism of Mr Rucastle (e.g. on 367) are only remotely reminiscent of Mr Rochester's eccentric treatment of *his* enterprising young governess, the connection is reinforced by other partially familiar motifs such as the sour-faced, tall, and strong wife of the drunkard housekeeper (367; cf. Grace Poole in Brontë's novel), the Romantic *Doppelgänger* theme (367, 371), or the "mad unreasoning terror" of the heroine caused by a mysterious prisoner (374). There is also an early version of Conan Doyle's notorious hound of the Baskervilles: "a giant dog, as large as a calf, tawny tinted, with hanging jowl, black muzzle, and huge projecting bones" (370), by now a classic Gothic motif which might also have been inspired by *Jane Eyre* (cf. the introduction of Rochester's dog).

Whereas the horrifying allusions mentioned above still merely hint at, and induce the reader to imagine, sensationalist alternatives to Holmes' final explanations, in "The Abbey Grange," such an alternative is actually spelled out in detail. Lady Brackenstall tells the investigators about yet another supposedly murderous band, namely the sinister Randalls (1161), a father and his two sons who allegedly beat her, smashed the skull of her husband, and callously toasted their crime with a bottle of his wine (1165). As this story shows, the horror of violence alone tends to be less memorable or sensational than that of the supernatural, which is perhaps why "The Adventure of the Creeping Man" emphatically suggests the latter as a possible explanation for the events it describes. The strange periodical metamorphosis of Professor Presbury, his bestial clashes with his wolf-hound, and his assistant's mention of the "phases of the moon" (1647) subtly remind the reader of the popular myth of the werewolf – although the professor is also described as "some huge bat glued against the side of his own house, a great square dark patch upon the moonlit wall" (1658). The horror alluded to in this second description is, in fact, more fully realised in the case of the "Sussex Vampire," whose implied initial hypothesis about what is happening in the Ferguson household falls into a well-known generic category. "Really we seem to have been switched on to a Grimms' fairy tale" (1556), says Holmes when first reading of Mrs Ferguson's behaviour, but, of course, popularisations of the vampire myth such as Bram Stoker's bestselling *Dracula* (1897) would have been the first association of contemporary readers. The dramatic setting of the housewife's bloodsucking (1561), her "wild, despairing look" (1562) and South-American origins (1568), the overnight affliction of the family pet (1567), the house in which a "smart maid" is "the only modern thing" (1570), Holmes' fixed gaze into, apparently, the "melancholy, dripping garden," the cherub-like beauty of the victim infant – all these Watsonian observations add vividness to Mr Ferguson's horrifying theory of his wife's Vampirism, until, like all the other sensational narratives or suggestions of narratives I have outlined, they are superseded by Holmes' conclusive version of events.

What about Holmes' solutions themselves, then? How do they actually differ from the narratives they replace and expose as inadequate? As should be too obvious to need detailed illustration, they are far more cogent than their competitors, cover more of the facts at hand – including seemingly trivial ones – and are based on rationally retraceable chains of cause and effect. The importance, accorded by them, to significant trifles and, again in Zola's words, the "absolute determinism" of things clearly conforms to the aesthetics of nineteenth-century realism. Broadly speaking, then, Holmes' micro-narratives seem to constitute quite plausible manifestations of the aesthetic outlook identified earlier in this essay, of the detective's role, that is to say, as Conan Doyle's fictional representative of nineteenth-century realism in the spirit of Balzac and Zola. However, there are certain problematic aspects of Holmes' solutions that still need to be addressed. For what about the realist emphasis on the commonplace? What about its artistic valuation of the everyday and typically human? Are these principles at all compatible with the exotic nature of Dr Roylott's crime in "The Adventure of the Speckled Band"? Or the Dr-Jekyll-and-Mr-Hyde-style experiment Holmes reveals in "The Adventure of the Creeping Man"? The teenager's scheme of infanticide in "The Sussex Vampire"? The stepfather's impersonation of a lover in "A Case of Identity"? Or the parental incarceration of a daughter in "The Copper Beeches"? Ultimately, I would argue, the answer to these questions is yes – though how exactly Conan Doyle achieves this effect requires some further analysis.

## VI

One of the strategies that help Conan Doyle to present as commonplace even the more unusual crimes he has Holmes uncover is that of introducing arcane, but conventionally trustworthy, scientific background knowledge. Scientific explanations are linked to realism not only because of their inspiring emphasis on observation and causal reasoning. Their necessary reference to empirically substantiated general laws also makes them highly effective "normalisers," so to speak. As is commonly known, scientific explanation subsumes individual events and phenomena under laws that, by definition, hold also for many other events and phenomena. It thus emphasises their typicality and detracts from their uniqueness and fear-inducing unfamiliarity. Take, for example, Holmes' identification of the deadly "speckled band." Once it is named and zoologically classified as "the deadliest snake in India," the "swamp adder" might still command the reader's respect, but despite Watson's highly emotive and mythically charged description of "the loathsome serpent" (256), Holmes' precise assessment of how long it took its owner to die from its bite (257), the training of the animal by conditioning with milk, and the general predictability of its behaviour (258) effectively deflate its earlier potential to horrify. Similarly, the behaviour of the creeping man is largely demystified by means of scientific explanation (see 1662), and Holmes' knowledge of foreign poisons and childhood psychology leave little room for the sensational at the end of "The Sussex Vampire." In the latter story, the detective even adduces a historical precedent – "a Queen in English history" (1574) – in order to downplay the unusual nature of the supposed act of Vampirism. Like in all the stories I am looking at here, however, and especially the ones in which science proper offers little help to the detective, the sense of the commonplace evoked by Holmes' solutions – as opposed to that of the "unnatural" or "supernatural" evoked by their narrative competitors – is most effectively achieved by yet another strategy of Conan Doyle's.

This strategy consists of having Holmes resort to the kind of explanation that, while not entirely unrelated to science (if one counts sociology), recalls even more directly the realist fiction produced in the nineteenth century. For familial domesticity does not only provide the characteristically realist settings of the stories I have selected. Its reputedly commonplace internal dynamics are also regularly revealed as the ultimate sources of the crimes or near-crimes committed in them, and thereby, even more strongly than mere settings would, recall the contemporary realist novel. Whereas the various fantastic horrors imagined or at least suggestively hinted at by Watson, Robert Ferguson, Helen Stoner, Violet Hunter, Trevor Bennett, and Lady Brackenstall all constitute intrusions from outside the closely guarded privacy of the Victorian family circle, the narrative realities Holmes replaces them with invariably arise from within. However exotic or elaborate the technical execution of these crimes, their situational origin and the motives behind them are conspicuously commonplace since they arise from quite common social and material conditions: those of the contemporary family system.

Perhaps the most striking example in this respect can be found in "A Case of Identity." As we have already seen, this very early story of Conan Doyle's contains the most substantial metafictional discussion of the Holmes *corpus*, and also with regard to the detective's explanation of events it is no less than paradigmatic. Initially, Mary Sutherland's problem looks like a case involving a number of mysterious external factors, factors unknowable to her and the impatient Watson, and hence not even imaginable as the sort of vaguely outlined horror we find in the other stories.[12] But then the detective cuts the mystery down to size. He does so, first of all, by explicitly denigrating Mary Sutherland's "little problem, which, by the way, is rather a trite one" (89). It might not quite qualify as a scientific regularity, but, as Holmes assures Watson, "you will find parallel cases, if you consult my index, in Andover in '77, and there was something of the sort at the Hague last year." Most importantly, though, Holmes reveals the social scope of the case to be rather less grand than it looked at first by identifying it as an entirely intra-familial intrigue. At the same time, Holmes reinterprets an act for which common material greed is explicitly eliminated as a motive (i.e. Hosmer Angel's disappearance; see 87) as, precisely, an act of common material greed (i.e. Angel's impersonation by Mr Windibank; see 96).

Material greed in itself would already be considered vulgar by gentlemen professionals such as Holmes, who worked, as Watson puts it in "The Speckled Band," "rather for the love of [their] art than for the acquirement of wealth" (227). Yet as a determining factor within the family household, its presence in Holmes' account of events constitutes yet another notable allusion to the realist tradition. Near the turn of the century, the insidious material pressures within the family household, within the supposed *sanctum* of kind-hearted affection in other words, were quite aggressively exposed in works by Gissing and Arnold Bennett (e.g. *New Grub Street* of 1891 and *Riceyman Steps* of 1923), and as Henry James notes in "Honoré de Balzac" (1878), money was already a high thematic priority of the founding father of European realism:

---

12 "I believe that [Mr Hosmer Angel] foresaw some danger [. . .] and what he foresaw happened" (87) is all the sensationalism we get from the baffled Miss Sutherland and Watson on this occasion, which might be one reason for the lastingly low reputation of the text. In Coren, "A Case of Identity" is even described as "perhaps the weakest of the Holmes stories" (73).

"'Things' for him are francs and centimes more than any others, and I give up as inscrutable, unfathomable, the nature, the peculiar avidity of his interest in them" (162). Balzac's interest in money and its attractions is clearly reflected in the motivational force he ascribes to it throughout his works – including those dealing predominantly with family life – and if Watson is surprised by seeing Holmes listen "with the greatest concentration of attention" to Miss Sutherland's account of her family's finances, this is only because the doctor does not share his friend's Balzacian outlook (81).

In "The Speckled Band," too, a precisely determined monetary *cui bono* forms the basis of Holmes' investigation (243), as it would probably have in "The Copper Beeches," had the relevant information been available before the conclusion (cf. 381). Yet in "A Case of Identity," there is an even more direct sign of the French realist's influence on the Holmes stories and the extent Holmes' narrative solutions are based on realist principles. It occurs in connection with the correspondence of Hosmer Angel: "'As to the letters,' [Holmes] continued, glancing over them, 'they are very commonplace. Absolutely no clue in them to Mr. Angel, save that he quotes Balzac once [. . .]'" (91). Klinger's corresponding footnote runs: "Why Holmes found Windibank's quotation of Balzac interesting is unknown" (91 n. 44), and Green's Oxford edition simply quotes a passage in which Conan Doyle seems to profess ignorance of the Frenchman's innumerable works (313).[13] Yet, bearing in mind Holmes' realist solution of

[13] While Conan Doyle's casual comments in *Through the Magic Door* (93) indicate his avoidance of Balzac, they do not positively rule out his having read any of that author's works in the past, and certainly not his having read or heard about some of them (which would be sufficient for my explanation). In any case, Conan Doyle's reference to the realist author would make no sense at all if he did not associate him with anything.

the case, it is actually possible to make sense of his remark. For, looking for situational and plot similarities in Balzac's work, one soon comes across *Eugénie Grandet* (1833), which Christopher Prendergast describes as "one of the first of Balzac's novels to be accorded the aura of 'classic' status" (xii). This famous realist narrative combines at least two plot elements that Holmes might have recognised. These are a) a miserly father preventing his daughter from marrying her penniless cousin since this would diminish the family income, and b) the daughter's life-shatteringly futile adherence to her promise of waiting for said cousin's return from abroad. The precise social circumstances differ, of course, but the correspondences to Mr Windibank's scheme of keeping his romantically susceptible step-daughter out of the marriage market should be obvious even from this skeletal summary. *Eugénie Grandet* clearly constitutes a very plausible source of inspiration – both to the step-father planning his deception and the detective reconstructing it.

"A Case of Identity" is paradigmatic of Holmes' domestic cases, and the way in which his Balzacian solution replaces Mary Sutherland's theory of an honest but endangered lover has close parallels in the other stories. In the sober eyes of the bachelor detective, the mystery of the "Sussex Vampire" boils down to the jealous frenzy of a damaged teenager, that of the "Speckled Band" to the materially motivated murder of a daughter by her step-father, that of the "Creeping Man" to an aging bridegroom trying to boost his virility, that of the "Abbey Grange" to the revenge killing of a violent drunkard by an admirer of his wife, and that of the "Copper Beeches," once again, to the greed-motivated ill-treatment of a daughter by her father. However sensationally exotic or horrifying the events of these stories might appear to the uninitiated, Holmes turns them into markedly realistic tales of intra-familial egotism, addictions, material greed, and sadly predictable desires. As Catherine Belsey puts it in the context of her own argument: “no hint of the fantastic or the implausible is permitted to remain once the disclosure is complete” (103).

To conclude, it might be worth noting that while this latter prohibition certainly allays the horrors felt by Watson, other bystanders, and any reader looking for epistemological reassurance, those of Holmes are barely affected. Stephen Knight expresses the standard criticism of the Sherlock Holmes stories when he states that their “embarrassing success depended on the hero’s power to assuage the anxieties of a respectable London-based, middle-class audience” (67). True as this may be, the hero does not manage to assuage his own anxieties, and thus there is at least the possibility of another kind of reading, one that resists Watson’s overall narrative guidance and sympathises rather with Holmes’ disillusioning realism. However satisfying the detective’s solutions of his domestic cases might appear to most onlookers, there is only limited closure for the detective himself. For, as we have seen, he is not horrified by any fantastic intrusions from the dark unknown, but rather by the sadly transparent *status quo* of domestic family life. In the passage from “The Copper Beeches” I have quoted at the start of this essay, he deplores the typical family home’s “isolation and [. . .] the impunity with which crime may be committed there” (363), and the outcomes of his domestic cases strongly confirm his suspicions. Most of them end on a doubtful note of immorality or illegality – despite his and Watson’s chivalrous interventions, that is – and they invariably expose abusive fathers or husbands. In “A Case of Identity,” most radically of all, the deceitful stepfather remains not only entirely unpunished, but Holmes feels not even capable of freeing Mary Sutherland from her “delusion” (100). If one looks past the sexist generalisation that ends the story, this unsettling result cannot help but suggest a profound criticism of contemporary social realities. As such, it and its counterparts in the other stories of my selection complicate overly simplistic views of Conan Doyle's conservatism and the subversive potential of his writings.

**Works Cited**

Altick, Richard D. "Mr. Sherlock Holmes and Dr. Samuel Johnson." *221B: Studies in Sherlock Holmes by Various Hands*. Ed. Vincent Starrett. New York: Macmillan, 1940. 109-28.

Balzac, Honoré de. "Preface to *The Human Comedy*." Trans. Petra Morrison. Kettle 140-53.

Barolsky, Paul. "The Case of the Domesticated Aesthete." *Virginia Quarterly Review* 60 (1984): 438-52.

Belsey, Catherine. *Critical Practice*. 2nd ed. London: Routledge, 2002.

Bennett, Arnold. Preface. *The Old Wives Tale*. Ed. John Wain. London: Penguin, 1983. 31-35.

Bernard, Claude. *Introduction à l'étude de la médecine expérimentale*. Paris: Ballière, 1865.

Blathwayt, Raymond. "Doyle." *Interviews*. London: A. W. Hall, Great Thoughts Office, 1893. 51.

Brontë, Charlotte. *Jane Eyre: An Autobiography*. London: Smith, Elder, 1847.

*Census of Great Britain, 1851*. London: Longman and Brown, 1854.

Chase, Karen, and Michael Levinson, eds. Introduction. *The Spectacle of Intimacy: A Public Life For the Victorian Family*. Princeton: Princeton UP, 2000. 3-17.

Conan Doyle, Arthur. "The Adventure of the Abbey Grange." Klinger 2: 1158-88.

___. "The Adventure of the Blanched Soldier." Klinger 2: 1482-510

___. "The Adventure of the Copper Beeches." Klinger 1: 351-83.

___. "The Adventure of the Creeping Man." Klinger 2: 1636-66.

___. "The Adventure of the Crooked Man." Klinger 1: 582-607.

___. "The Adventure of the Red Circle." Klinger 2: 1272-99.

___. "The Adventure of the Speckled Band." Klinger 1: 227-63.

___. "The Adventure of the Sussex Vampire." Klinger 2: 1555-80.

___. "A Case of Identity." Klinger 1: 74-100.

___. *The Hound of the Baskervilles*. Klinger 3: 383-628.

___. *Memories and Adventures*. London: Hodder and Stoughton, 1924.

___. "Mr Stevenson's Methods in Fiction." *National Review* Feb. 1890: 650.

___. "A Scandal in Bohemia." Klinger 1: 5-40.

___. *The Sign of Four*. Klinger 3: 209-382.

___. *A Study in Scarlet*. Klinger 3: 3-208.

___. *Through the Magic Door*. London: Smith, Elder, 1907.

Coren, Michael. *Conan Doyle*. London: Bloomsbury, 1995.

"A Dinner to Dr. Doyle." *Critic* 1 Aug. 1896: 79.

Eagleton, Terry. *Criticism and Ideology*. London: New Left, 1976.

Green, Richard Lancelyn, ed. *The Adventures of Sherlock Holmes*. By Arthur Conan Doyle. Oxford: Oxford UP, 1993.

Hennessey, Rosemary, and Rajeswari Mohan. "The Construction of Woman in Three Popular Texts of Empire: Towards a Critique of Materialist Feminism." *Textual Practice* 3 (1989): 323-59.

James, Henry. "Honoré de Balzac." Kettle 154-74.

Jann, Rosemary. "Sherlock Holmes Codes the Social Body." *ELH* 57 (1990): 685-708.

Kettle, Arnold, ed. *The Nineteenth-Century Novel: Critical Essays and Documents*. London: Heinemann, 1972.

Klinger, Leslie S., ed. *The New Annotated Sherlock Holmes*. 3 vols. New York: Norton, 2005-2006.

Knight, Stephen. *Form and Ideology in Crime Fiction*. London: Macmillan, 1980.

Levine, George. *The Realistic Imagination: English Fiction from Frankenstein to Lady Chatterley*. Chicago: U of Chicago P, 1981.

McDonald, Peter D. *British Literary Culture and Publishing Practice, 1880-1914*. Cambridge: Cambridge UP, 1997.

Ousby, Ian. *Bloodhounds of Heaven: The Detective in English Fiction from Godwin to Doyle*. Cambridge, MA: Harvard UP, 1976.

Poe, Edgar Allan. *Tales of the Grotesque and Arabesque*. Philadelphia: Lea and Blanchard, 1840.

Porter, Dennis. *The Pursuit of Crime: Art and Ideology in Detective Fiction*. New Haven: Yale UP, 1981.

Prendergast, Christopher. Introduction. *Eugénie Grandet*. By Honoré de Balzac. Trans. Sylvia Raphael. Oxford: Oxford UP, 1990. vii-xxiv.

Stashower, Daniel. *Teller of Tales: The Life of Arthur Conan Doyle*. New York: Henry Holt, 1999.

Zola, Emile. "The Experimental Novel." Trans. Belle M. Sherman. Kettle 302-29.

# Algernon Blackwood's Modernist Experiments in Psychical Detection

George M. Johnson
Thompson Rivers University

**Abstract:** Algernon Blackwood has been inaccurately labeled as a ghost story writer, but his self-declared fundamental interest was in articulating the signs and proofs of extended capacities such as telepathy and prevision that lie hidden in humankind. His project of extending the boundaries of realism to encompass these powers he shares with the modernists; he is thus more accurately viewed as one of the first moderns to realize the imaginative potential of the new psychology and psychical research. Blackwood's psychic detective stories demonstrate this since they adapt several formal properties, as well as subject matter of Society for Psychical Research psychical case studies, as gathered and classified in leading psychological theorist Frederic Myers' magnum opus *Human Personality and Its Survival of Bodily Death* (1903). Blackwood's 1911 novel *The Centaur* most imaginatively engages with S.P.R. case studies and elevates the psychic detection genre onto a profoundly metaphysical plane.

2008 marks the centenary of the "birth" in print of the most famous psychical detective in English fiction. Despite his longevity, many will struggle to identify who that character may be. Algernon Blackwood's Dr. John Silence arguably holds this distinction and yet he claims only a cult following today, unlike his "cousin" Sherlock Holmes.[1] There are a number of reasons for Silence's slip into relative obscurity, perhaps most notably the difficulty critics have had in categorizing his creator Algernon Blackwood, all too frequently pigeon-holing him as a ghost story writ-

[1] Interestingly, during his heyday Silence, like Holmes, received sometimes bizarre requests for help, and according to biographer Mike Ashley, Blackwood responded to the cases of psychic affliction that intrigued him (*Starlight* 136).

er,[2] or at best a supernaturalist, albeit "the foremost British supernaturalist of the twentieth century," according to E. F. Bleiler (x). However, Blackwood's talents are much more diverse than these labels would suggest: his novels frequently depict the fantasy lives of children, or are mystical odysseys; his stories include nature tales, in which nature is a powerful living force, psychological stories depicting dual personalities and idées fixes, fantasies of escape from mundane reality, thrillers, and, of course, detective stories of the psychical variety, exploring possession, prevision and thought-transference, among other phenomena. He himself claimed: "My fundamental interest, I suppose, is signs and proofs of other powers that lie hidden in us all; the extension, in other words, of human faculty" (qtd. in Penzoldt 229). With this interest he shares the project of many of his modernist contemporaries, including D. H. Lawrence and Virginia Woolf, in attempting to extend the boundaries of realism in fiction, to capture "this incessantly varying spirit," as Woolf put it, this "semi-transparent envelope, or luminous halo, surrounding us from the beginning of consciousness to the end"[3] ("Modern" 33). Blackwood is more accurately viewed as one of the first moderns to articulate the imaginative potential of the new psychology, psychical research and more esoteric mystical ideas.[4]

---

[2] Blackwood himself noted the restrictions placed on him by being labeled the "Ghost Man" (Kunitz 147), and, ironically, claimed never to have seen a ghost (Ashley, *Algernon* 5).

[3] Woolf also wrote that her era was "one which seeks the supernatural in the soul of man, and the development of psychical research offers a basis of disputed fact for this desire to feed upon" ("Across" 219; cf. Johnson, *Dynamic* 150-57, 176-205).

[4] Hillaire Belloc in a perceptive early review of *John Silence* recognized that Blackwood's presentation of the English ghost story was "startlingly modern in its methods and in the scientific basis upon which that method reposed" (68).

Blackwood's forays into psychic detection can be used to demonstrate this, since in these stories he engaged with discourses in psychology and psychical phenomena by those at the forefront of debate in pre-Freudian England, the psychical researchers. Specifically, he adapted several formal properties, as well as subject matter of Society for Psychical Research psychical case studies, as gathered, classified and theorized about in such works as Frederic Myers' magnum opus *Human Personality and Its Survival of Bodily Death* (1903). Although Blackwood's involvement in S.P.R. investigations of haunted houses, as well as his independent psychical investigations have been documented (Ashley, *Starlight* 35), his interrogation of psychical discourse has not been systematically analyzed, and in fact has occasionally been denied. Peter Keating, for instance, in his social history of the English novel, *The Haunted Study* (1989), incorrectly states that the S.P.R. did not play "any part" in Blackwood's "neglected talent that found expression in *Jimbo* (1909), *The Human Chord* (1910), *The Centaur* (1911) and *The Prisoner in Fairyland* (1913)" (361). The extent of Blackwood's innovations on the S.P.R. case study will be made clear by examining several of the stories in his earliest collections, *The Empty House* (1906) and *The Listener* (1907), as well as those in *John Silence: Physician Extraordinary* (1908), and the more ambitious novel, *The Centaur* (1911). Although traditionally viewed as a fantastical odyssey, this novel can be seen afresh as a psychic mystery probing the death of Mother Earth to modern consciousness owing to the negative impact of modern civilization. *The Centaur* represents Blackwood's most imaginative adaptation of the S.P.R. case study and, I would argue, elevates the genre of psychic detection onto a profoundly metaphysical plane.

Blackwood was not the originator of the psychical detection sub-genre, but a glance at his most significant Victorian forerunner, Joseph Sheridan Le Fanu, will suggest the leap forward that Blackwood took. Le Fanu links together his psychical stories (collected in *In A Glass Darkly*, 1872) using the character of Dr. Martin Hesselius, an affluent German physician and self-styled "medical philosopher" (180). An idealist, he believes that "the entire natural world is but the ultimate expression of that spiritual world from which, and in which alone, it has its life" (181). The cases range from the "spectral illusion" of a sinister monkey induced by imbibing green tea, to revenge hauntings, to a vampire tale. However, they are posthumously presented by Hesselius' medical secretary. Le Fanu's use of this frame narrative does create complexity and ironies, as Valentina Gabusi and Jack Sullivan have pointed out; readers perceive the story from at least two different perspectives, including the supernatural and rational, and these are not reconciled, thus mirroring the ambivalence of the Victorians towards the supernatural. However, as stories they rely mainly on exposition rather than on dramatic scenes that unfold through psychic detection. Although this man praises his employer's "work of analysis, diagnosis and illustration" (179), the reader discovers that Hesselius does not actually engage in any psychical detection as such but has merely received reports narrated by others (cf. Penzoldt 251 n. 23). The partial exception is the most famous tale, "Green Tea," in which Hesselius provides an arm-chair diagnosis of the victim's affliction, but even then fails to intervene to save his client, who commits suicide. In the somewhat dissatisfying conclusion, Hesselius merely states that "I had not even commenced to treat Mr. Jennings' case" (206-07). In striking contrast to this, Blackwood's psychic detectives either experience the psychical phenomena themselves or actively engage in aiding victims, making Blackwood's stories much more dynamic than Le Fanu's.

Nevertheless, Le Fanu does broach the tension between materialist and preternatural explanations in a couple of stories, "Green Tea" and "The Familiar" (187-88, 218, 225), a dialectic that Blackwood exploits fully and which is one of the most significant features of S.P.R. psychical case studies. In these, either the person experiencing the psychical phenomenon or a witness to it typically claims previous disinterest in psychical phenomena before becoming convinced of its veracity. The strategy is presumably used as a means of establishing the objectivity of the witness and the strength of the evidence. For example, in a case of clairvoyance collected by Myers, one M. H. Gray states, "The circumstances were most prosaic, and I a matter-of-fact individual, with little interest and less faith in psychical phenomena," and yet Grey becomes convinced of the experience, described as "So strange and so real" (*Human* 2: 414). Blackwood elaborated on and dramatized this feature by having a skeptic confront someone convinced of the psychic nature of a mystery, propose a psychological or materialist explanation, and then realize the limitations of it or come to believe in the psychic event.

In "With Intent to Steal," a case of possession,[5] Blackwood generates dramatic tension by making the narrator protagonist the skeptic. He only agrees to participate in Jim Shorthouse's psychical investigation because his curiosity is provoked by Shorthouse's taciturnity, he is flattered by the request from this older man of wide experience, and impressed by his conviction (120, 123). Nevertheless, since the experience belongs "to an order of

[5] Ashley claims that Blackwood not only drew on the S.P.R. Brockley Court case involving a white monk who possessed unsuspecting guests of the house, but also may have investigated it himself (*Starlight* 115).

things I had always rather ridiculed and despised" (120), the narrator's tone continues to be skeptical and even (self-consciously) sneering (123). Here Blackwood uses the dialectic not only for expository purposes, to gradually fill in details of the case, but also to eliminate other possibilities proposed by the narrator, such as that the case constitutes an open-and-shut suicide (122). Eventually the narrator comes to know "positively" that they face an evil presence, the spirit of a Black magician, in the barn where they have been staked out (139). Ironically, however, he also comes to see Shorthouse as a source of weakness and has to carry out a dramatic rescue of the psychical researcher by grappling with him on a rafter to prevent the possessed man from committing suicide.

The tables are turned in "The Empty House" where a much younger Jim Shorthouse is the skeptic and his Aunt Julia, "with a mania for psychical research" (277), the instigator of a nocturnal examination of a haunted house.[6] Once again, though, the investigator persuades the skeptic by flattery and the earnestness of the request (278). In this third-person story, limited to Shorthouse's perspective, Blackwood generates tension by having Shorthouse express worry that his Aunt will be incapable of maintaining self-control, and then to show him as unable to prevent her succumbing to the house's evil female presence (278, 289). Shorthouse proposes several explanations for his Aunt's increasingly odd behaviour, including that she has possibly become a physical medium channelling the evil force, while at the same time battling against "depletion of his vital forces" himself, which is "the chief horror of the experience" (287, 288). Only by taking direct action

[6] According to Ashley, this story was also based on an investigation, of a haunted house near Brighton, that Blackwood carried out himself – in this case before it was brought to the attention of the S.P.R. (*Starlight* 35-36).

against the enemy (and by supplying his Aunt with a nip of brandy) does Shorthouse manage to extract himself and his Aunt from the peril.

In a couple of other early stories the dialectic occurs between materialist doctors and visionaries, a dynamic that Blackwood developed fully in *The Centaur*. "Smith: An Episode in A Lodging House" repeats to a point the pattern of "With Intent to Steal" in that the experimenter engages the skeptic through flattery and curiosity – and in the skeptic's greater vitality, enabling him to act at the key moment and save the visionary. In this case, however, the investigator, Smith, seems to be a participant in uncanny events and to possess extraordinary powers including telergy (195).[7] He flatters the skeptic, a medical student "in the heavy, unquestioning state of materialism" (195), by soliciting the doctor's knowledge of Hebrew (187). The main difference, though, is that the doctor never ceases to view Smith, a fellow boarder, as a suspicious intruder, who "was somehow making use of me against my will" (195). This greatly enhances tension in the story, as does the doctor's vehemence in attributing his experience to "delusion" of a "gigantic force [. . .] an invisible being who could crush me as easily as I could crush a fly" (203, 200). Once again, the skeptic doctor's "amazing vitality" and his fearlessness in acting (206, 212) cause him to save Smith, though unwittingly.

Whereas this doctor implicitly rejects or at least distances himself from his experience by quitting the boarding-house as quickly as possible, the similarly "prosaic, matter-of-fact, materialistic doctor" of "May Day Eve" is utterly transformed by his "consciousness-expanding" journey to visit a folklorist friend, one of

[7] According to Myers, telergy is "the force exercised by the mind of an agent in impressing a percipient, – involving a direct influence of the extraneous spirit on the brain or organism of the percipient" (Myers, *Human* 1: xxii).

Blackwood's numerous physically large visionaries whose stature seems to increase with their visions (170, 189). The doctor sets out to take a book to the folklorist that "utterly refuted all his tiresome pet theories of magic and the powers of the soul" (166). En route he begins to experience the "world around me as something alive," in other words the sentient quality of nature, which initially merely gives him insight into "certain curious mental cases" (175) but eventually evokes the "unreasoning conviction…that I had hitherto been spending my life in the pursuit of false knowledge, in the mere classifying and labelling of effects, the analysis of results, scientific so-called" (182). Ironically, when the doctor reaches the folklorist's place, the old man refers to him as a "case" and provides the "explanation" that on May Day eve elemental beings have power over the minds of men, especially extremists like him (187). Almost against his will, he then agrees to go outdoors with the folklorist to "see more" (188).

Blackwood's use of this dialectic, which not only bears affinity with the psychical case study structure but also alludes to the great philosophical debates of the late nineteenth century between idealism and materialism, or positivism, generally proves effective in generating tension in the short story's condensed form, since Blackwood doesn't have the space to become too didactic. Psychical case studies on the whole are typically fairly condensed, thus lending themselves to treatment in short story form. Nevertheless, they do raise large issues like this, along with others such as the question of survival of human personality after death, or reincarnation, and they engage with phenomena that defy comprehensive rational explanation or at least occlude or problematize meaning; in so doing they typically open up more gaps or questions than are resolved.

On one level, rumour and legend riddled with gaps is the very stuff of psychical fiction and Blackwood employs them to heighten anticipation, as in "With Intent to Steal," where Shorthouse deliberately withholds information in order to engage the skeptic but also to protect him. In this case the skeptic recognizes the strategy, claiming that Shorthouse "knew a great deal more than he meant to tell," and acquiesces to it, stating that "I [. . .] was not sure that I wanted to hear too much beforehand" (129). What little Shorthouse does say about the evil force they face tends to emphasize its extraordinary nature: "It is no mere family ghost that goes with every ivied house in England of a certain age; it is something real and very malignant" (128). In "The Empty House," the Aunt is more forthcoming, supplying a skeleton of information about the century-old murder that occurred in the house, but that is all. She claims that "I've not been able to get more details of the story" and that recent occurrences in the house have "been most cleverly hushed up" (278). "The Woman's Ghost Story" provides a clever twist on the employment of gaps, since the narrator, a self-declared "'psychical researcher', and a woman of new tendencies" (66), declares at the outset: "I'll give you just the essentials and you can make of it what you please" (65), thus preparing readers for inconclusiveness. About the haunted house she has chosen to investigate, she says merely: "The story was a good one – satisfied me, at any rate, that it was worth investigating; and I won't weary you with details as to the woman's murder and all the tiresome elaboration as to *why* the place was *alive*" (65). At the denouement we discover the possible reason for her sketchiness, since the investigator has herself been tested by the house owner, who has supplied her with a false story in order to prevent her from being biased by her previous knowledge. She, for her part, withholds details of her encounter with a lonely male ghost who has requested and received a kiss from her, making her feel a "momentary ecstasy" (73). This phenomenon of the persistence of a personality with feelings beyond death cannot, of course, be rationally explained.

On another level, the more profound gaps tend to appear at the close of the stories, as in "The Woman's Ghost Story," and this characteristic parallels the open-endedness typical of modernist short stories. In "Keeping His Promise," Blackwood provides only partial resolution, in that Field's sister reveals in a letter that he died on the very night that he appeared before his friend, Marriott, the story's protagonist. The story thus falls into the category of crisis apparition, a type extensively documented by Myers and the S.P.R. and thus easily recognizable to a contemporary audience.[8] Nevertheless, this "explanation" still defies reason, and it does not begin to account for the continuous breathing heard by Marriott, or for the fact that the meal Marriott witnessed Field consume remains untouched, although Marriot suggests that these phenomena were hallucinations (314). Furthermore, Blackwood gives no response from his characters to the information about the date of death, leaving it to readers to make their own assessments. "The Empty House" similarly omits any reaction from the investigators once they rush from the house at the story's close; the focus throughout has firmly been on articulating the vicissitudes of fear, rather than on filling in details of the apparition and its history, or even broaching the issue of how spirits might persist to reenact a crime and haunt a house. Not only does "May Day Eve" not attempt to resolve the issue raised of the sentience of nature, but Blackwood leaves the doctor on the threshold of a whole new ad-

[8] Ashley claims that "Keeping His Promise" was based on the crisis apparition involving a pact reported by Lord Brougham in 1799 and summarized by Myers (*Human* 2: 43).

venture and possibly a new way of seeing the world, thus evoking open-endedness on many levels simultaneously.

Perhaps the most striking example of a story blossoming with possibilities at its close occurs in "Ancient Sorceries," one of the John Silence stories, although not one in which Silence plays the most active role. He does draw out from Arthur Vezin his horrifying experience of a witch's Sabbath while on vacation, but at the denouement Silence dramatically increases ambiguity about the story's status by suggesting that "the entire affair took place subjectively in the man's own consciousness" (81); Silence does theorize about the dynamic that has occurred, one based on Myersian discourse about the subliminal (a term Myers coined): "Subliminal uprushes of memory like this can be exceedingly painful, and sometimes exceedingly dangerous. I only trust that this gentle soul may soon escape from this obsession of a passionate and tempestuous past. But I doubt it. I doubt it" (83). However, he also seems unable to resolve the man's dilemma and envisions further trouble, claiming, "'the end of his trouble is not yet. We shall hear of him again. It is a case, alas! I can do little to alleviate'" (82). Vezin's fate is not revealed.

Aside from structural correspondences, Blackwood's stories share affinities in characterization and thematic preoccupations with psychical research and particularly its case studies. Blackwood's most famous character, Dr. John Silence, has been trained as a medical doctor but practices as a psychic doctor, a "soul-doctor" (8); as such he embodies several characteristics of the psychical researchers themselves, some of whom, like Frederic Myers' brother, Arthur, and Pierre Janet, were also medical doctors. Blackwood repeatedly asserts that Silence is a scientifically trained psychic who has carried out experiments (*John* 19, 31,

117, 118), and thus not a believer in spiritualism.[9] Also similarly to many psychical researchers, he believes in telepathy (3) – another term coined by Frederic Myers – that human personality persists beyond death (20, 42, 170), and, as we have seen, in subliminal uprushes of memory (83). Unlike the typical materialist doctor of the day, Silence does not attempt to exert control over the will of his patients, nor does he hold the view that insanity is a discrete category warranting being locked up in an asylum. Although aware of the dangers to his subjects' sanity presented by the mysterious phenomena afflicting them, like the psychical researchers he is sympathetic to subjects' plights and advocates listening to their impressions and even fancies, as well as their "certainties" (10). Despite the similarities between Silence and the psychical researchers, we are told that "[f]or the modern psychical researcher he felt the calm tolerance of the 'man who knows'" (2), perhaps reflecting an anxiety of influence on the part of Blackwood. (Ambivalence towards psychical research was quite common among period fiction writers who assimilated its discourses, from Henry James to Aldous Huxley).[10]

Nevertheless, Blackwood's presentation of apparitions aligns well with one of Myers' main findings derived from case studies of hauntings, that apparitions do not correspond to preconceived notions of them (*Human* 2: 5). Myers discovered that most

---

9 Myers defined spiritualism or spiritism as a " religion, philosophy, or mode of thinking, based on the belief that the spirits of the dead communicate with living men" (*Human* 1: xxi).

10 Perhaps most famously, Henry James claimed in 1908 that "the new type [of ghost story] indeed, the mere modern 'psychical' case, washed clean of all queerness as by exposure to a flowing laboratory tap, and equipped with credentials vouching for this – the new type clearly promised little" (James 169) when he himself had drawn on the famous Morton S.P.R. case, summarized by Myers (*Human* 2: 388-9), in "The Turn of the Screw," and on other cases in several other stories (Johnson, "Survival").

hauntings are not precipitated by "some great crime or catastrophe" (*Human* 2: 68), but are purposeless and seemingly random. Apparitions tend not to be evil, only occasionally mischievous; on the contrary, claims Myers, "Haunting phantoms, incoherent and unintelligent may seem restless and unhappy. But as these rise into definiteness, intelligence, individuality, the phantoms rise also into love and joy" (*Human* 2: 78). Peter Penzoldt in *The Supernatural in Fiction* notes that Blackwood's "apparitions fill us with awe, while those of so many others fill us with horror akin to disgust" (232). Blackwood's description of the elementals encountered by the doctor in "May Day Eve" provides a good example:

> The faces that met me were fine, vigorous and comely, while burning everywhere through their ripe maturity shone the ardours of youth and a kind of deathless enthusiasm. Old, yet eternally young they were, as rivers and mountains count their years by thousands yet remain ever youthful; and the first effect of all those pairs of eyes lifted to meet my own was to send a whirlwind of unknown thrills about my heart and make me catch my breath with mingled terror and delight. (179)

As Blackwood's ghosts become more individualized they occasionally resemble Myers' description, as in "The Woman's Ghost Story."[11] Although the story's apparition had been a misanthrope who committed suicide, and the female psychical researcher initially feels terrified of him (despite his appearing "well-dressed, youngish and good-looking" [66]), she discovers that he is desperate for compassion and love. Eventually she pities and

---

[11] Mike Ashley notes that the story "reads as though it were written from one of Blackwood's psychic explorations" (*Starlight* 124).

kisses him, giving her momentary ecstasy and releasing him, even though she had no connection with him when he was alive (73).

One of the most prevalent themes in Blackwood's psychical tales is loss of vitality and, indeed, fear of loss of self. This is to be expected, and is certainly present, in his cases of possession, such as "With Intent to Steal," where Shorthouse says, "I feel my vitality going rapidly" (144) while in the presence of evil. After his recovery from possession, he adds that he had "lost all sense of his own identity" (160). During Dr. Silence's investigation of a case of possession in "A Psychic Invasion," he too "began to lose memory – memory of his identity, of where he was, of what he ought to do" (38). However, the theme occurs in almost every one of Blackwood's psychical cases. It is most graphically depicted in "May Day Eve" when the narrator has a vision of two contrasting beings after his personality has been shaken to its foundations by his new perceptions (182). The first is of a loathsome caged creature "dully satisfied with its prisoned cage behind the bars, utterly unconscious of the vast world about it, grunting with pleasure" and the second of a goddess with refined countenance (184). He then comes to the painful recognition that "they were born of my own being, and were indeed *projections of myself.* They were portions of my own consciousness, projected outwardly" (185). The narrator also states that "I had of course read much concerning the changes of personality, swift, kaleidoscopic" (176), as had Blackwood, who claimed that as a young man he devoured "every kind of book I could find on psychology" (*Episodes* 102).

Blackwood's preoccupation with this theme would certainly appear to reflect late nineteenth-century fascination with the nature of selfhood. Frederic Myers was a leading participant in the burgeoning discourse on this topic, and his threshold theory of the subliminal in particular called into question the substantiality of the self, although Myers did suggest that the soul unified the individual, a point that went largely unnoticed. He wrote: "I regard each man as at once profoundly unitary and almost infinitely composite, as inheriting from earthly ancestors a multiplex and 'colonial' organism – polyzoic and perhaps polypsychic in an extreme degree; but also as ruling and unifying that organism by a soul or spirit absolutely beyond our present analysis" (*Human* 1: 34). Myers theorized that

> the stream of consciousness in which we habitually live is not the only consciousness which exists in connection with our organism. Our habitual or empirical consciousness may consist of a mere selection from a multitude of thoughts and sensations, of which some at least are equally conscious with those that we empirically know. I accord no primacy to my ordinary waking self, except that among my potential selves this one has shown itself the fittest to meet the needs of common life. ("Subliminal" 301)

Below the threshold of the ordinary, empirical consciousness, which he named the supraliminal, was psychical action that he called subliminal. The spectrum of consciousness in the subliminal extended from automatic physiological processes no longer required as part of memory in order to survive, to psychic impressions "which the supraliminal consciousness is incapable of receiving in any direct fashion," such as telepathic and clairvoyant messages ("Subliminal" 306). This subliminal consisted of "an aggregate of potential personalities, with imperfectly known capacities of perception and action, but none of them identical with the assumed individuality beneath them" (308). Myers preferred the term subliminal to secondary self, used by a number of his contemporaries, which gave the impression that there could only be one other self. The number of potential personalities and streams of consciousness was apparently limitless. Myers rejected the idea of unconscious mental events, since he believed that all psychic events could potentially figure in a stream of consciousness. Also, although the subliminal could be diseased, it was not necessarily inferior to the supraliminal. On the contrary, Myers believed that messages from the subliminal could indicate expansion and evolution of the personality, as found in the visions of genius (317). Overall, Myers' conception of the subliminal was not reductive, but exploratory, emphasizing potential and extensions of capacity.

Myers' unique contribution was to integrate into psychology and thus legitimize the evidence for extensions of the powers of human consciousness, including telepathy, clairvoyance, psychic possession, and automatic writing, a project remarkably akin to Blackwood's stated "fundamental interest" in the extensions of human faculties in fiction. The extent to which Blackwood interrogated Myers' and others' psychical findings and in particular developed the imaginative possibilities of the psychical case study and psychical detection can be demonstrated by examining *The Centaur*, Blackwood's flawed masterpiece and personal favorite (Ashley, *Starlight* 164, 172).

One of *The Centaur*'s most striking features is its large scale, that is, the range of philosophical, psychological and metaphysical issues it engages, an effect enhanced by Blackwood's quotation of numerous philosophers, psychologists, psychical researchers and poets in the epigraphs to chapters, directly in the text and even in footnotes. His employment of this apparatus has the mark of an enthusiast attempting to lay out his vision in the most convincing way possible, to increase the veracity, the believability, the "realism" of the phenomena explored; this strategy is simultaneously the novel's fascination and also its downfall. Mike Ashley rightly emphasizes that Blackwood drew the basic concept for the novel from Gustav Fechner, that the Earth is a sentient being, the landscape her face, and that human beings have lost contact with this Mother Earth (*Starlight* 164). Certainly Blackwood frequently repeats this idea, invokes Fechner, draws on William James' interpretation of Fechner, and even plants a biography of Fechner within the novel's pages (*Centaur* 111-12). Nevertheless, several other significant concepts, the dynamic of the novel and its characterization owe much more to psychical research than to Fechner. The novel possesses all the elements of the psychical case study, all the earmarks of psychic detection, including the materialist/visionary dialectic, gaps, ambiguities, and mysteries on several levels, the character of the psychic doctor, the benevolence of the apparition and the haunting, as well as, paradoxically, fear of loss of self.

Most fundamentally, the novel constitutes an exploration of extensions of human personality in time and space and postulates that Mother Earth has a similar capacity:

> We know to-day [. . .] that the human personality can extend itself under certain conditions called abnormal. It can project portions of itself, show itself even at a distance, operate away from the central governing body. In exactly similar fashion may the Being of the Earth have projected portions of herself in the past. Of such great powers or beings there may conceivably be a survival... a survival of a hugely remote period when her Consciousness was manifested, perhaps, in shapes and forms long since withdrawn before the tide of advancing humanity... forms of which

> poetry and legend alone have caught a flying memory and called them gods, monsters, mythical beings of all sorts and kinds.... (68)

This discourse engages several of Myers' concepts. As a means of proving the survival of personality beyond death, Myers' main aim, he postulated what he called a metetherial realm, "the spiritual or transcendental world in which the soul exists" (*Human* 1: xix).[12] What he termed the supernormal, that is extensions of human capacity like telepathy, were "survivals from the powers which that spirit once exercised in a transcendental world" (*Human* 2: 267). Other such extensions include what Myers termed psychical excursion, where an invading spirit modifies a certain portion of space, and psychorragy, a breaking loose of a psychical element that is able to produce a phantasm, which is what Blackwood describes in the above passage. As Carlos Alvarado notes, "In the higher end of the excursive or psychorrhagic spectrum Myers speculated on the possibility of ecstasy, or the entrance to a spiritual world and to 'communities higher than any which this planet knows'" (7; cf. also *Human* 2: 297). Blackwood shows his protagonist, O'Malley, experiencing psychorragy and entering into one such community, of mythological beings called centaurs, himself manifesting as one of these elemental beings, or *urmenschen*, survivals from a more spiritual time (*Centaur* 59). For the most part, Blackwood figures this as an extreme subliminal adventure: "Through regions of their sub-liminal consciousness, which transcends the restricted physical expression of it called personality as the moisture of the world transcends a drop of wa-

[12] Blackwood's protagonist O'Malley voices this belief at the beginning of the novel when he says: "The Cosmos, in a word, for him was psychical, and Nature's moods were transcendental cosmic activities" (*Centaur* 5).

ter, deific presences pass to and fro" (154). Drawing on the subliminal, "a vast amount the race has discarded unwisely and prematurely" can be recovered (169). However, Blackwood also engages with Myers' concept of the supernormal, or "superconsciousness," to evoke man's potential; the perfect man will exercise both subliminal and supernormal (169). Nevertheless, the novel postulates a danger in this subliminal adventuring, that the dissociation involved might be overwhelming and result in death (103, 175). Following the lengthy description of O'Malley among the centaurs, it is suggested that "that blending with the Earth's great Consciousness was but a flashing glimpse after all. The extension of personality has been momentary" (284), thus casting the adventure as a modernist psychological moment. And yet O'Malley never recovers from it since he cannot articulate his experience nor can he integrate back into so-called civilization.

Blackwood generates tension in *The Centaur* mainly through its complex case study structure, particularly through the dialectic between materialist explanation and mystical experience. Multiple observers investigate several cases. The frame narrator, an ordinary office worker, pieces together his mystical friend O'Malley's experience, by "observing [O'Malley's] creative imagination actually at work" (49). This narrator serves to diffuse our disbelief and condition our responses, in his distinguishing the "literal" facts of O'Malley's adventure, for instance (228). O'Malley, too, observes his fellow travellers on ship, the Russian and his son, and is intrigued by their mysterious case, as is O'Malley's friend, Dr. Stahl, the ship's physician: "there *was* this competition on the part of the two friends to solve [the case], from opposing motives" (34). Furthermore, O'Malley closely observes the Doctor, speculating about the ambiguities in his personality and questioning him about experiences that parallel his own (104). Nevertheless, the principal psychic investigator is Dr. Heinrich Stahl, a more complex version of Dr. John Silence. He very deliberately places O'Malley under his microscope (56)[13] in order "to observe [O'Malley] – your psychical being – under the stress of certain temptations," namely his contact with the Russian, an *urmensch*, who has also numbered among Stahl's many case studies, while he worked at "the German equivalent for the Saltpêtrière" (58).

Stahl possesses a "mind of opposite type" (74) to the mystic O'Malley, and throughout the novel they clash, as when O'Malley accuses Stahl, saying "If you had your way you'd take away my beliefs and put in their place some wretched little formula of science that the next generation will prove all wrong again" (100). Ultimately they are viewed as "two eternally antagonistic types that will exist as long as life itself" (329). Nevertheless, Stahl is portrayed as a divided and contradictory figure, a "scientific mystic" (165). On the one hand, he seems degenerate, or at least decadent, being described as "[b]ald-headed, slovenly, prematurely old, his beard stained with tobacco and snuff, undersized" (27) and as a poet (70). The insinuation is that he has been corrupted by civilization; he is "thick-coated with the civilization whence he came" (293). On the other hand, he emerges as advanced and intuitive about his subject, "meeting the great dream halfway" (314), a confessor figure who proposes a talking cure for O'Malley (286, 308) and who keeps a "half-paternal, half-professional" attendance over the Irishman (139). Most significantly, it emerges that Stahl is nothing like an objective scientist since he too had come under the influence of the Russian while treating him, to the extent that Stahl craved leaving his body to merge with the earth, a threatening experience he reduces to the medical label of "suicidal

[13] This trope appears throughout the novel: cf. 58, 63, 187.

mania" (319). O'Malley has earlier speculated that there must be mysteries associated with Stahl's past, that Stahl might have had a visionary experience and that that might account for his having left the prestigious hospital and having become a lowly ship's doctor (104). His question, "Had this 'modern' man, after all, a flaming volcano of ancient and splendid belief in him, akin to what was in himself, yet ever fighting it?" turns out to be prescient (104). And yet, Stahl's eventual confession only raises more questions, as O'Malley recognizes: "the confession had not been complete, he felt. Much had been held back" (327).

The mysteries of Stahl's past and his motivation constitute just one set of a series of mysteries raised and left open-ended. The Russian's boy collapses on the ship's deck, the "scientific verdict" being syncope (160), and yet just prior to this O'Malley observes the lad's spirit leaping from the deck crying "Chiron!" and pawing the air like a swimming animal (158). When the Russian himself similarly mysteriously disappears once the ship reaches the port of Batoum, "O'Malley knew that to search for his friend by the methods of the ordinary detective were useless" (180). The most significant mystery involves the nature of O'Malley's experience upon reaching "the first Garden" in the Central Caucasus (255). That the experience cannot be explained is anticipated when we are told that "Since the beginning of the world such transcendental experiences had never been translatable in the language of 'common' sense," and that not only was there a "gaping hiatus" in O'Malley's written account, but also that his account spoken to the narrator consisted of "fragments" (174, 175, 235).

Despite this, the mystical experience, the haunting such as it is, appears to be a positive, ecstatic experience for O'Malley: "He had found the heart of the Earth, his mother. Self-realization in the perfect union with Nature was fulfilled. He knew the Great At-one-ment" (263). During it, he hears the exquisite piping of Pan, and the Russian appears along with cosmic beings that take the shape of centaurs, the "Lapithae"; O'Malley becomes one, flying along with them "upon all fours" (258). Even though centaurs have a nasty reputation in mythology, here they are described as "living, splendid creatures" (255). Nevertheless, foreboding about them has been planted earlier in the novel by the Russian, who claimed that "To see them is to die" (190). When Stahl supplies the evidence that the Russian died on June 15th, the day, O'Malley realizes, "I saw him come to me from the trees – the day we started off together to the Garden" (296), the mystery is not solved but rather re-cast as "a spiritual adventure to the last," or what the psychical researchers would call a crisis apparition.

Throughout the novel the mystical paradox has been expressed that loss of Self is a necessary precondition to know the Divine, "that the personal self must be merged in a larger one to know peace" (176, cf. 239 also), and yet in the aftermath of O'Malley's experience Stahl argues, from his own personal experience, that this sense of expanded consciousness represents "a beginning of unbalance that might end in insanity, the thin wedge of a dissociation of the personality" (318). O'Malley rejects this explanation, remaining "to the last convinced that death would merge him in the being of the Earth's consciousness" (336). Though the narrator presents as misguided and a tragedy O'Malley's attempts to communicate his mystical experience of the Simple Life to men "occupied by the machine-made gods of civilization" (336), O'Malley's fate remains open-ended. He does suffer "a deep and poignant sense of loss" (285) upon returning to modern life and gradually sinks into illness. The official diagnosis by yet another doctor is that O'Malley is dying "[f]rom lack of living pure and simple," that it is a case of nostalgia, or as we might say today post-traumatic stress disorder (340). Nevertheless, when a blind beggar appears and plays the pipe outside O'Malley's window, he is entranced; the narrator witnesses something "rushing past" him from the window, and then two large and spreading figures vanishing into the fog (347), an event replicating to a degree the departure of the Russian boy's spirit. Here, at the novel's denouement, the suggestion is that Pan has come to collect his fellow *Urmensch*; O'Malley's body is left behind, lifeless. And yet, just before introducing this final episode, the narrator suggests that in his delusion O'Malley "made the outer world confirm some imagined detail of his inner dream" (345). Has O'Malley finally lost his sanity, or gained the freedom to participate in his visionary world? The mystery of O'Malley's vision and of his demise remains unresolved as, of course, does the metaphysical mystery, of whether spirit exists and whether it can depart the body and persist in another realm. Interestingly, the psychic detective, Stahl, disappears from the novel before its conclusion, perhaps signifying that his medical explanation can only go so far, that his observation of O'Malley is only useful up to a point, though Stahl does accurately predict that "the world is not yet ready to listen" to O'Malley (331).

O'Malley's experience on returning to the modern world does imply yet another mysterious death, that of Mother Earth to "an age of machinery, physical luxury, and superficial contrivances" (285). O'Malley's encounter with an American on the returning ship underlines this: "Scenery for him was evidently a commercial commodity, or it was nothing. It was the most up-to-date nation in the world that spoke – in the van of civilization – representing the last word in progress due to triumph over Nature" (300). O'Malley, as a most unconventional psychic detective himself, comes to realize that the mystery of this death cannot be solved "from the outside" (336) by proselytizing, but that "To reach their hearts, the new ideas must rise up from within. I see the truer way. I must do it *from the other side*. It must come to them in Beauty" (336).

This large mystery, this tragedy, gives *The Centaur*, Blackwood's most metaphysical exercise in psychical detection, perhaps its greatest relevance to a contemporary audience, as an early environmental fable; it is unfortunate that Blackwood himself felt compelled to proselytize about the mystical vision, to provide so much evidence that it could occur in reality, instead of showing it unfolding with the eloquence which he demonstrates during O'Malley's actual out-of-body experience. That technique would have aligned him even more closely with his contemporary modernists, yet he must have felt some didacticism necessary because of the unusual terrain he traversed – his blending of mystical odyssey, psychic mystery and psychological case study. With *The Centaur* Blackwood clearly elaborated on psychical research case studies and on his earlier tales of psychic detection, extending the form to its imaginative limits.

**Works Cited**

Ashley, Mike. *Algernon Blackwood: A Bio-Bibliography*. New York: Greenwood, 1987.

___. *Starlight Man: The Extraordinary Life of Algernon Blackwood*. London: Constable, 2001.

Alvarado, Carlos S. "On the Centenary of Frederic W. H. Myers's *Human Personality and Its Survival of Bodily Death*." *The Journal of Parapsychology* 68 (Spring 2004): 3-43.

Belloc, Hilaire. Rev. of *John Silence, Physician Extraordinary*. *The Morning Post* 17 Sept. 1908: 2. Rpt. in Jones, Stephen and Kim Newman, ed. *Horror: One Hundred Best Books*. New York: Carroll and Graf, 1988. 67-68.

Blackwood, Algernon. "Ancient Sorceries." *Complete John Silence* 44-83.

___. *The Centaur*. London: Macmillan, 1911.

___. *The Complete John Silence Stories*. Ed. and introd. S. T. Joshi. New York: Dover, 1997.

___. "The Empty House." *The Empty House and Other Ghost Stories*. 1906. London: John Baker, 1964. 1-31.

___. *Episodes Before Thirty*. London: Cassell, 1923. Revised ed., London: Peter Nevill, 1950.

___. "Keeping His Promise." *The Empty House and Other Ghost Stories*. 1906. London: John Baker, 1964. 91-118.

___. "May Day Eve." 1907. *The Insanity of Jones and Other Tales*. Harmondsworth: Penguin, 1966. 166-88.

___. "Smith: An Episode in a Lodging House." *The Empty House and Other Ghost Stories*. 1906. London: John Baker, 1964. 186-217.

___. "A Psychic Invasion." *Complete John Silence* 1-43.

___. "With Intent to Steal." *The Empty House and Other Ghost Stories*. 1906. London: John Baker, 1964. 119-60.

___. "The Woman's Ghost Story." 1907. *The Insanity of Jones and Other Tales*. Harmondsworth: Penguin, 1966. 65-74.

Bleiler, E. F. Introduction. *Best Ghost Stories of Algernon Blackwood*. New York: Dover, 1973. v-x.

Gabusi, Valentina. "The Mirroring Frame: Narrative Device and Reflected Victorianism in *In a Glass Darkly*." *Le Fanu Studies* 3.2 (Nov. 2008). 16 Jan. 2014 <http://www.lefanustudies.com/mirroring.html>.

James, Henry. *The Art of the Novel: Critical Prefaces*. New York: Charles Scribner's, 1934.

Johnson, George M. *Dynamic Psychology in Modernist British Fiction*. Houndmills: Palgrave Macmillan, 2006.

Keating, Peter. *The Haunted Study: A Social History of the English Novel 1875-1914*. London: Secker and Warburg, 1989.

Kunitz, Stanley J., and Howard Haycraft, eds. "Algernon Blackwood." *Twentieth Century Authors: A Biographical Dictionary of Modern Literature*. New York: Wilson, 1942.

Le Fanu, Joseph Sheridan. *Best Ghost Stories of J. S. Le Fanu*. Ed. and introd. E. F. Bleiler. New York: Dover, 1964.

Myers, Frederic W. H. *Human Personality and Its Survival of Bodily Death*. 2 vols. New York: Longmans, Green, 1903.

___. "The Subliminal Consciousness. Chapter 1. General Characteristics of Subliminal Messages." *Proceedings of the Society for Psychical Research* 7 (1892): 298-327.

Penzoldt, Peter. "Algernon Blackwood." *The Supernatural in Fiction*. London: Peter Nevill, 1952. 228-53.

Sullivan, Jack. *Elegant Nightmares. The English Ghost Story from Le Fanu to Blackwood.* Athens, Ohio: Ohio University Press, 1978.

Woolf, Virginia. "Across the Border." *The Essays of Virginia Woolf 1912-1918*. Vol. 2. Ed. Andrew McNeillie. London: Hogarth, 1987. 218-19.

___. "Modern Novels." *The Essays of Virginia Woolf 1919-1924*. Vol. 3. Ed. Andrew McNeillie. London: Hogarth, 1988. 30-37.

___. "Modern Novels." *The Essays of Virginia Woolf 1919-1924*. Vol. 3. Ed. Andrew McNeillie. London: Hogarth, 1988. 30-37.

# Devolved Forms: Aesthetic Solutions to the Contentious Style of Arthur Machen's "The Great God Pan"

Paul Fox
East Georgia College

**Abstract:** Arthur Machen's novel "The Great God Pan" has been critically questioned due to its perceived structural incoherency and its lack of individuated characters. Rather than a confused detective novel, I believe Machen's story to be a deliberate representation of the dominant aesthetic values of the Victorian *fin de siècle*, patterned purposefully by the author to compose in narrative form a particular impression of reality.

> ET DIABOLUS INCARNATUS EST. ET HOMO FACTUS EST.[1]
> – Arthur Machen, "The Great God Pan"

Arthur Machen's "The Great God Pan" was first published by the Bodley Head press as part of its Keynote series in December of 1894 and was such a popular success that a second edition was quickly printed and distributed in February of the following year. The text's critical reception was mixed, but the novel was certainly not ignored as had been several of Machen's earlier works. The reaction of the journals and newspapers made a name for both the author and his story, many of the reviews adding to the interest the public was already showing in the novel. Oscar Wilde and several of the leading figures of the Decadent movement in literature praised the book. John Lane's Bodley Head press was infamous for publishing the more scandalous sort of literature, texts from which other houses would shy away, and Lane's decision to

[1] "And the Devil was made flesh. And he was made man."

publish Machen's story certainly played a large role in the subsequent popularity of both the press' Keynote series and Machen himself.

"The Great God Pan" is divided into eight sections, the first of which, "The Experiment," had been published in 1890 as a short piece in the journal *The Whirlwind.* This episode describes the visit of a Mr. Clarke to his friend Dr. Raymond's house where a scientific experiment occurs. Raymond operates on his adopted daughter Mary's brain to allow her to see the reality of existence behind the material world, what he says the Ancients referred to as "seeing the god Pan" (2). The experiment has only the briefest moment of success as Mary wakes from unconsciousness with a look of ecstasy on her face. But this look is quickly replaced by one of horror, and on Mr. Clarke's departure she has become an idiot.

After this initial episode the narrative jumps ahead in time, and describes various and seemingly unconnected incidents and characters until the story's conclusion. The final section of "The Great God Pan" is entitled "The Fragments" and this title could easily be taken as a critical description of the structure of the entire story. Machen's narrative traces the various incidents and tales told by a number of gentlemen, which, only at the conclusion of the text, are shown to be connected and are revealed to be the singular history of the life of a Miss Helen Vaughan. Several of the gentlemen characters, if one can call them such as they are scarcely differentiated in terms of their characters and personalities, are in search of Helen and her past. A spate of mysterious suicides among the upper-class men of London becomes the final spur to identifying Helen as the instigator of these deaths, although the manner in which she does so is never described by Machen. She is discovered to have travelled from the countryside of Wales where she grew up, married into a good society family, escaped to South America with the family's money, returned to England under the name of Mrs. Beaumont, and she has left a trail of deaths in her wake. The individuals who become amateur sleuths in the story do not really know what they are looking for, are unsure even if a crime has been committed. All they are sure of is that there is an intriguing story to be uncovered. The impetus to discover this narrative is for them, in truth, largely an aesthetic one, and even the epidemic of suicides in London adds only a more intriguing nuance to the tale for several of the detectives.

The character who appears most often in the story is a Mr. Villiers, but even at the conclusion he is not in possession of the entire history of Helen Vaughan and her various aliases. Villiers, along with Clarke who had witnessed the experiment that initiated the tale, finally confronts Helen and offers her the choice of hanging herself (Villiers brings with him the finest hempen rope which he has purchased for just this eventuality) or being arrested. Helen chooses the former option and in a horrific series of metamorphoses devolves through various stages to protoplasmic jelly, then reascends the evolutionary ladder before finally expiring. Clarke and Raymond share a brief correspondence at the conclusion of the story that reveals that Helen was in fact the child of Mary, born nine months after the latter "saw Pan."

The fantastic nature of Machen's story certainly was one of the prime reasons for its sensational reception. And "The Great God Pan" has retained its popularity over the last century to a great extent. It is printed in virtually all collections of later Victorian Gothic fiction, and often finds itself critically mentioned alongside the more famous texts of the *fin de siècle*. The story of Helen Vaughan, the mysterious rash of suicidal mania among London's society gentlemen, and the laborious amateur detective work of a number of inquiring individuals, was popular enough, as the critic Kirsten Macleod details, to spawn "numerous parodies" (52). But despite the enthusiasm for the story readily shown by these imitators and in the cash-box of the Bodley Head, the text had been attacked from its publication, and continues to be critically questioned today, for a number of stylistic and structural reasons.

One of the initial problems that critics cited with the story was its relationship to audience expectation. "The Great God Pan" was conceived by its author, and appreciated by many critics, as a romance in the line of Robert Louis Stevenson's extraordinarily popular tales. Stevensonian romance enjoyed a huge readership among the young, and while the generic appeal of Machen's story suggested that the same audience would find his tale enthralling, the subject matter was in no way suitable for non-adults. Macleod states that "[f]or these critics, the treatment of advanced subject matter in a popular form represented a disturbing disruption of genre conventions that constituted in their minds a Decadent text" (123-24). An unconventional story was one thing to critics, but the intrusion of adult themes into the genre most appealing to the young, was something that many of them found utterly unacceptable. The identification of Machen with the Decadent movement did not help his cause. Just how much he owed to the broad interest and popularity in Decadence was evident when his story *The Three Imposters*, published by John Lane as part of the Keynote series in 1895, received scant notice from the critics. Earlier that year Oscar Wilde had been imprisoned and Wilde's downfall immediately caused a critical and popular decease for any author or artist associated with the Decadent movement. Machen, along with various critics of his work, certainly blamed the failure of *The Three Imposters* on the timing of its release (Gekle 74).

If the style of "The Great God Pan" was a problem of genre for its contemporary critics, it is critically questioned today in terms of technique and structure. The critic Mark Valentine in his biography of Machen summarizes what he deems to be the story's major flaws when he writes that

> it has two technical weaknesses that can deter a casual reader. It is structured as a set of separate episodes which ultimately are seen to interlock and inform one another, but until this connection becomes clear there is an impression of fragmentation, of lack of focus. And it describes the activities of various gentlemen who each play some part in the story but do not have distinctive characters, so it is possible to become confused by the role of each. (25)

S. T. Joshi puts it rather more succinctly when he writes that the story is "extremely clumsy in construction" (22). The devolution of the story's whole into seemingly unconnected parts and the collapse of characters' identities into virtually undifferentiated voices have been the two concerns to which critics have returned again and again. Obviously in a narrative of detection a reader expects the presentation of a crime to be solved and the logical advance toward that solution. At the conclusion of the story any unanswered questions in the detective's methodological process are resolved. The presentation of individuated characters is a primary concern for authors of the detective genre as criminal motivation is a based in characters' histories.

Machen would seem to have contravened the fundamental tenets of the genre in his narration of Helen Vaughan's story. No one detective in "The Great God Pan" possesses the entire catalogue of details that is presented to the reader in the course of the story.

Many aspects of the more horrific episodes are left implied and unspecified, just as conversations are broken off at the moment some detail seems about to be revealed. This is the stylistic ploy most remarked upon by contemporary critics. Kelly Hurley is representative of this viewpoint when she writes that "rhetorical obfuscation, this refusal to name, finds its parallel in a variety of narrative strategies which serve to disrupt the smooth transmission of the story" (14). Robert Mighall sees Machen's narrative lacunae paralleled in the conversations of his characters when he says that "Helen Vaughan is represented largely through the effect she has on others, an effect which is registered by their inability to describe her" (200-01). Kirsten Macleod even sees Machen's style as being an authorial flirtation with his audience, stating that the author "teased his readership with omissions and gaps, checking himself, and failing to deliver just when the narrative seems about to offer up salacious details" (126). Perhaps the most obvious example of the "refusal to name" and the narrative "omissions" is evident when we realize that the horrific crimes committed by Helen are never actually revealed, only their results.

I would suggest that the solution to the questions raised by Machen's style and the structure of "The Great God Pan" can be resolved by examining the author's aesthetic, an aesthetic upon which Machen had deliberated, and employed quite purposefully in the patterning of his text. It was a view of art similar to that of his Decadent contemporaries, one developed from the work of Walter Pater, specifically Pater's extraordinarily influential *The Renaissance: Studies in Art and Poetry*, first published in 1873 as *Studies in the History of the Renaissance*. In the "Conclusion" to these studies, Pater presented his readers with a dynamic view of existence and the artistic manner in which the fleeting nature of one's experience could be ordered. Concerning life, the aesthete should

> [f]ix upon it in one of its more exquisite intervals, the moment, for instance, of delicious recoil from the flood of water in the summer heat. What is the whole physical life in that moment but a combination of natural elements to which science gives their names? [. . .] Our physical life is a perpetual motion of them. [. . .] This at least of flame-like our life has, that it is but the concurrence, renewed from moment to moment, of forces parting sooner or later on their ways. (150)

This view of existence as constituted moment by moment through a dynamic motion of forces is one rearticulated by Dr. Raymond in the opening section of "The Great God Pan." In attempting to explain to Clarke the ontological reality behind the veil of the material world, Raymond says that he first understood things when "the great truth burst upon me, and I saw, mapped out in lines of light, a whole world, a sphere unknown" (3). This confluence of dynamic influences into a moment's realization explains not only Raymond's sudden recognition, but what is recognized: the nature of reality itself. It is one made up, as Pater had written, "of forces parting sooner or later on their ways (150). Accepting that it is virtually impossible to describe his discovery in literal terms, Raymond goes on to employ the metaphor of electric wires transmitting currents from one location to another across the country in split seconds. He continues his explanation saying:

> Suppose that an electrician of today were suddenly to perceive that he and his friends have merely been playing with pebbles and mistaking them for the foundations of

> the world; suppose that such a man saw uttermost space lie open before the current [. . .]. As analogies go, that is a pretty good analogy for what I have done. (3)

Existence then is composed of energies coming together momentarily and separating once more in their continual motion. To make sense of this chaotic flux Pater had suggested that one must "fix upon" the moment (150). It is only in this artfully, and artificially, fixed moment that life's flow can be comprehended. Without the ordering power of art, existence is a chaos of fleeting impressions. What Peter Dale writes of Pater's aesthetic, I would suggest, holds equally for Machen's own: "art strives to express in as pure a way possible that inherent formalizing tendency of mind, to exhibit nakedly the structure by which the mind in the act of perception holds the manifold of phenomena together" (223). Machen's fragmented narrative is a succession of moments that only make sense when seen as a composite whole. "The Great God Pan" portrays, in literary form, Pater's aesthetic, both the fragmentation of existence into distinct moments and the impression one receives of their relationship, one which occurs for the reader only in the final narrative moment of the text. It is the reader, unlike Machen's characters each of whom owns only a part of the history of Helen Vaughan, who composes the text into a meaningful and ordered whole. For Machen, then, the ultimate detectives are not his gentlemen amateurs, but the readers themselves.

In the slight regard for individuated characterization in the portrayal of Messrs. Villiers, Clarke, Austin, Drs. Phillips and Matheson, Machen also reveals the influence of the Paterian aesthetic, albeit inflected by Oscar Wilde's own unique interpretation of it in his sole novel, *The Picture of Dorian Gray*. Pater had written in the "Conclusion" to *The Renaissance: Studies in Art and Poetry* that it is "with the passage and dissolution of impressions, images, sensations, that analysis leaves off – that continual vanishing away, that strange, perpetual, weaving and unweaving of ourselves" (152). In other words, Pater states that the dynamic forces of the external world are equally apparent in the individual. In Wilde's novel Dorian considers the

> shallow psychology of those who conceive the Ego of man as a thing simple, reliable and of one essence. To him, man was a being of myriad lives and myriad sensations, a complex multiform creature that bore within itself strange legacies of thought and passion. (107)

For both Pater and Wilde then, man is himself composed of forces which alter in their combination each moment, weave and unweave the individual. Pater makes it clear that these forces which constitute each man momentarily extend beyond him into the external world (150). For Machen, the mystery of Helen Vaughan is the external dynamic which composes his characters, and each appears similar to the other because the same narrative and existential forces have merged at that moment to give each his identity. Each episode is a moment in narrative time, one in which Machen artificially "fixes" the characters of his detectives so that they might be comprehended by the reader. For it is precisely Helen's crime that she is, like Dorian's conception of man, living a life which is "multiform" and that bears in it "strange legacies," those of the ancient and barbaric rites of her father Pan. Machen's characters may appear dully undifferentiated in contrast to Helen Vaughan, but it is because art must render identity in the artifice of Pater's "fixed" moment. The men regard themselves as individuals, no matter if they are simply a "fixed" type of London society. To do otherwise, to live as Helen does in the flux of existence, is to give oneself up to chaos. Each of Machen's gentlemen detectives relies on his sense of self to understand Helen's history, and Machen's naming of each man as an individual contrasts with their own difficulty in ascribing identity to Helen who has gone under so many aliases.

The full horror of the reality of existence is revealed at Helen's end. A Dr. Matheson has been brought along by Villiers and Clarke to record her final moments, and he describes them thus:

> The skin, and the flesh, and the muscles, and the bones, and the firm structure of the human body that I had thought to be unchangeable, and permanent as adamant, began to melt and dissolve. [. . .] For here was some internal force, of which I knew nothing, that caused dissolution and change. [. . .] I saw the form waver from sex to sex, dividing itself from itself, and then again reunited. Then I saw the body descend to the beasts whence it ascended, and that which was on the heights go to the depths, even to the abyss of all being. [. . .] I saw a Form, shaped in dimness before me, which I will not farther describe. (46)

What Matheson witnesses echoes an experience of Clarke's earlier in the text. Affected by the anaesthetic fumes used by Dr. Raymond prior to the operation on Mary, Clarke seems to remember a childhood experience in the woods when "for a moment of time he stood face to face there with a presence, that was neither man nor beast, neither the living nor the dead, but all things mingled, the form of all things but devoid of all form" (6).

These are fine examples of how Machen and his characters refuse to accommodate the reader with a full description of what is witnessed in the story. Matheson's recounting of Helen's dissolution is by far the most detailed of any of the horrors narrated in the text. And Clarke's description of "the form of all things but devoid of form" might operate as a signature to the aesthetic intentions of Machen himself. He sought to present a story that described the indescribable, that portrayed what, because of its fleeting existence, could not be truly represented without aesthetic falsification. In structuring the stories as a succession of fragments Machen portrayed the chaotic nature of existence, personified in the character of Helen, and avoided attempting to linguistically describe what is impossible to contain in language. It is in the disintegration of a unified narrative that we see Pan truly represented, not in the horrified silences, insinuations and implied crimes of Helen. At the end of the story the aesthetic power to make sense of chaos is afforded the reader who finally holds all the narrative fragments of the story at one and the same time. Susan Navarette writes that

> [t]he omissions and ellipses of Machen's story disclose an essentially decompositive strategy, betraying language's constitutional vulnerability to the entropic forces that surround and beset it as they simultaneously induce the emotional and intellectual short-circuits in which reason gives way to elemental emotions – to fear, anxiety, and shame. Though we suffer an emblematic death in those spaces, however, we are productive in them as well, for we must become the cocreators of an evolving horror that, in blasting speech, renders speechlessness expressive. (201)

It is true that the structure of the story reflects the chaos of reality in the dissolution of Helen Vaughan, but language is not "vulnerable" in the face of this chaos. Language pertains to a completely different plane of existence, one which artificially "fixes" things and operates under the aesthetic illusion that meaning is static, objective and "real." Machen's gentlemen detectives are named, separated from each other by language, while the reality of their characters is one which sees little differentiation in the totality of the text. Art and language hide the horrible reality of undifferentiated chaos. That horror does not "blast" speech in the sense that Navarette suggests, rather speech is incapable of fully communicating the lack of fixity that constitutes the horror of unveiled existence itself. It can go so far, and no further. The reader in the text, as I have suggested, becomes a creator along with the author, but not of the unspeakable, rather of the means of containing the unspoken at the conclusion of the tale. As Hurley remarks of the variety of letters, diaries, notes and drawings that are viewed by Machen's characters, "There's a compulsion to represent, as the almost obsessive proliferation of interpolated manuscripts indicates, but at the same time the novel abjures utterance" (48). What is unspoken, however, is woven deliberately, and becomes the fundamental structure of the story itself, one to be uncovered in the act of reading.

The reader in their detection of the correspondences between fragments can create the meaning of Machen's text only with the concluding "fragment" of the final section. Navarette suggests that when "the text falters, we falter as well and are drawn into its decline" (199). My reading of "The Great God Pan" is one where the text is not a faltering one, but where lacunae are deliberately placed by the author, where language does not "falter" but can only accept the impossibility of speaking the unspeakable. It is in the *pattern* of the text that the reader uncovers Machen's depiction of chaotic dissolution, and it is a pattern to which only the reader has full access. In contrast to being passively drawn into a textual "decline," I would suggest that Machen's audience is actively engaged by the author in creating the solution to the horrible questions raised by the life and death of Helen Vaughan.

Identity's dissolution in the chaotic flow of reality is the true crime in "The Great God Pan". Matheson's description of Helen's death throes, her passing up and down the ladder of evolution, is horrific specifically because it shows the absolute fluidity of identity and existence. Machen makes a mockery of science in his story, rubbing salt into the wounds of the empiricist by having a scientist speak the words which make a nonsense of the belief in the permanence of the body and its physical structure. Matheson, like so many other gentlemen who have become involved with Helen Vaughan, will die an early death, in his case from apoplexy. The shock of witnessing evidence of the chaos that informs life is too much for the constitution of any individual, indeed it undermines a belief in that constitution itself.

In naming Helen, in uncovering her history, the detectives are able to momentarily give her an identity, to "fix" her in the broader narratives with which they have become involved. Her connection to deaths in the countryside of her childhood is revealed; her part in the death of her husband is uncovered; her role in the early demise of an artist travelling in South America is connected to the other discoveries; and Mrs. Beaumont is finally believed to be the same woman going under a different alias, the woman who seems to lie at the heart of the suicidal mania that is gripping the city. Her ultimate identity, the offspring of the idiot Mary and her having "seen the god Pan," is stated in the final words of the text. Behind all the events wherein Helen has wrought some destruction in the everyday lives of individuals is her father. At several points in the story someone mentions her "playmates," presumably the satyrs of Pan's party.

It is, and has been, a critical compulsion to reveal the actual events that cause the deaths and madness of individuals who have fallen in with Helen. The shock of the reviewers, those who saw a corruption of Stevensonian romance in Machen's text, was based in a belief that illicit couplings took place throughout the novel, the ancient rites and revels of Pan. However, the text itself never actually states that such a thing takes place in Helen's story. We don't know exactly how Mary was impregnated; we are just told she bore a daughter nine months after the failed experiment. The gentlemen who commit suicide leave no notes explaining why they do so, but they are known to have been in Mrs. Beaumont's company the evenings before they took their own lives. The child who witnesses Helen in the woods "playing with a 'strange naked man'" (11) is unable to give any more detailed descriptions about the type of sport being enjoyed. But it has been an almost critical constant that the activities of Helen are sexual in nature.

There is one instance where a more explicit suggestion of sexual acts occurs, and almost on the closing page of the story. It is one of the final fragments of the tale, one in which Clarke is writing to Dr. Raymond and describing his visit to the countryside where Helen grew up. Clarke is visiting the scenes of the earliest, strange events in Helen's life, at least those that have come to his notice. He examines a small pillar at a museum, a Roman artefact that has recently been unearthed from the woodland where Helen is first thought to have indulged in introducing a friend to her father in some orgiastic ritual. On the pillar is an inscription that the curator tells Clarke suggests a rite which is a mystery to scholars. The Latin text on the pillar is worn and Clarke must construe what is missing. The text is given as

DEVOMNODENT*i*
FLA*v*IVSSENILISPOSSV*it*
PROPTERNVP*tias*
*qua*SVIDITSVBVMB*ra*

> "To the great god Nodens (the god of the Great Deep or Abyss), Flavius Senilis has erected this pillar on account of the marriage which he saw beneath the shade." (49)

Once more the lacunae of the text must be filled in by a reader, although in this instance it is Clarke who takes on that responsibility. It is as if, at the story's conclusion, Machen is giving the reader one last signpost to what has been his textual intention and his expectation that his audience become the detectors of Helen's crime. The meaning of the marriage witnessed by Flavius Senilis is presumed by Clarke, and has been equally accepted by most critics, to be a rite similar in kind to those which Helen introduced her friends, her husband, and the society guests she received as Mrs. Beaumont in London.

Certainly the rites of Pan are fundamental to any reading of Helen's story, but to reduce "Pan" to any one thing is both a linguistic, and in Machen's story, an ontological, crime. Pan is "everything" and in the text Machen makes it clear that the figure of Pan informs not only the narrative, but the structure of his narrative, his characterization of the detectives, the dissolution of Helen Vaughan, and the reality of existence expressed in allegorical form by Dr. Raymond in the opening section of the text. Robert Mighall is one of the few critics who appreciate the rhetorical structure of Machen's text and the fact that to suppress it in favor of psychosexual readings is to demean the entire purpose of the author's craft. He writes that

> [u]ltimately there is no sexual secret at the heart of Machen's text. It cannot be named because it doesn't exist. At the heart of the text stands *The Great God Pan*. There is no secret at all, for all (Pan) is the secret. The book is a "Chinese puzzle" with no centre. For critics to search for a truth that is "clearly sexual" merely shows how effectively Machen [. . .] deployed the trope of the ineffable. (207)

Mighall's metaphor of the "Chinese puzzle" refers to an early section in "The Great God Pan" where one of the gentlemen suggests that the strange story of Helen's husband he has just heard is only the beginning of stranger tales to come: like a "nest of Chinese boxes; you open one after another and find a quainter workmanship in every box" (17). Mighall rightly assesses the basis of the text to be Pan, or "all." When Hurley writes that "'The Great God Pan' [. . .] is a 'presence' impinging upon human realities, but not explicable within human symbolic systems" (13) she dramatically underestimates the relationship of Pan to reality. Human reality *is* Pan, not one which Pan "impinges" upon, and it cannot be fully expressed in language precisely because it is never static; it is the ultimate *pan-daemonium*. The marriage witnessed by Flavius Senilis is the collapsing of form into chaos, the agglomeration of "all things mingled" as Clarke described it in the opening section of Machen's story (6). The rites enacted by Helen and those witnessed by Flavius Senilis are only vaguely suggestive of what this chaos is, for language cannot represent it, only the aesthetic patterning of fragments and rhetorical lacunae that Machen creates in his story.

Villiers comes closest to expressing what Machen patterns in his text, to speaking the unspeakable. In doing so, Villiers also appreciates the impossibility of language describing what he has come to understand existence to really be. Speaking to Austin he says:

> We know what happened to those who chanced to meet "The Great God Pan", and those who are wise know that all symbols are symbols of something, not of nothing. It was, indeed, an exquisite symbol beneath which men long ago veiled their knowledge of the most awful, most secret forces which lie at the heart of all things; forces before which the souls of men must wither and die and blacken, as their bodies blacken under the electric current. Such forces cannot be named, cannot be spoken, cannot be imagined except under a veil and a symbol, a symbol to the most of us appearing a quaint, poetic fancy, to some a foolish tale. But you and I, at all events, have known something of the terror that may dwell in the secret place of life, manifested under human flesh; that which is without form taking to itself a form. (43)

The "exquisite symbol" which veils the horrible forces constituting reality is, for Machen, art. His deployment of a structure of fragments to construct his novel depicts, in symbolic form, the structure of reality itself. Since language cannot express the dynamic chaos of reality, only a broader linguistic pattern can. The formless takes form repeatedly, as Dorian Gray had realized, as Pater had formulated in his "Conclusion" to his Renaissance studies. Art is the veil that makes life livable, which allows for the negotiation of chaotic existence. Beneath the surface of all things, including every human, is the reality of the god Pan. And if Pan is the underlying reality of everything in existence, then Machen is portraying existence itself as criminal. Every character partakes in the crime, everyone is party to the chaotic confusion that Helen reveals in her death throes. Her ascent up the evolutionary ladder from the depths of the devolved forms to which she sank make it clear that, to Machen, the Liberal belief in inexorable progress was a sham, that reality was a great deal more chaotic than science wished to believe. The only means to surviving the disintegrating forces of reality is, for Machen, an aesthetic one. The gentlemen detectives of "The Great God Pan" finally triumph and destroy Helen because they succeed in fixing her identity, in connecting the various episodes of her life into a narrative whole. If none of them really have the full story, they have all, at least, constructed a history of Helen which operates as a complete narrative.

Machen's audience must follow the same process through which the author's detectives have "fixed" Helen's story. Like Villiers in his investigation of Mrs. Beaumont, the readers must "cast out a good many lines" (40), in other words be sensitive and receptive, in a Paterian sense, to the influences and impressions that exist in the text. In doing so, they capture the truth of Machen's impressions, an understanding of what is at stake if their reading goes awry, and their own part in the tale of the crime which Helen represents. For a reader to give in to the temptation to shirk what is for Machen an aesthetic responsibility is to be swept along into the chaos which is "The Great God Pan". To construct meaning of the numerous fragments of life narrated by the various characters is to aesthetically fix chaos, to understand Helen, and to keep Pan in his artfully rendered Chinese box.

## Works Cited

Dale, Peter Allan. *The Victorian Critic and the Idea of History.* 1977. Cambridge, Massachusetts: Harvard UP, 1979.

Gekle, William Francis. *Arthur Machen: Weaver of Fantasy*. Millbrook, New York: Round Table, 1949.

Hurley, Kelly. *The Gothic Body: Sexuality, Materialism and Degeneration at the* Fin de Siècle. Cambridge: Cambridge UP, 1996.

Joshi, S. T., ed. *The Three Imposters and Other Stories*. By Arthur Machen. Hayward, CA: Chaosium, 2000. Vol. 1 of *The Best Weird Tales of Arthur Machen*.

___. *The Weird Tale*. Holicong, Pennsylvania: Wildside, 2003.

Machen, Arthur. "The Great God Pan." Joshi 1-50.

___. *The Three Imposters*. Joshi 101-234.

Macleod, Kirsten. *Fictions of British Decadence: High Art, Popular Writing and the* Fin de Siècle. New York: Palgrave Macmillan, 2006.

Mighall, Robert. *A Geography of Victorian Gothic Fiction: Mapping History's Nightmares*. Oxford: Oxford UP, 1999.

Navarette, Susan J. *The Shape of Fear: Horror and the* Fin de Siècle *Culture of Decadence*. Lexington, Kentucky: UP of Kentucky, 1998.

Pater, Walter. *The Renaissance: Studies in Art and Poetry*. Ed. Adam Phillipps. Oxford: Oxford UP, 1986.

Valentine, Mark. *Arthur Machen*. Bridgend, Wales: Seren-Poetry Wales, 1995.

Wilde, Oscar. *The Picture of Dorian Gray. Collin's Complete Works of Oscar Wilde*. Centenary ed. Glasgow: Harper Collins, 1999. 17-159.

## Double Lives, Terrible Pleasures: Oscar Wilde and Crime Fiction in the *Fin de Siècle*

Nick Freeman
Loughborough University

**Abstract:** This essay examines the influence of Oscar Wilde on the crime fiction of the 1890s and 1900s. It argues that Wilde was important in two ways. He formulated in his fiction, drama, and epigrams a beguiling theory of the criminal as artist, one which was eagerly taken up by writers such as E. W. Hornung and Clifford Ashdown. However, he was also the focal point of wider anxieties about masculinity during the period, especially after the publication of *The Picture of Dorian Gray* (1890-1891) and his sentencing for Gross Indecency in May 1895.

After he has murdered Basil Hallward, the artist who sought to immortalise his beauty upon canvas, Dorian Gray does what any self-respecting decadent anti-hero would do: he attends a party. It is only "a small party, got up rather in a hurry" and his hostess is far from prepossessing. Nonetheless, Dorian makes an impressive entrance, "exquisitely dressed, and wearing a large buttonhole of Parma violets" (Wilde, *Picture* 127). Nobody realises that he has recently "passed through a tragedy as horrible as any tragedy of our age," and even he is astonished by his poise. The obscene juxtaposition of crime and high society gives him an exquisite thrill and "for a moment" he feels "keenly the terrible pleasure of a double life" (128).

Four years later, the terrible pleasures of Wilde's own double life were to be exposed to the public gaze in the most humiliating fashion. Wilde had seen his nights with London's male prostitutes as "feasting with panthers," but the jury at the Old Bailey saw only a squalid parade of intimidated or openly dishonest rent boys, panders, and go-betweens. The married playwright who composed piquant fairy tales for his two young sons emerged as a reckless and sordid hedonist given to frequenting houses of assignation, and to extravagant expenditure on food, wine, and silver cigarette cases.

Lord Henry Wotton, the suave amoralist who exercises so fatal an influence upon Dorian Gray, had hailed insincerity as "merely a method by which we can multiply our personalities" (*Picture* 107). In a London courtroom, insincerity resembled nothing so much as vulgar deceit. Wilde's plight was worsened further by his casual untruths about his age and the defence's exhumation of epigrams such as "If one tells the truth, one is sure, sooner or later, to be found out" ("Phrases" 1244). It was obvious that the man responsible for "The Decay of Lying" (1889) was not to be trusted. Wilde (mis)represented himself as a sentimental pedagogue, and Edward Carson delighted in exposing the inconsistencies of his position. It was one thing to quip that "[t]he well-bred contradict other people. The wise contradict themselves" ("Phrases" 1244), quite another to expect a late-Victorian lawyer to sympathise with such views. "Wilde was being forced to conduct his case within the framework of an externally imposed moral universe whose authority and value he utterly repudiated," writes Alison Hennegan:

> The key words – beauty, morality, art, goodness – which Carson hammers home time and again, menacingly, sneeringly, incredulously, mean utterly different things to the two men and, despite brilliant parries as dramatic as anything the London stage could offer, Wilde was slowly and relentlessly cornered in a setting where only Carson's reading of those words was permitted. (188)

A plank bed and prison gruel beckoned.

The late-Victorian cultural world Wilde inhabited was one that delighted in the maintenance of alternative identities. William Sharp was Fiona MacLeod, Henry Harland the acidic "Yellow Dwarf" of *The Yellow Book*. Arthur Symons was "Silhouette," the *Star*'s theatre reviewer. Mary Chavelita Dunn was the altogether more memorable George Egerton, Frances McFall was the scandalous Sarah Grand, Pearl Craigie the Catholic novelist John Oliver Hobbes. Swinburne assumed the unlikely guise of Mrs Horace Manners. As befits a man who put only his talent into his work and his genius into his life, Wilde disdained such tactics. His double life went far beyond a literary pseudonym, and its exposure was ultimately calamitous. Its revelation sent shock-waves through British society, but it was a revelation for which the reading public had been subliminally prepared for over thirty years, and one which Wilde himself had enjoyed hinting at in his fiction and society comedies. Fed by an inexhaustible public appetite for such tales, English sensation novels, and their off-shoot, detective stories, had exploited the narrative possibilities of duality since the 1860s, evoking a world of concealed, contested, and negotiated identities and the festering secrets that they masked. Victorian writers had quickly realised how the city, particularly the vast metropolis of London, was central to fiction of this type, and they excelled in exploiting it as the setting for narratives of disguise, duplication, and intrigue. From Wilkie Collins' *The Woman in White* (1859-1860) to Conan Doyle's "The Man with the Twisted Lip" (1891, collected 1892) and beyond, amateur investigators and consulting detectives sought to unravel tangled skeins of imposture, and restore an order in which things (and people) were as they seemed to be. Even novels which could never be classed as "sensational" in the Collins or Braddon sense showed themselves keenly attuned to the dramatic power of secrets, revelation, and concomitant social ruin: witness the downfall of eminent citizens such as Bulstrode in George Eliot's *Middlemarch* (1871-1872) or Michael Henchard in Thomas Hardy's *The Mayor of Casterbridge* (1886). Finally, Robert Louis Stevenson's *Strange Case of Dr Jekyll and Mr Hyde* (1886), whose title mimicked the truncated language of newspaper headlines, literalised the conceit of the double life by pitting its titular characters against one another in what was ultimately internecine warfare. The novella helped to enshrine the idea of the gentleman with "something to hide" in late Victorian fiction, and was an obvious influence on Wilde, not least in its depiction of an enclosed homosocial world. Wilde's protagonists, Dorian and Lord Henry, were wittier and more suave than Stevenson's, however, and their crimes were never made explicit, unlike Hyde's shocking murder of Sir Danvers Carew. As a result, their glamour and panache were untarnished by the reality of their offences.

A burgeoning popular press displayed a similar delight in stories where guilty secrets or dubious pasts caught up with apparently blameless citizens. Patrick Brantlinger, Richard Altick, and Thomas Boyle have demonstrated the complex symbiotic relationship between the sensation novel and sensational journalism, noting their similarities of form as well as content. Dramatic criminal investigations such as the exposure of the daring burglar Charles Peace in 1877 (Honeycombe 1-4), the search for the missing clergyman Benjamin Speke in 1868 (Liddle 89-104), the long-running saga of the Tichbourne Claimant and the bizarre one of mistaken identity surrounding Adolph Beck loomed large in both "respectable" newspapers and in the popular press where, in the words of H. G. Wells,

> vilely drawn pictures brought home to the dullest intelligence an interminable succession of squalid crimes, women murdered and put into boxes, buried under floors, old men bludgeoned at midnight by robbers, people thrust suddenly out of trains, happy lovers shot, vitrioled and so forth by rivals. (*Tono-Bungay* 37)

Inevitably, such rich raw material was quickly echoed in fiction, with the most famous outrage, the vicious murder of a number of prostitutes by "Jack the Ripper" in the autumn of 1888, spawning an enduring industry of its own. The belief that the killer was actually a "toff," a lawyer or doctor with a fatal penchant for "slumming" still exerts a morbid fascination on the reading public of the Western world, and much ink has been spilled in speculation as to his (or indeed, her) identity.[1]

With the exception of the Ripper murderers, all these stories have one common feature. The double life brings not the thrilling *frisson* but the anxiety of discovery: a stark fear of exposure, humiliation, and ruin overwhelms Dorian's "terrible pleasure." As Stephen Knight has shown in *Form and Ideology in Crime Fiction* (1980), a fundamentally conservative genre such as the late-Victorian detective story uses the disruption of order to generate excitement and suspense and its restoration to bring narrative closure and reader satisfaction. Similarly, newspapers emphasised that criminals would be and were caught and punished, however ingenious, daring, and readable their crimes. In fact and fiction

[1] Even Hornung's Raffles has his theories about the murderer's identity, airing them in "Gentlemen and Players" (*The Amateur Cracksman*, 1899). "[I]t's my conviction that Jack the Ripper was a really eminent public man, whose speeches were very likely reported alongside his atrocities" (*Collected Raffles* 38), he says. In a later story, "The Raffles Relics" (*A Thief in the Night*, 1905), he quips that Charles Peace was the "greatest of the pre-Raffleites" (*Collected Raffles* 414) during a tour of Scotland Yard's Black Museum.

alike, the Victorian reader knew, or at least was encouraged to believe, that the villain may wriggle on the hook but there can be no escape: discovery is inevitable. With the obvious exception of the Ripper killings, unsolved cases rarely attracted sustained press coverage, for, as George Gissing realised, "Nothing [is] so abhorred by the multitude as a lack of finality in stories, a vagueness of conclusion which gives them the trouble of forming surmises" (93). Wilde's downfall, or the exposure of Sir Percival Glyde's despicable scheme in *The Woman in White*, offered satisfying, final, and, according to one's moral stance, deserved conclusions, as well as the comforting endorsement of a providential universe in which, as Wilde quipped, "the good [end] happily, and the bad unhappily. That is what Fiction means" (376).

Wilde's sentencing made this neat opposition of "good" and "bad" characters obvious for those conservatives who saw him as the leader of an unsavoury and even dangerous cult. For them, his imprisonment marked a watershed in the sexual and class politics of the *fin de siècle*, and a vigorous "counter-decadence" became increasingly vocal as the 1890s progressed. However, those more sympathetic to Wilde's sexuality and/or his artistic doctrines were sceptical of moral polarities that seemed convenient rather than true. "The criminal classes are so close to us that even the policeman can see them," Wilde wrote in November 1894. "They are so far away from us that only the poet can understand them" ("Few Maxims" 1243). In "Phrases and Philosophies for the Use of the Young," published the following month, he warmed to this theme. "Wickedness is a myth invented by good people to account for the curious attractiveness of others," he theorised (1244), and the notion that "curious attractiveness" resided somewhere beyond the bounds of "respectable" society is echoed surprisingly frequently in late-Victorian and Edwardian literature. When Wilde was publishing his "A Few Maxims for the Instruction of the Over-Educated," he slyly distanced himself from the "criminal classes" to which he now belonged, claiming that they deserved the homage of art rather than the lash of the law, yet he openly admitted the fascination they held for him. Intrigued by the relationship between crime and creativity in his own life and in that of Thomas Griffiths Wainewright, the subject of "Pen, Pencil and Poison" (1889). Wilde was moving towards an exciting theoretical basis for crime fiction. This drew upon what Richard Lancelyn Green styles the "literature of roguery," a "distinctive genre" that "runs in an unbroken line from Chaucer, through the Tudor 'cony-catchers,' Elizabethan picaresque, *The Beggar's Opera*, Defoe and Fielding to the 'Newgate novels' of the 1830s" (xxiii), but it differed from it in crucial ways. Wilde was not interested in the crime story as a morally simple cautionary tale: he would famously maintain that "[a]ny preoccupation with ideas of what is right or wrong in conduct shows an arrested intellectual development" ("Phrases" 1245). He argued instead that crime was inextricable from art, and a means of personal development as well as of resisting corrupt or unjust authority. It is notable that his defending counsel, Sir Edward Clarke, endeavoured to the last to keep them separate, and ultimately, in the words of the prosecution, "preserve Wilde by means of a false glamour of art" (qtd. in Coates, *Trial* 167).

Unfortunately for Clarke, the two were to prove stubbornly indivisible. In Robert Hichens' *The Green Carnation* (1894), a parody of Wilde that veers so close to pastiche that one wonders if the satirist is occasionally taking dictation from his purported target, the Wildean Esmé Amarinth announces:

> There are only a few people in the world who dare to defy the grotesque code of rules that has been drawn up by that fashionable mother, Nature, and they defy – as many women drink, and many men are vicious – in secret, with the door locked and the key in their pockets. And what is life to them? They can always hear the footsteps of the detective in the street outside. (109)

Such characters are persecuted, as Amarinth sees it, not simply because they break the laws of nature but because they resist, albeit in secret, the processes of social assimilation. The gilded fop would have little sympathy for Althusserian critique, but his words expose nonetheless the ideological and repressive apparatus of the state. In Wilde's work, this exposure is best accomplished not by the highwaymen, courtesans, or thief-takers of earlier fiction, but by cool aesthetes from the privileged sectors of society. From "Lord Arthur Savile's Crime" (1887) to *The Importance of Being Earnest* (1895), Wilde experimented with a very different notion of the criminal protagonist, the gentleman-about-town, exploring the gulf between appearance and reality that preoccupied him throughout his creative life.

"No crime is vulgar, but all vulgarity is crime," Wilde announced ("Phrases and Philosophies" 1244), influenced to an extent by the aesthetic position of Thomas De Quincey's "On Murder Considered as One of the Fine Arts" (1827). Wilde had offered comic murder in "Lord Arthur Savile's Crime" and the shocking killing of Hallward in *Dorian Gray*, but his subsequent work moved away from sensational outrages.[2] Probably informed

---

[2] "The Ballad of Reading Gaol" (1898) deals with the consequences of a crime of passion, but is more interested in these than in the details of the crime itself. The poem's repeated assertion that "[e]ach man kills the thing he loves" further compli-

by his own skirmishes with blackmailers, his plays became preoccupied with secrets and their exposure, and with the moral manipulation of their audience. In *An Ideal Husband* (1895) for instance, Mrs Cheveley's blackmail of Sir Robert Chiltern seems to be regarded as considerably worse than the politician's own dubious dealings, while in *The Importance of Being Earnest*, Wilde hints at what two clever, personable and privileged young men might achieve, albeit within the confines of romantic comedy. The play's young heroes are essentially harmless, yet encourage theatre audiences to condone a variety of dishonest behaviour, from sanctioning visits to bogus invalids to the maintenance of alternative identities. Theatregoers were also encouraged to take delight in bereavement and other once-taboo comic topics. Jack (that is, Ernest) and Algernon are not criminal in the way that Dorian Gray or Mrs Cheveley are criminal, but they are nonetheless subversive. Working within the established formulae of light-hearted romance, Wilde was able to appear socially conformist while in truth drawing attention to the artificiality of the rituals and compromises on which the prosperous society of the Home Counties was based. The conception of crime as witty, stylish, and entertaining had been seen to some extent in Robert Louis Stevenson's *The New Arabian Nights* (1882), but Wilde's greater cultural visibility, not to mention the increasingly menacing rumours swirling about him, meant that he was the writer chiefly responsible for envisioning it in this way. When H. G. Wells began his 1894 short story "The Hammerpond Park Burglary" with the epigrammatic flourish, "It is a moot point whether burglary is to be considered as a sport, a trade, or an art" (*Complete* 294), it seemed almost an act of homage.

cates the relationship between the criminal, the prisoner, and the supposedly lawful citizens beyond the prison walls.

Although many hoped that his imprisonment would destroy the Decadent movement, Wilde's influence continued to manifest itself. Stylistic echoes can be found in the comedies of Ada Leverson and E. F. Benson, the macabre fantasies of Saki, the provocative social agitation of Grant Allen's *The British Barbarians* (1895) (see Nick Freeman), the early stories of Ronald Firbank and the Gothic nightmares of Somerset Maugham's *The Magician* (1908). Perhaps most striking however is the way in which Wilde's conception of artistic crime and his fascination with double lives resurfaced in the fiction of E. W. Hornung, Arthur Morrison, Clifford Ashdown, and others.

Several problems faced writers who followed Wilde's approach to crime writing. The first was simply getting work published in the aftermath of his downfall: open defiance of moral convention was unlikely to find a publisher even though the informal system of censorship represented by the library monopoly had all but collapsed by the mid-1890s. The second was that by and large, the reading public had become used to crime fiction operating within conventions of form and content that were flouted only at the cost of sales and the unlikely renewal of contracts. The third was the overwhelming success of Conan Doyle's Sherlock Holmes. In February 1890, his second adventure, *The Sign of Four*, had appeared in the American *Lippincott's Magazine*, followed, in July, by *Dorian Gray*. Both offered versions of the hero as aesthete, but it was Conan Doyle's story which had the greater influence, inspiring a plethora of rival sleuths.[3] Some of these, Robert Barr's Sherlaw Kombs, for example, parodied the great

---

[3] Holmes soon lost his associations with decadence, both in his habits and in the illustrations in the *Strand* by Sidney Paget.

detective.[4] Others, such as M. P. Shiel's extravagant Prince Zaleski, played up aspects of his personality or, as Arthur Morrison did with the deliberately understated Martin Hewitt, toned them down and embodied "[t]he detective as ordinary man" (Symons 90). Either way, Conan Doyle's creation was impossible to avoid, leading Hornung to joke that "[t]hough he might be more humble, there's no police like Holmes" (Conan Doyle, *Memories*; qtd. in Rowland 138). A Conan Doyle copyist could sell fiction to magazines such as the *Strand*, *Pearson's*, *Cassell's*, *Harmsworth's* or the *Windsor* (Greene 13), but a more ambitious writer was likely to balk at such derivative performances.

So, with this in mind, how were writers to adjudicate between the competing claims of the marketplace and their own innovative approach to narratives of felony? Morrison, Hornung, Ashdown, and Grant Allen all began by breaking a fundamental commandment of Conan Doyle, who, in his autobiography, *Memories and Adventures* (1924), recalled telling Hornung, his brother-in-law, that his Raffles stories were "rather dangerous in their suggestion" and that it was wrong to make "the criminal a hero" (qtd. in Rowland 138).[5] Hornung's cricketing cat-burglar, Allen's trickster Colonel Clay, Ashdown's opportunistic adventurer, Romney Pringle, and Morrison's murderous inquiry agent, Horace Dorrington, all live outside the law, even if the latter occasionally purports to act in its interests in pursuing "a gentlemanly line of business and villainy" (Morrison 306). Nonetheless, they tend to be sympathetic figures, with Raffles an especially appealing creation of enduring popularity. For them to find publishers and, in the

---

[4] These are listed at length by Watt and Green in *The Alternative Sherlock Holmes* (2003).

[5] For a useful round-up of criminal heroes in fiction of this period, see Kemp, Mitchell, and Trotter 81-82.

case of Raffles, enthusiastic support, during a time of cultural realignment is a perhaps surprising aspect of late-Victorian literary history.

The chief method by which writers were able to serve two masters simultaneously was to make the criminal intelligent, charming, witty, and, on the whole, violent only in exceptional circumstances. Such figures were then unleashed on victims who were far removed from their readers (see Watson 45-52). A prosperous middle-class businessman living in a London suburb may have been anxious about burglary – though it is worth noting that recorded crime fell continually between 1860 and 1914 – and would scarcely have endorsed a "hero" who preyed on the typical inhabitants of the commuter belt. However, he was quite prepared to see Raffles and his ilk prey upon other morally dubious individuals, especially if that dubiousness could be linked to popular prejudice against, for instance, Jews or arrogant colonial businessmen. As Joseph Kestner notes, such tactics allow the apparent "criminal" to exact "a form of justice on behalf of the culture" (*Edwardian* 47), or, in another way, act out its jealousy and semi-submerged aggression in a "safe" context. Raffles robs the illicit diamond buyer Rueben Rosenthall in "A Costume Piece" (1899), the rascally fence and blackmailer Angus Baird in "Wilful Murder" (1899), and the Jewish moneylender Dan Levy in *Mr Justice Raffles* (1909).[6] Colonel Clay torments Sir Charles Vandrift, a South African financier throughout *An African Millionaire* (1897), while in Ashdown's "The Assyrian Rejuvenator" (1902), Pringle outsmarts a villainous Jew who peddles a dubious line in patent medicines. Even Dorrington is preferable to Mallows, the duplic-

[6] As Lancelyn Green notes, Rosenthall is clearly based on Barney Barnato (Barnett Isaacs Barnato, 1852-1897), a Jewish South African diamond magnate of unsavoury reputation (147 n.).

itous businessman behind the fraudulent Avalanche Bicycle and Tyre Company, who attempts to gas him in an enamelling oven when threatened with exposure or worse, having to share his profits.

Another popular tactic was to have the criminal act to redeem a debt of honour. Conan Doyle was not above stories of this kind, allowing Holmes and Watson to technically break the law in the service of a greater good, "The Adventure of the Abbey Grange" and "The Adventure of Charles Augustus Milverton" (1904, collected 1905) being typical examples.[7] Still another stratagem was Hornung's favourite: the reduction of criminal acts to the status of playful challenges in which individual nerve and derring-do distract the reader from the implications of lawbreaking. The combination of these meant that criminals were not a threat to society at large, and allowed their adventures to be enjoyed without the worrying suggestions of complicity that troubled Conan Doyle.

Nevertheless, cultural convention, not to mention faith in the police and judiciary dictated that criminals, however educated and engaging they may have been, and however harmless their crimes to the wider public, could not be allowed to openly disport themselves as being above the law. These criminal bachelors, educated bourgeois deviants who devote their undoubted intelligence and daring to self-advancement rather than the good of the state, were forced therefore to maintain dual identities or double lives, and

[7] Patterns of influence are far from one-way here. "Charles Augustus Milverton," originally entitled "The Adventure of the Worst Man in London" (Haining 162), is obviously indebted to Hornung's "Wilful Murder." This suggests that Conan Doyle was very much alive to developments in popular fiction and taste, and kept a keen eye on his rivals. One might also note frequent engagement with wider fashion. "The Adventure of the Copper Beeches" (1891, collected 1892) opens with Holmes identifying himself, albeit indirectly, as "the man who loves art for its own sake" (Conan Doyle 316).

live in permanent fear of discovery. "To follow Crime with reasonable impunity you simply *must* have a parallel, ostensible career," Raffles tells Bunny. "Fill the bill in some prominent part, and you'll never be suspected of doubling it with another of equal prominence" (*Collected Raffles* 38). Perhaps Wilde believed that a highly visible life as a husband, father, playwright and social butterfly would conceal his other activities? Either way, Raffles suggests the urbane heroes of his comedies, in that he shares the trappings of establishment respectability in, for instance, belonging to London clubs, yet represents a challenge to the very institutions and authorities that he seems to represent.

Raffles has particularly close links to Wilde, links memorably exploited by Graham Greene in his play, *The Return of A. J. Raffles* (1975). To begin with, Hornung himself was a friend of the dramatist, and was even bold (or foolish) enough to have his son christened Oscar in May 1895 (Rowland 76).[8] He was also friends with the eccentric criminologist and cricketer George Ives, a campaigner for homosexual law reform and associate of Wilde's who, like Raffles, and indeed, Ernest Worthing, had rooms in the Albany. Lancelyn Green offers persuasive evidence for Ives as in part the model for Raffles (xxiv-xxvi), though points out that Hornung's relationship with him was not close, and revolved around their shared passion for sport rather than any of Ives more esoteric interests.

There are a number of other associations and parallels between Raffles and Wilde. Though he has emerged from the supposedly "manly" world of the English public school, Raffles has been educated at Wilde's *alma mater*, Oxford, which was far more susceptible to subversive aesthetic doctrines than other universities of

[8] More prudently, the boy was also named Arthur after his godfather, Conan Doyle.

the period: he quotes Swinburne on several occasions in "The Fate of Faustina" (1901). The influence of Oxford aestheticism lingers in his rooms, which are "charmingly furnished and arranged, with the right amount of negligence and the right amount of taste" (*Collected Raffles* 8), and he prefers books and reproductions of Pre-Raphaelite paintings to sporting memorabilia. In "A Jubilee Present" (1901) he homages George Du Maurier's famous *Punch* cartoon of an aesthetic couple attempting to live up to their blue china (*Collected Raffles* 160). Like Wilde, he enjoys consuming large quantities of expensive Egyptian cigarettes, perhaps sharing Lord Henry's belief that "[a] cigarette is the perfect type of a perfect pleasure. It is exquisite, and it leaves one unsatisfied" (*Dorian Gray* 67). He even assumes the alias "Maturin" when hiding from the police: the Gothic novelist, Charles Maturin, author of *Melmoth the Wanderer* (1820), was Wilde's great-uncle, and Wilde used the name Sebastian Melmoth during his exile (see Rowland 71-81). In all, Raffles "might have been a minor poet instead of an athlete of the first water," since "there had always been a fine streak of aestheticism in his complex composition" (*Collected Raffles* 8). Even before embarking on a career of crime, therefore, Raffles is already leading a double life in some respects by alternating between the supposedly antipathetic roles of aesthete and sportsman.

Wilde may have concealed his relationships with young men from his wife and the authorities, but he did not disguise his identity when he was with them. This was less because his image had been widely reproduced for over a decade than because he was carelessly honest in the company of disreputable characters. Only a man with so positive a view of human nature or a misguided notion of personal invulnerability would have had his name engraved on expensive cigarette cases gifted to passing acquaintances. Raffles, by contrast, lives in a web of disguises. He is Raffles the cricketer and Raffles the aesthete, as well as the daring burglar of Bunny's breathless narration and the professional Cockney villain who, to reduce the risk of blackmail by his fence, "drive[s] all [his] bargains in the tongue and raiment of Shoreditch" (*Collected Raffles* 29).

Hornung's hero illustrates particularly well the ways in which an author could exploit the notion of the double life for the purposes of entertainment. He is charismatic, daring and honourable, even, in "A Jubilee Present," fiercely patriotic (*Collected Raffles* 168-69), but the fact remains that he is a skilled and experienced safe-breaker who is addicted to both the excitement and the material rewards of his profession. He and Bunny are also ruthless on occasion, notably in the treatment of the schoolboys who try to prevent a burglary in "The Wrong House" (1901), a story which appalled Colin Watson in *Snobbery with Violence* (1971). The tales have "a wit that consistently questions the assumption that crime fiction must always be respectable in its ethic," observes Stephen Knight (*Crime Fiction* 70), but the moral codes of the era and its fiction decreed that Raffles could not be allowed to remain at liberty since he had become, as Wilde before him, a sustained thorn in the flesh of authority. He is therefore cornered in "The Gift of the Emperor" (1899), flees to Italy where he battles the altogether more dangerous villains of Naples' murderous secret society, the Camorra, in "The Fate of Faustina," and is finally redeemed by becoming a soldier and dying in the Boer War after unmasking a spy in "The Knees of the Gods" (1901). "I am grateful to the General for giving me today," he says, mortally wounded. "It may be the last. Then I can say only it's been the best – by Jove!" (*Collected Raffles* 273). Hornung here seems to allow Raffles to be swallowed up by the militaristic ideologies that seized the British imagination in the aftermath of Mafeking in May 1900, but his death is not quite the capitulation it appears to be. Another collection of stories, *A Thief in the Night*, appeared in 1905 and a novel, *Mr Justice Raffles* followed four years later. There were also film and theatrical adaptations, not to mention sequels by other hands.

The result was that although the character had been seen to be punished, he had also escaped punishment by being reanimated and returned to the 1890s of his heyday. Peter Rowland points out that by setting *Mr Justice Raffles* in 1899, Hornung "makes nonsense of the dating of the previous tales" (190). However, one might ask whether these chronological loopholes do not also suggest the temporal confusion of *Dorian Gray*, which, if it is to conclude in the 1890s, must surely have begun far earlier than seems possible from the opening chapters (see Sutherland, "Why" 196-201). One might also note how the persistent mythologisation of "the Beardsley period" allowed Wilde to continue spouting *bon-mots* at the Café Royal, uninterrupted by the sordid indignities of arrest and imprisonment, let alone actual death.[9]

Joseph Kestner argues that by the end of the nineteenth century, crime writing had become a way by which society was able to address the "disturbance and destabilization" caused by contemporary political and social anxieties from nationalism, anarchism, and feminism, to "gender redefinition [. . .] social class, international diplomacy, race deterioration and imperial policy" (*Edwardian* 7). Accordingly, he reads Ashdown's two collections of Romney Pringle stories (1902, 1903) as dramatising tensions in Anglo-French and Anglo-American relations, though he notes too the persistent suggestion that gentlemanliness is essentially a

[9] The phrase is Max Beerbohm's, but it is chiefly known through being the title of Osbert Burdett's *The Beardsley Period: A Study in Perspective* (1925).

masquerade, a performance (Kestner 47, 57). Pringle is a reputedly wealthy and cultured man, as well as, like Dorian Gray, a connoisseur of precious stones. It is therefore surprising that Kestner does not pursue the links between him and Wilde's duplicitous heroes, either here or in his earlier *Sherlock's Men* (1997), though the latter signals useful intersections between Conan Doyle's world of embattled imperial masculinity and the decadent movement (see especially 1-39).

Pringle poses as an underemployed literary agent – a cultural in-joke at a time of a rapidly proliferating print media – and is a master of disguise. As Knight points out, he also has "genuine criminal skills" (Knight, *Crime Fiction* 71) in key-cutting and forgery. He is quick-witted, courageous, and, unlike Raffles, far from patriotic where questions of national welfare are concerned. In "The Submarine Boat" (1903), Pringle fails to prevent a French spy stealing military secrets, but is comforted by the large sum of money he has tricked out of the French intelligence service: at one point he is forced to "abandon all hope of a counterplot for the honour of his country, to say nothing of his own profit" (Ashdown, "Submarine" 7). He impersonates policemen not, as Raffles did in "A Costume Piece," to rescue a stricken friend, but to advance his own criminal activities in robbing a German blackmailer. He also profits from the debates surrounding the presentation of sexual matters in English fiction in the wake of novels such as Moore's *Esther Waters* (1894) and Hardy's *Jude the Obscure* (1895). In "The Assyrian Rejuvenator," the bogus medicine appears to be an Edwardian forerunner of Viagra, and one chiefly resorted to by army officers of advancing years. Such subversive stories offer a satire on English martial (and marital) vigour: the less than glorious resolution of the South African conflict means that Pringle will never believe that war can cleanse a stained moral character.

Pringle's haunts are the cosmopolitan eateries of Soho, where his command of French stands him in good stead on several occasions. Less ostentatious and improvident than Wilde, the rogue literary agent nonetheless owes much to his creations. He even, as Wilde did in his lengthy prison letter to Lord Alfred Douglas, leaves a self-justifying account of his adventures, a set of memoirs that walk the line between fact and fiction. "Whether, as might be imagined from their intimate record of the chief actor's career, they were derived from the notes of actual experience, or whether they were simply the result of imagination, they are here presented exactly as left by the author," the preface to *Further Adventures* announces (qtd. in Kestner, *Edwardian* 46).[10] The tales are clearly intended to be published, with Kestner commenting that this is "either a gesture of egoism on Pringle's part" or a "rebuke to the society which so easily fell to his transgressive behaviour" (*Edwardian* 47). Here again one can detect the influence of Wilde, who had blurred the lines between reality and invention in "The Decay of Lying" and indeed, during his appearances in the dock at the Old Bailey. Pringle's "telling the truth" eventually "finds him out", yet it is at too great a remove for the forces of law and order to seek redress for his crimes. Indeed, a number of his acts cannot be verified, either through the disappearance of key personnel (French spies, German blackmailers) or the understandable reluctance of elderly men to admit their sexual failings.

Raffles and Pringle are the most Wildean rogues of their time, since Allen's Colonel Clay has a justifiable grievance against Vandrift that simplifies the stories' moral basis, while Horace

[10] The House of Stratus reprint of *Further Adventures* omits the preface.

Dorrington is too serious a criminal to fit easily within such a paradigm. Like Pringle, he is intelligent, cunning, skilled in disguise and forgery, and has considerable reserves of courage and bravado. He also leads a double life in which he is as likely to commit crimes as solve them. However, his apparently humble origins, lack of wit and, most obviously, his willingness to kill in the pursuit of his aims prevent him from being truly Wildean. If Dorrington's character and activities place him at a crucial distance from such notions of crime, one should note that Morrison (1863-1945) himself was an adroit leader of the double life; a man who covered his tracks so successfully that his early life was not properly documented until Peter Keating's research of the 1960s.[11] John Sutherland describes him as "morbidly secret" ("Arthur" 447), and such was his sleight-of-hand that he was able to deny his humble origins when writing fiction such as *Tales of Mean Streets* (1894) and *A Child of the Jago* (1896) that was heavily informed by personal experience, while at the same time concealing an impressive knowledge of oriental art that, had he publicised it, would have compromised his gritty stance with its suggestions of aestheticism. Like Wilde, Morrison delighted in dramatising his secrets, and it is telling that the one story which shows Dorrington engaged in legitimate detective work, "The Case of Mr Loftus Deacon," exploits his creator's enthusiasm for Japanese ceramics and lacquerware. Morrison eventually published a respected scholarly work, *The Painters of Japan*, in 1911.

Secrets and double lives were crucial ingredients of late-Victorian and Edwardian crime fiction, but important differences should be recognised between Wilde's example and the work of Hornung and others. First of all, until R. Austin Freeman pio-

---

[11] This was eventually published as the introduction to the 1971 Panther edition of *A Child of the Jago*.

neered the "inverted story" (Symons 89) in *The Singing Bone* (1912), secrets were essential to all stories of crime and detection since without a secret, a mystery, or a puzzle, the stories themselves could not exist. Hence once Raffles is exposed, he has to redisguise himself so that he can commit crimes while posing as somebody else, and the pursuit and unmasking that generates narrative tension can begin again. Wilde had a more substantial and ultimately more damaging personal secret than most, and a greater fascination with the workings of secrecy itself (as shown in "The Sphinx without a Secret" [1887] and elsewhere), but he did not have a monopoly on narratives of concealment in this period. From Wilkie Collins to Henry James to the serried ranks of Victorian melodramas, the keeping of dangerous secrets is a crucial dramatic device. Where Wilde and those who followed him were radical was in manipulating readers so that they would not want the secrets to be exposed. This radical rejection of traditional narrative concerns, in which suspense was valued above its resolution, was allied to unconventional moral positions in which readers sympathised (or even, in extreme cases, identified with) criminals. Raffles' nemesis, Inspector Mackenzie, is a sharp-witted and accomplished detective, but the reader always hopes that the daring burglars will slip through his fingers. This is not simply because Hornung exploits latent English prejudice against the Scots. It is also because the pleasure of the text derives, at least in part, from sharing a secret with a criminal rather than with the authorities. If a theatre audience laughs at a quip in *The Importance of Being Earnest*, it colludes with Wilde's "curiously attractive" characters. If a reader hopes Pringle will succeed in tricking his victims, and even, in his final adventure, escaping from prison, then s/he is mounting a challenge to the established order, even if only momentarily.

The most notable difference between Wildean criminality and its various incarnations in the crime writing of the *fin de siècle* however lies in the nature of Wilde's personal crimes. However he may have theorised secrets or dramatised murder and blackmail, he was ultimately convicted of sexual offences in line with Section Eleven of the 1885 Criminal Law Amendment Act. As such, his crimes could not be discussed in polite society. The writer Beverley Nichols records how as a teenaged boy in the early years of the 1914-1918 war his father beat him for reading *Dorian Gray.* When he asked what Wilde had done, he received a piece of paper on which his father had written in Latin, "The horrible crime which is not to be named" (Connon 40). One would have thought that any writer who ventured into creative territory associated with Wilde would have been at pains to demonstrate that his heroes were either romantically inclined heterosexuals (as indeed is Colonel Clay) or else celibate, as Holmes is despite his fascination with Irene Adler in "A Scandal in Bohemia" (1891, collected 1892). Yet this is not the case. Women are invariably absent from these stories.

One explanation for this is that such tales were often aimed at a male readership who wanted excitement rather than romance: their escapist rejection of quotidian realities made them appealing reading for adolescents of all ages. As Julian Symons writes of Holmes, Conan Doyle "was not in the least misanthropic or misogynistic but he recognised in his readers (and no doubt felt himself) the need for Holmes to be a man immune from ordinary human weaknesses and passions" (71). Another is that domesticity and normality actively impede characters' propensities for adventure. Mrs Watson is a means of signalling a key difference between Holmes and his assistant rather than being a character in her own right or even a point of interest: if Holmes needs to catch a train in a hurry, disappear into an opium den disguised as a drug addict (as he does in "The Man with the Twisted Lip") or simply head to down Dartmoor at short notice, he needs the freedom to be able to do so. Nonetheless, these practical reasons are only partially convincing.

Henri Labouchère's well-meant but poorly thought through addition to the Criminal Law Amendment Act placed male friendships under intense scrutiny.[12] "Any male person who, in public or in private, commits, or is party to the commission of, or procures the commission by any male person of any act of gross indecency, with another male person, shall be guilty of a misdemeanour," it read, the key words being "in private." Not for nothing was it soon known as the "Blackmailers' Charter," and, should its terms be applied to fiction, all manner of characters would find themselves at risk. Holmes and Watson, snug in the bachelor rooms at 221B Baker Street, Bunny, dropping in on Raffles in the Albany at all hours of the day or night, or even Pringle, sitting alone in French restaurants wearing artfully applied make-up, all risk their behaviour being misconstrued, and Dorrington would surely have been alive to the possibilities of blackmail. A growing legion of critics – Eve Kosofsky Sedgwick, Christopher Craft, Elaine Showalter, D. A. Miller, Jonathan Dollimore, Alan Sinfield, Joseph Bristow – has alerted us to the queer undercurrents of Victorian society, and, in the case of, for example, Neil Bartlett's *Who was that Man?* (1988), Ed Cohen's *Talk on the Wilde Side* (1992), or Sinfield's *The Wilde Century* (1994), the significance of the Wilde trials in the formation of modern gay identity. Julian Sy-

[12] The main purpose of the Criminal Law Amendment Act was the increased protection of young women following the scandal of W. T. Stead's sensational exposure of the late-Victorian sex industry, "The Maiden Tribute of Modern Babylon" (1885).

mons could suggest back in 1974 that "there are suggestions of a platonic homosexual relationship" (94) between Raffles and Bunny, and more forensic and ingenious modern readings leave one wondering how their antics could ever have been tolerated by a heteronormative society consumed with anxiety, even paranoia, about the nature and performance of "manliness." Their verbal and physical affection, their preference for each other's company over that of women, their inhabitation of an exclusively masculine world of Turkish baths, clubs, and cricket pavilions, not to mention their rejection of marriage and the family do not, it seems, mark them as deviant to their readers. The self-contained Pringle and Dorrington, unswayed alike by romance or desire are too aloof to be drawn into homoeroticism, yet they are clearly moulded from commoner clay than Conan Doyle's superman. Women appear in the Pringle stories only as marriage tokens, and are almost entirely absent from Dorrington's papers. Because both Ashdown and Morrison frame their stories as a series of cases or adventures assembled after the disappearance of their heroes, their personal lives remain unexplored, but it seems clear that they move in predominantly masculine environments despite the notable presence of women in both late nineteenth-century espionage and serious crime (see Morton).

Late-Victorian and Edwardian crime stories were occasionally censured for their moral content, that is, their unconventional attitudes towards the law, but their sexual content was not remarked upon despite, or rather, because of, the sensitivity of the cultural climate in the aftermath of Wilde's downfall. Raffles and Bunny are social equals, public school men, the nature of whose friendship is determined by their class rather than their sexual proclivities. Such at least is the comforting fiction that the two are "chums" rather than lovers. It is, one might suggest, unthinkable for a reader of *Cassell's* or the *Strand* to map the revelations of the Wilde case onto thrilling escapism. Pringle sits in Soho restaurants to pick up snippets of information rather than other men; Dorrington and Hicks seem to have a purely professional partnership. Perhaps too determined an attempt has been made to "out" a certain type of Victorian bachelor, from Dickens' Eugene Wrayburn to Hornung's Bunny Manders, but one cannot ignore the intensely homosocial atmosphere of many *fin-de-siècle* crime fictions. Neither can one suppress the thought that Raffles' advice about having a "parallel, ostensible career" seems, from a contemporary critical perspective, a clever smokescreen: the safe-crackers are too busy cracking safes to have time for romantic entanglements, least of all with each other. It is also telling that the relationship between Raffles and Bunny is far more vividly realised than those with female characters in stories such as "The Fate of Faustina."

Wilde's influence therefore permeates the crime stories of the 1890s and 1900s in two significant respects. The first is a daring reformulation of crime as an art and the criminal as a hero, a stance that drew audiences into at least briefly subversive moral positions. The second is a far more speculative set of associations about the homosocial, the homoerotic, double lives and secrets that shows a particular type of man resisting the pressures of conformity with every means at his disposal. The extent to which the stories of Freeman, Hornung, and even Conan Doyle were influenced by the fate of Wilde cannot now be known, but one wonders if Edward Carson enjoyed them.

## Works Cited

Allen, Grant. *An African Millionaire*. London: Grant Richards, 1897.

Ashdown, Clifford [i.e. R. Austin Freeman and John Pitcairn]. *The Adventures of Romney Pringle*. 1902. Philadelphia: Oswald Train, 1968.

___. "The Assyrian Rejuvenator." 1902. *The Rivals of Sherlock Holmes: Early Detective Stories*. Ed. Hugh Greene. London: Penguin, 1974. 124-39.

___. *The Further Adventures of Romney Pringle*. 1903. London: House of Stratus, 2001.

___. "The Submarine Boat." *Further Adventures* 1-17.

Bartlett, Neil. *Who Was That Man? A Present for Mr Oscar Wilde*. London: Serpent's Tail, 1988.

Burdett, Osbert. *The Beardsley Period: A Study in Perspective*. London: John Lane, 1925.

Coates, Tim, ed. *The Strange Story of Adolph Beck*. London: The Stationery Office, 1999.

___. *The Trials of Oscar Wilde, 1895*. London: The Stationery Office, 2001.

Cohen, Ed. *Talk on the Wilde Side*. London: Routledge, 1992.

Conan Doyle, Arthur. *The Sign of Four*. 1890. *Penguin* 89-158.

___. "A Scandal in Bohemia." 1891. *Penguin* 161-76.

___. "The Man with the Twisted Lip." 1891. *Penguin* 229-44.

___. "The Adventure of the Copper Beeches." 1891. *Penguin* 316-34.

___. "The Adventure of the Abbey Grange." 1904. *Penguin* 635-49.

___. "The Adventure of Charles Augustus Milverton." 1904. *Penguin* 572-81.

___. *Memories and Adventures*. London: Hodder & Stoughton, 1924.

___. *The Penguin Complete Sherlock Holmes*. London: Penguin, 1981.

Connon, Bryan. *Beverley Nichols: A Life*. London: Constable, 1991.

Criminal Law Amendment Act 1885 (-). *Swarb.co.uk – uk law online*. Vers. 3. 8 Jan. 2007. 15. Jan. 2007 <http://www.swarb.co.uk/acts/1885Criminal_Law_AmendmentAct.shtml>.

Freeman, Austin. *The Singing Bone*. London: Hodder & Stoughton, 1912.

Freeman, Nick. "'Intentional Rudeness'? Grant Allen and the Cultural Politics of 1895." *Grant Allen: Literature & Politics at the Fin de Siècle*. Ed. William Greenslade and Terence Rogers. Aldershot: Ashgate, 2005. 111-28.

Gissing, George. *Charles Dickens: A Critical Study*. 1898. London: Gresham, 1903.

Green, Richard Lancelyn. Introduction. *Raffles: The Amateur Cracksman*. By E. W. Hornung. London: Penguin, 2003. xvii-xlvii.

Greene, Graham. *The Return of A. J. Raffles: An Edwardian Comedy in Three Acts Somewhat Loosely Modelled on E. W. Hornung's Characters in "The Amateur Cracksman."* London: Bodley Head, 1975.

Greene, Hugh, ed. *The Rivals of Sherlock Holmes: Early Detective Stories*. 1970. London: Penguin, 1974.

Haining, Peter, ed. *London after Midnight*. 1996. London: Warner, 1997.

Hennegan, Alison. "Personalities and Principles: Aspects of Literature and Life in *fin-de-siècle* England." *Fin de Siècle and Its Legacy*. Ed. Mikuláš Teich and Roy Porter. Cambridge: Cambridge UP, 1990. 170-215.

Hichens, Robert. *The Green Carnation*. 1894. London: Robin Clark, 1992.

Honeycombe, Gordon. *The Murders of the Black Museum 1870-1970*. London: Hutchinson, 1982.

Hornung, E. W. *The Amateur Cracksman*. 1899. Rpt. as *Raffles: The Amateur Cracksman*. Ed. Richard Lancelyn Green. London: Penguin, 2003.

___. *The Collected Raffles*. London: J. M. Dent, 1985.

___. "A Costume Piece." 1899. *Collected Raffles* 37-54.

___. "The Fate of Faustina." 1901. *Collected Raffles* 169-86.

___."Gentlemen and Players." 1899. *Collected Raffles* 22-37.

___. "The Gift of the Emperor." 1899. *Collected Raffles* 118-40.

___. "A Jubilee Present." 1901. *Collected Raffles* 156-69.

___. "The Knees of the Gods." 1901. *Collected Raffles* 255-74.

___. *Mr Justice Raffles*. London: Smith, Elder, 1909.

___. "The Raffles Relics." 1905. *Collected Raffles* 409-25.

___. *A Thief in the Night*. London: Chatto & Windus, 1905.

___. "Wilful Murder." 1899. *Collected Raffles* 69-82.

___. "The Wrong House." 1901. *Collected Raffles* 243-55.

Kemp, Sandra, Charlotte Mitchell, and David Trotter, eds. *Edwardian Fiction: An Oxford Companion*. Oxford: Oxford UP, 1997.

Kestner, Joseph A. *Sherlock's Men: Masculinity, Conan Doyle, and Cultural History*. Aldershot: Ashgate, 1997.

___. *The Edwardian Detective, 1901-1915*. Aldershot: Ashgate, 2000.

Knight, Stephen. *Form and Ideology in Crime Fiction*. Basingstoke: Macmillan, 1980.

___. *Crime Fiction 1800-2000: Detection, Death, Diversity*. Basingstoke: Palgrave Macmillan, 2004.

Liddle, Dallas. "Anatomy of a 'Nine Days' Wonder': Sensational Journalism in the Decade of the Sensation Novel." *Victorian Crime, Madness and Sensation*. Ed. Andrew Maunder and Grace Moore. Aldershot: Ashgate, 2004. 89-104.

Morrison, Arthur. *A Child of the Jago*. 1896. Ed. P. J. Keating. London: Panther, 1971.

___. *The Dorrington Deed-Box*. 1897. Rockville, MD: James A. Rock, 2002.

___. "The Case of Mr Loftus Deacon." *Dorrington Deed-Box* 199-254.

___. *The Painters of Japan*. London: T. C. & E. C. Jack, 1911.

Morton, James. *Gangland: The Early Years*. London: Time Warner, 2003.

Orwell, George. "Raffles and Miss Blandish." 1944. *Critical Essays.* 1946. London: Secker & Warburg, 1954. 163-78.

Rowland, Peter. *Raffles and His Creator*. London: Nekta, 1999.

Sinfield, Alan. *The Wilde Century: Effeminacy, Oscar Wilde and the Queer Moment*. London: Cassell, 1994.

Stead, W. T. "The Maiden Tribute of Modern Babylon." 1885. *The Fin de Siècle: A Reader in Cultural History c.1880-1900*. Oxford: Oxford UP, 2000. 32-38.

Stevenson, Robert Louis. *Strange Case of Dr Jekyll and Mr Hyde*. London: Longmans, Green, 1886.

Sutherland, John. "Arthur Morrison." *The Longman Companion to Victorian Fiction*. London: Longman, 1988. 447-48.

___. "Why Does This Novel Disturb Us?" *Is Heathcliff a Murderer? Puzzles in Nineteenth-Century Literature*. Oxford: Oxford UP, 1996. 196-201.

Symons, Julian. *Bloody Murder*. 1972. Rev. ed., Harmondsworth: Penguin, 1974.

Watson, Colin. *Snobbery with Violence: English Crime Stories and Their Audience*. London: Eyre & Spottiswode, 1971.

Watt, Peter Ridgeway, and Joseph Green. *The Alternative Sherlock Holmes: Pastiches, Parodies and Copies*. Aldershot: Ashgate, 2003.

Wells, H. G. "The Hammerpond Park Burglary." 1894. *The Complete Short Stories of H. G. Wells*. London: Ernest Benn, 1927: 294-301.

___. *Tono-Bungay*. 1909. Ed. John Hammond. London: Dent, 1994.

Wilde, Oscar. "The Sphinx Without a Secret." 1887. *Complete Works*. London: Harper Collins, 1994: 205-08.

___. "The Decay of Lying." 1889. *Complete Works* 1071-92.

___. "Pen, Pencil and Poison." 1889. *Complete Works* 1093-1107.

___. *The Picture of Dorian Gray*. 1891. *Complete Works* 17-159.

___. "A Few Maxims for the Instruction of the Over-Educated." 1894. *Complete Works* 1242-43.

___. "Phrases and Philosophies for the Use of the Young." 1894. *Complete Works* 1244-45.

___. "The Ballad of Reading Gaol." 1898. *Complete Works* 883-99.

# The Medical Detective and the Victorian Fear of Degeneration

Aaron Parrett
University of Great Falls

**Abstract:** Advances in biology and medical science in the nineteenth century prompted the proliferation of theories about the "degeneration" of the human organism over time and the resurgence of atavistic types of human beings who posed a threat to the genteel and "civilized" races. These fears of degeneration were exploited in much of the popular literature of the era, including the genre of detective fiction. Often the crime or treachery in such stories involved medicine—either as a tool in the hands of a *medicus scelestus*, or as a method contributing to the solution of a crime. This essay examines the six short stories by L. T. Meade and Robert Eustace published in *Strand* (1903) known as The Sorceress of the Strand series as examples of how the medical detective confronted the perceived threat of degeneration. The essay argues that these stories represent a unique crystallization of Victorian apprehensions about race, culture, gender, and the (d)evolutionary power of nature.

Two years before Darwin's *Origin of Species* (1859) appeared, the French physician Bénédict Augustin Morel conceived of a kind of evolution in reverse, known as "degeneration," which he developed as a theory in 1857 in his *Traité des dégénérescences physiques, intellectuelles et morales de l'espèce humaine* (*Treatise on the Physical, Intellectual, and Moral Degeneration of the Human Species*). The notion of degeneration soon became a frequent theme in the popular literature of the second half of the nineteenth century, including the burgeoning Victorian genre of detective fiction.

The concept of degeneration merged with the ideas presented in *Origin of Species*, and dovetailed even more with those contained in Darwin's later volume, *The Descent of Man* (1871) to bolster a pioneering branch of sociology that would become known as criminology. Nowhere was this coupling more complete than in Cesare Lombroso, author of the widely influential *L'uomo delinquente* (*Criminal Man*, 1876), and the sociologist most often identified as "the father of criminology." Lombroso was influenced not only by Darwin, but by Morel, and Max Nordau, and to a lesser extent Arthur de Gobineau and Pierre-Paul Broca. Trained as doctor, and having taken his degree in surgery from the University of Genoa in 1859, Cesare Lombroso distilled from a mash of these myriad thinkers his conception of *homo delinquens*, a subspecies of the human being that was congenitally predisposed toward violence and criminality. Leonard Savitz writes that Lombroso viewed *homo delinquens* as "a 'throwback,' a reversion to past races of mankind, who was born out of time and would have been normal had he been born at some earlier point in time" (xi). The criminal type thus resembled "primitive races" and children in that, like them, he was characteristically self-absorbed, inquisitive but not necessarily reflective, and typically cruel – as Lombroso put it in his introduction to *Criminal Man*, "an atavistic being who reproduces in his person the ferocious instincts of primitive humanity and the inferior animals" (Lombroso, *Criminal* xxv). In the text proper, Lombroso wrote that "the criminal is an atavistic being, a relic of a vanished race," his cruelty and viciousness arising from the lack of a moral sense (135).

In summarizing the widespread acceptance and popularity of the Positivist School (*La Escuela Positiva*), as it came to be known, Savitz writes that "Lombrosianism was thought to be a normal and natural adaptation of Darwinism to criminology and appealed to a public already intrigued and impressed with evolutionary thought" (xvii). Criminality was hereditary, and its ubiquity could be taken as evidence for the larger problem of degeneration. Lombroso himself, for example, succinctly characterized the phenomenon of crime in this way: "the aetiology of crime, therefore, mingles with that of all kinds of degeneration: rickets, deafness, monstrosity, hairiness, and cretinism, of which crime is only a variation" (136).

In aesthetic terms, "degeneration" became one of the rationalizations for the literary movement known as Decadence, in which decay and the inevitability of death in all aspects of life absorbed the imaginations of late nineteenth- and early twentieth-century artists and writers. The aesthetic vision of much Victorian detective fiction demonstrates a fusion of *decadence*, as conceived of by the literary imagination, and *degeneration*, as conceived of by the scientific imagination. This fusion finds expression in many of the works of Victorian detective fiction, including Conan Doyle's Sherlock Holmes Canon, as well as the writings of often neglected writers such as L. T. Meade and two of her collaborators, Robert Eustace and Clifford Halifax, whose later short stories will be the focus of this essay.

The critic Désiré Nisard is said to have coined the term 'decadence' in 1834 in reference to his French poetic contemporaries whose style he deemed a wretched approximation of earlier masters – in the same way that the first-century Roman poet Lucan typified what Julian North calls the "debased aftermath" of the Golden Age of Roman Literature (86). North describes Nisard's view of the decadents as "backward-looking" intellectuals "imitating the curious detail of former ages [. . .] in a spirit of stale erudition," language that recalls Lombroso's derogation of criminals as anthropological throwbacks to a more primitive species (86).

Medical science was struggling through a difficult adolescence in the nineteenth century, and its development would color each one of the various threads that would be brought together to compose the weave of the Victorian detective genre. In the first place, crime became conceived of as a disease or a degenerative aberration of nature's mechanism of evolution, thus providing a formal *explanation* of the phenomenon of crime. The rationalism of scientific investigation as it emerged in the nineteenth century offered a compelling model for medically-minded criminologists and detectives, with its emphasis on data and forensics, its meticulous obsession with details of evidence and accumulation of facts leading toward the solution of a crime. In this way, the *form* of the medical examination became the model for the form of the detective investigation, especially as depicted in the Victorian detective story. And as Nancy Hoffman remarked in an article for the *Journal of the American Medical Association*, "doctors make excellent protagonists as detectives because they are trained in drawing inferences: diagnosis is the fine art of medical sleuthing" (74).

But a secondary and more speculative aspect of the scientific approach, largely inspired by Darwin's second great work on evolution, *Descent of Man*, soon emerged: human beings became conceived of as "types," and their specific features or behaviors as evidence for the combination of such types. On the one hand, such speculation gave rise to the optimistic if horribly misguided platform of the eugenicists, while on the other hand, it stirred the fears of those who discerned an undeniable disjunction between nature and culture to which men like Morel and Lombroso gave the name 'degeneration.' Not only did medical doctors conceive of criminality as a disease, but certain "types" were naturally predisposed to contracting it. Medical doctors referred to the concept of degeneration to explain motive whenever they were called upon to use their expertise in the exposition of crimes involving a particular medical aspect, certainly a common event in Victorian detective fiction.

Accordingly, the form of the detective story in the Victorian period quite often resembles the form of the medical romance – a genre still popular today that consists of the usual elements of a popular romance, though with a medical doctor in the role of the hero. L. T. Meade was adept at many genres, including the medical romance and the detective story, and hence similarity of narrative technique and descriptive features are especially evident in her Sorceress of the Strand cycle. In fact, both medicine and detection become excellent expositions of what Lawrence Frank, in his discussion of the Holmes Canon, calls "narrative science" – that is to say, speculative but plausible recovery of causes based on the residue of their effects (172).

In practice, this meant that in addition to providing detectives with a theory of criminality, and detective authors a form for narrating the work of the detective, medicine could also provide for them a practical method worth emulating. The detective found his finest exemplar in the medical practitioner who studied symptoms (clues) and used reason to develop a diagnosis (hypothesis), leading to treatment (a solution to the mystery) and a hopeful prognosis.

As a not altogether ironic consequence, the most dangerous fictional criminals (as perhaps in real life) would become those villains who exploited their medical expertise in their nefarious pursuits. Trained as a physiologist, the title character in H. G. Wells' *The Island of Doctor Moreau* (1896) is perhaps the most famous example, but L. T. Meade's character Madame Sara, whom I shall discuss presently, is a far more sinister example of the nineteenth-century *medicus scelestus*. By the end of the century, and well into the first decades of the next, these three related notions came to underpin the close associations between medicine and detective literature: medical biology providing an explanation for criminality; the medical practitioner providing a method for detectives to emulate; and the degenerate doctor providing the most horrible criminal type imaginable. With these underlying correspondences, similarities of form and style would naturally follow.

Medical science influenced the form of the detective story in two specific and important ways: First, it offered a model for the investigation of the *corpus delicti*, that is, the *body* of the crime, and second, it legitimated intuitive judgments of suspects' characters. Pyrhönen points out that the criminal's character and behavior "become increasingly important in the genre" (19). Doctor Watson in the Conan Doyle stories, and both Dr. Halifax and the physician Vandeleur in L. T. Meade's stories, frequently identify or recognize the criminal element in the visage or features of their antagonists. It is no accident that such an approach developed during the age of phrenology and other physiognomic pseudoscience. While Lombroso's approach, meanwhile, has been largely debunked in the late twentieth century by such luminaries as Stephen Jay Gould (*The Mismeasure of Man*, 1981), his influence is readily apparent in detective literature between 1880 and 1920. Conan Doyle has been criticized for perpetuating some of the chauvinisms of the colonial period, including depicting foreigners (especially dark-skinned) in atavistic terms, but it will be seen that Meade and her collaborators are just as guilty of the same charge.

The Victorian detective story thus underwrites a double-edged aesthetic: it extols both the rationalist order of things that the positivist is forever at pains to demonstrate and announce by way of "narrative science," and at the same time it seeks evidence of the hidden criminal nature in its outward, physiological manifestations – a swarthy complexion, reptilian eyes, or the like.

All of this may be amply discerned in the work of the writer Elizabeth Thomasina Toulmin-Smith (1854-1914), known from her title pages as L. T. Meade. Meade was undoubtedly one of the most prolific women writers of the late nineteenth and early twentieth centuries. Though she wrote dozens of quasi-detective and mystery stories, she is remembered (when she is remembered at all) for her hundreds of children's stories – in particular a huge body of stories for teenage girls. In collaboration with Dr. Clifford Halifax (pseudonym of Edgar Beaumont, 1860-1921) and Dr. Robert Eustace (pseudonym of Dr. Robert Eustace Barton, 1868-1943), Meade authored a series of medical mysteries that offer a unique opportunity to explore the intersection of late Victorian fears of "degeneration" and the role of the medical investigator, whose response to the threat is both therapeutic and ambiguous. Both Beaumont and Barton have faded into relative obscurity. Eustace has become especially *perdu*, though according to Everett Bleiler, he was well-known for supplying authors as late as the 1930s (including Dorothy Sayers) with "scientific background, ideas, and plots" upon which they would build their stories (308).

The form of the medical detective story incorporates a series of critical elements: the protagonist or hero is inevitably a doctor or in some way intimately connected to one; the crime in some way involves a medical crisis – often, for example, the criminal poisons or otherwise incapacitates those who stand in the way of the crime (usually robbery); as a consequence, the solution to the crime somehow involves a medical investigation. It is in the exposition of this last point that we are most apt to witness the influence of theories of degeneration, insofar as the criminals invariably afford evidence for their employment.

One example, from 1896, *Dr. Rumsey's Patient*, has Meade and Halifax detailing how the protagonist Doctor Rumsey interprets symptoms in terms of an inheritable brain disease:

> [I]t is my duty to tell you frankly that this condition of things, if not immediately arrested, will lead to a complete atrophy of your mental system, and you, in short, will not long survive it. You told me once very graphically that you were a man who carried about with you a dead soul. I did not believe you then. Now I believe that nothing in your own description of your case has been exaggerated. (179)

In this early story, the crisis of degeneration is restricted to the form of an organic malady from which, if proper steps are taken, the patient may be restored. A survey of Victorian detective literature will reveal that foreigners are naturally more susceptible to disease than their robust English counterparts.

The ending of *Dr. Rumsey's Patient* is perhaps meant to recapitulate humanity's triumph over the otherwise inevitable extinction that would result from unchecked degeneration, with its closing lines offering a tidy summary: "you have learned the bitter and awful lesson of how a man may fall, rise again, and in the end conquer" (305). In the nineteenth century, as in the twenty-first, the nature of the relationship between human beings and nature is ambiguous: culture and technology are disdained for interfering with the natural order (a point of view engendered by Social Darwinism), and yet both literary-minded as well as scientifically-minded writers were beginning to discern ways in which culture and technology might enhance nature in order to "guide" human evolution in eugenically favorable ways.

In Meade's short stories, Halifax is sometimes presented as a doctor narrating his own adventures, and in other cases merely an author presenting the adventures of other medical personnel. The aesthetic element is often somewhat Gothic (as in the case of Edgar Allan Poe, one of the earliest practitioners of the genre), and stories are as much exhibitions of physiognomy as they are explications of medical "deduction." As such, they are revealing examples of Lawrence Frank's notion of narrative science. Like the geologist forced to "narrate" temporally remote events based only on sedimentation, for example, the criminal detective is called upon to recapitulate a crime by extrapolating back in time based only on examination of artifacts, or what we more commonly call 'evidence.'

Meade and Eustace collaborated on a series of medico-detective stories published in *Harmsworth Magazine* between April 1899 and June 1901, of which the most compelling entry is "The Great Pink Pearl," offering perhaps the most revealing example of formal overlap between the fields of medicine and detection. To briefly summarize the story: a young colonialist obtains a huge pearl worth a fortune that marks him as a target for mercenary thieves. When he is attacked, he makes a narrow escape with the pearl in his pocket, crawling to a surgeon who operates to save him even as the attack ensues. As the thieves close in, the doctor sews the great pearl into the fellow's open chest wound just seconds before he is himself killed. The patient survives, but is compelled to undergo hypnosis in order to remember the dying doctor's explanation of where he hid the pearl. Thus, the form of the two genres achieves perfect overlap: the crime is thwarted by heroic medical measures, and the recovery of the pearl (i.e., the solution to the mystery) is achieved through nineteenth-century medical technology: anesthetic surgery and Mesmerism.

But the most interesting narratives concocted by Meade came between October 1902 and March 1903, when she and another collaborator, Robert Eustace, published a series of six rather unusual detective stories celebrating not a paragon of rational investigation such as Holmes, but rather a diabolical and inveterate criminal known as Madame Sara. Gathered together in 1903 in the collection called *The Sorceress of the Strand*, these stories offer an alternative aesthetic to the Sherlockian fascination with articulate rationality and definitive culpability. As Jennifer Halloran writes in a 2002 essay on the Madame Sara collection,

> Unlike traditional detective stories, where the detective's foregone defeat of the criminal offers readers a narrative of social order and control, the Madame Sara stories provide a dystopic view of a society in which the aberrant criminal can be contained only provisionally. (176)

The inherent xenophobia of the Victorian era is well-known but particularly apparent in these tales in which the "degenerate" criminal achieves her apotheosis and, as Halloran puts it, is dangerously "poised to penetrate and contaminate British society" (178).

Meade's collaborations with Eustace (and to a similar extent her collaborations with Halifax) offer a different slant on the differential aesthetic that obtains wherever "advanced" or civilized races are depicted in contrast to "degenerate," primitive, or atavistic ones. Halloran argues that what is precisely so disturbing about a protagonist such as Madame Sara is that she bears traits of the exotic "other" (she is part Indian and part Italian) at the same time that she embodies "the pinnacle of intellect, and beauty, which was supposed to be conferred upon the 'superior races'" (191).

A common theme in colonial literature explores the frightening consequences that might ensue should "primitive" tribes gain the technological benefits of civilization without meanwhile possessing the requisite "civilized" ethics – and Madame Sara, with her arsenal of medical gadgetry ("delicate needle-pointed instruments of bright steel, tiny lancets, and forceps," for example, and an array of batteries for "administering static electricity," not to mention a "chloroform and ether apparatus" ["Madame Sara" 327]) in this way epitomizes the degenerate doctor.

Such chauvinism appears throughout Meade's medical stories, both those she wrote in conjunction with Halifax and those she wrote with Eustace. Doctor Halifax repeatedly encounters those we are to understand as villains in the stories, making overt reference to their unsavory features. A few examples from the collection *Stories from the Diary of a Doctor* (1894) should suffice to make the point. In the story "Very Far West," for example, Halifax notes that

> I was startled by the fixed gaze of the man who sat by her side. His closely-set dark eyes were fixed on me. He seemed to look me all over. There was a sinister expression in the thin lines of his closely-shut lips. The moment I glanced at him he turned away. I felt a sudden sense of repulsion. I have had something of the same feeling when I looked full into the eyes of a snake. (58)

Clearly Halifax's scrutiny of the fellow reveals an animal, and not simply one on the order of a lower mammal – a dog, say, who might very well turn away when stared at – but rather a *reptile*. The dark eyes, the thin lips, the absolute absence of emotion in the visage of the fellow all clearly indicate that order of nature which is wholly alien to the human, and yet because the man so closely resembles a human being, the effect is all the more chilling. The terror borne of the simultaneous recognition of otherness *and* family resemblance, according to many critics of colonial literature, is precisely what lies behind the invariably vicious treatments natives experience at the hands of the colonialists.

In Meade's stories, so-called professionals are not unique in their ability to offer such fleeting assessments of human character: even a layperson, it turns out, can discern a person's depth of moral rectitude and intellectual prowess. When Lenora Whitby, the main character in "Very Far West," solicits the help of Dr. Halifax, she notes, "You look clever. The moment I saw your face, I knew you were clever. The moment I looked at your hands, I saw capabilities in them. You have got the hands of a good surgeon" (65). Miss Whitby, it turns out, is an attractive treacherous criminal who has lured Dr. Halifax into her ostensibly sick father's house so that she can rob him. Though Halifax comes out the unsatisfied victim, he had been sage enough to observe at first glance that "she was wonderfully beautiful [but] a strange sensation of admiration mixed with repulsion came over me, as I stood by the hearth and watched her" (68).

Hence, without being able to avail himself of the data he instinctively gathers, Halifax is nevertheless attuned enough to the criminal "type" to sense that something is amiss. Like Adam in Eden, Halifax is bewitched by the beauty of an otherwise sinister female, even though he had earlier seen her consorting with a man resembling a serpent. Miss Whitby stands as a clear prototype for Madame Sara. The emphasis on physiology as a foundation for behavior and moral (or amoral) status finds expression in much of Meade's detective fiction.

Given Meade and her collaborators' tendency to follow the chauvinistic habits of the era in depicting foreigners as dangerous throwbacks to savagery and the primitive, pre-moral stage of human development, her presentation of Madame Sara is especially remarkable in that her villainess becomes, like Milton's Satan, a kind of superhuman hero. Madame Sara is never apprehended or defeated by those who pursue her. In the science of medicine and dentistry she outstrips her pursuers, and she is De Quincey's dream girl: a murderess who lists her day job as either '*parfumeuse*,' or – in an even more Dorian Gray-ish turn of phrase – 'beauty restorer.'

In the Madame Sara stories, Meade and Eustace have brought to the stage all of the topical elements I cite here: the detectives as well as the criminals practice medicine both as arts and sciences, and the crimes are treated on both sides as aesthetic phenomena. What is unique in their contribution to the genre is their creation of the "first female psychopath," in Jack Adrian's phrase – "the extraordinarily malevolent Madame Sara" (108). In my view, Madame Sara represents the logical extension of Victorian apprehension about degeneration in a literary manner that demonstrates the convergence of aesthetics and science, or science at least as it was interpreted by the Positivist school of criminology.

Madame Sara represents the sinister specter of the degenerate type, insofar as she is by birth an exotic hybrid of Indian and Italian, and yet she possesses a beauty and range of intelligence that surpasses in every respect her English counterparts; in every respect, that is, except the moral realm. Our narrators describe in great detail her medical acumen and reputation as a surgeon. From the story "Madame Sara," Halloran takes the line "she occasionally performs small surgical operations" coupled with "she does what is necessary for them" (314) to suggest that Madame Sara is, among other things, a back alley abortionist (Halloran 184).

In short, the most alarming aspect of Madame Sara's presentation is that she in no way adheres to the classical, Lombrosian description of the criminal type: she presents herself instead with the "innocent, frank gaze of a child" (315), and she exhibits an intellect that clearly surpasses that of her antagonists, since she repeatedly eludes them and proves the victor. In fact, it is precisely her triumph over them that accords with the fear associated in the Victorian period with degeneration and decadence. Madame Sara exceeds the finest qualities of the English among whom she moves socially, but her genetic disposition has left her absolutely devoid of a moral sense. Her atavism may be seen in her childlike, sociopathic approach to human relations. Moreover, she announces clearly her amorality, and displays with pride the implements of her dastardly trade: as she demonstrates her medical equipment to Dixon Druce, she says, "These are my secrets. By means of these I live and flourish." Almost a full century before Michel Foucault popularized Bacon's maxim, she informs Druce that "Knowledge is power" (318), and that through the power of her intellect she means to secure her position among the power brokers in the world. In practical terms, this means exploiting her knowledge of non-European toxin sources to perfect undetectable poisons, which she uses frequently and successfully throughout the six volume series of stories.

Madame Sara possesses uncanny scientific aptitude, and her knowledge of chemistry rivals that of Professor Piozzi, her attempted victim in "The Talk of the Town," the fourth story in the series, in which he is described as the world's "greatest experimental chemist" (67). Like Madame Sara, however, the professor is Italian, which creates an important point of contrast: as Vandeleur puts it, "the man is a foreigner; he has not got an Englishman's knack of keeping his temper under control," a degenerate trait that does not afflict Madame Sara, though she also is a foreigner (70). Once more, the exotic "other," inhabited by superior intelligence and an absence of conscience, makes Madame Sara a truly horrific antagonist.

In the fifth installment in the saga, "The Bloodstone," Madame Sara victimizes a once attractive young woman named Violet Bouverie in order to steal a world-famous gem known as "the bloodstone." Vandeleur confesses his amazement at "a healthy English girl being shattered by nerves," though it is clear that she is, to put it bluntly, in the process of decay: "She is losing her looks; she gets thinner and older-looking by the day" (199). The cause of her degenerative distress, naturally, is Madame Sara, who has contrived not only to steal the gem while it is housed at the Bouverie mansion, but to pin the crime on Violet. This episode does not require Madame Sara to employ her incredible medical knowledge, but instead depends on her fluency in Arabic and her personal acquaintance with certain Persian luminaries. "I was at Teheran for a time many years ago," she admits to Dixon Druce, "and I was a special friend of the late Shah's" (204).

Madame Sara's intrigue is, however, revealed in the story by way of a medical experiment. Violet's illness, it turns out, is precisely the thing by which her innocence can be proved. Vandeleur reports that "the medicine I have been giving her happens to contain large doses of iodine of potassium," and that "the drug is eliminated very largely by the mucous membranes, and the lachrymal gland, which secretes the tears" (211). Since the main piece of evidence linking Violet to the theft is a handkerchief identified as her own, Vandeleur runs chemical tests on it to show that it contains no traces of "iodine of potassium," thus demonstrating that it was a plant, and that Madame Sara has struck again.

The final installment, "The Teeth of the Wolf," demonstrates most saliently the ramifications of the Victorian fascination with degeneration. Accordingly, it most clearly illustrates the dimension of bigotry that accompanies such distorted evolutionary thought. In this episode, the immediate crisis involves a young woman named Laura Bensasan whose dastardly mother is in cahoots with Madame Sara to force her to marry "a horrible misshapen little man – a dwarf of the name of Rigby," who Vandeleur describes with contempt as "half Jew, half Greek" (279). It so happens that Laura's mother is the world's preeminent animal trainer, whose specialty is wolves. Mrs. Bensasan differs from her daughter in the extreme: whereas Laura is young and beautiful, the mother exhibits a grotesque appearance to match her unflinching cruelty to the animals she "trains." Druce describes her unflatteringly: "the brow was low, the eyes very large and very brilliant, but I thought them altogether destitute of humanity. The nose was thick, with wide nostrils, and the mouth was hideous, cut like a slit across her face" (281). To top it off, her mouth is beset with false teeth manufactured by Madame Sara that actually imitate those of the wolves she trains.

Rigby appears even more horrible, his face marked by "hillocks and excrescences, the forehead bulging forward, the eyes going back very deeply into their sockets [. . .] his face covered with a thick black moustache and short beard" (282). In short, the two characters are undeniably atavistic, "throwbacks," in Lombroso's phrase to a lower order on the scale of animal development. Mrs. Bensasan admits as much to Druce, when she remarks that "that great wolf seems part of me. Once, in some primeval age, we must have been akin" (283).

This singular series of stories concludes with the death of Madame Sara, her throat torn out by a Siberian wolf. Just before she is attacked, she fires fatal gunshots into Mrs. Bensasan, who confesses the complex crime the two of them had planned as the life drains from her. It seems fitting that Madame Sara should elude human apprehension, only to succumb to the attack of a wild beast that – like her – is devoid of moral capability.

The character of Madame Sara is a unique and fascinating figure for a host of reasons: in spite of her undeniable criminality, she stands as woman impossible for her male antagonists to subdue and thus embodies a feminism that challenges the nineteenth-century sexual order; in spite of her lack of an Anglo-Nordic heritage, she exhibits a dramatically superior intelligence, exceedingly successful social graces, and striking beauty – thus undermining the chauvinism of her day. Except for her petty pecuniary interest, she would appear much less malevolent and more at home in the Nietzschean world of Olaf Stapledon's delightful *Odd John* (1935).

Most vexing, of course, is her utter lack of ethical compunction – the single degenerative atavism that marks her most dangerous. The formal aesthetics of the Victorian detective story require a criminal who looks the part, but Madame Sara opens a fissure in this mold. By surpassing her pursuers in medical, scientific, and social finesse, Madame Sara nullifies the whole slate of aesthetic assumptions requisite to the detective story, not the least of which is that the detective should, through ratiocination, triumph. Accordingly, the Madame Sara stories represent a unique crystallization of Victorian apprehensions about race, culture, gender, and the (d)evolutionary power of nature.

## Works Cited

Adrian, Jack. Afterword. *The Detections of Miss Cusack*. By L. T. Meade and Robert Eustace. Ed. Douglas G. Greene and Jack

Adrian. Shelburne, Ontario and Sauk City, Wisconsin: The Battered Silicon Dispatch Box, 1998. 107-10.

Bleiler, Everett F., ed. *A Treasury of Victorian Detective Stories*. New York: Charles Scribner's Sons, 1979.

Breuer, Hans-Peter. "Darwinism in Victorian Letters." *Literature and Medicine* 6 (1987): 128-38.

Darwin, Charles. *The Descent of Man, and Selection in Relation to Sex*. London: John Murray, 1871.

_____. *On the Origin of Species by Means of Natural Selection, or The Preservation of Favoured Races in the Struggle for Life*. London: John Murray, 1859.

Frank, Lawrence. *Victorian Detective Fiction and the Nature of Evidence: The Scientific Investigations of Poe, Dickens, and Doyle*. New York: Palgrave Macmillan, 2003.

Greene, Douglas G., and Jack Adrian, eds. *The Detections of Miss Cusack by L. T. Meade and Robert Eustace*. Shelburne, Ontario and Sauk City, Wisconsin: The Battered Silicon Dispatch Box, 1998.

Gould, Stephen J. *The Mismeasure of Man*. Scranton, Pennsylvania: W. W. Norton, 1981.

Greene, Douglas G. "The Only Women: The Female Sleuth in Fiction." *Baker Street Journal* 53.2 (Summer 2003): 6-13.

Halloran, Jennifer A. "The Ideology Behind *The Sorceress of the Strand*: Gender, Race, and Criminal Witchcraft." *English Literature in Transition, 1880-1920* 45.2 (2002): 176-94.

Hoffman, Nancy Y. "The Doctor and the Detective Story." *JAMA* 224.1, 2 Apr. 1973: 74-77.

Kestner, Joseph A. *Sherlock's Sisters: The British Female Detective, 1864-1913*. Aldershot, England: Ashgate, 2003.

Lombroso, Cesare. *Criminal Man, According to the Classification of Cesare Lombroso*. Reprint of 1911 English ed. Montclair, New Jersey: Patterson Smith, 1972.

_____. *L'uomo delinquente*. Milan: Hoepli, 1876.

Meade, L. T., and Dr. Halifax. *Dr. Rumsey's Patient*. New York: Hurst, 1896.

Meade, L. T., and Clifford Halifax. *Stories from the Diary of a Doctor*. Facsimile reprint of 1895 ed. of Philadelphia: Lippincott. New York: Arno, 1976.

Meade, L. T., and Robert Eustace. "The Blood-Red Cross." Russell 328-41.

_____. "The Bloodstone." *Strand Magazine: An Illustrated Monthly* 25 (1903): 198-212.

_____. "The Face of the Abbot." Russell 342-55.

_____. "Madame Sara." Russell 313-27.

_____. "The Talk of the Town." *Strand Magazine: An Illustrated Monthly* 25 (1903): 67-80.

_____. "The Teeth of the Wolf." *Strand Magazine: An Illustrated Monthly* 25 (1903): 279-90.

_____. "The Great Pink Pearl." *Harmsworth Magazine* June 1901: 395-402.

Morel, Bénédict Augustin. *Traité des dégénérescences physiques, intellectuelles et morales de l'espèce humaine*. Paris: J. B. Baillière, 1857.

Morton, Peter. *The Vital Science: Biology and the Literary Imagination 1860-1900*. London: George Allen & Unwin, 1984.

North, Julian. "Defining Decadence in Nineteenth-Century French and British Criticism." *Romancing Decay: Ideas of Decadence in European Culture*. Ed. Michael St. John. Aldershot, England: Ashgate, 1999.

Peterson, Audrey. *Victorian Masters of Mystery*. New York: Frederick Ungar, 1984.

Pyrhönen, Heta. *Murder from an Academic Angle: An Introduction to the Study of the Detective Narrative*. Columbia, SC: Camden House, 1994.

Reade, Winwood. *The Martyrdom of Man*. 1872. Humanist Library. London: Pemberton, 1968.

Russell, Alan K., ed. *Rivals of Sherlock Holmes: Forty Stories of Crime and Detection from the Original Magazines.* Selected by Alan K. Russell. Secaucus, NJ: Castle, 1978.

Savitz, Leonard D. Introduction. *Criminal Man, According to the Classification of Cesare Lombroso*. Montclair, New Jersey: Patterson Smith, 1972.

Sayers, Dorothy. Introduction. *The Omnibus of Crime*. New York: Doubleday, Doran, 1929.

St. John, Michael. *Romancing Decay: Ideas of Decadence in European Culture*. Aldershot, England: Ashgate, 1999.

Stapledon, Olaf. *Odd John*. London: Methuen, 1935.

Thoms, Peter. *Detection and Its Designs: Narrative and Power in 19th-Century Detective Fiction*. Athens, Ohio: Ohio UP, 1998.

Wells, H. G. *The Island of Doctor Moreau*. London: William Heinemann, 1896.

Wolfgang, Marvin E. "Cesare Lombroso." *Pioneers in Criminology*. Ed. Hermann Mannheim. 2nd ed. Montclair, New Jersey: Patterson Smith, 1972. 232-91.

# The Science of Detection: Geology and Aesthetics in Victorian and Edwardian Detective Fiction

Helen Sutherland
University of Glasgow

**Abstract:** In this essay I argue that Victorian and Edwardian detective fiction both arose from, and offered a critique of, the intellectual and aesthetic currents of the day. In the first part of the essay the focus is upon Sherlock Holmes, a detective whose outlook is scientific and whose methodology is similar to that of geology and palaeontology, and I suggest that this imposes a particularly strict form of mimesis upon the stories. I then consider some ways in which this mimesis is undercut by the introduction of elements of the fantastic, before exploring Holmes' relationship to the Aesthetic Movement of the late nineteenth century.

In the second part of the essay, I consider G. K. Chesterton's creation of Father Brown as an antithesis to Holmes, arguing that as a Christian apologist, Chesterton's teleological view of life releases his methodology from any geological underpinning, lifting the stories from a moral to a spiritual plane, resulting in a different type of story. Finally, I suggest that these detectives stand at the head of two distinct traditions, each of which can be traced throughout the twentieth century.

A close kin to sensation fiction, and written for the newly literate mass market, detective stories have a reputation for superficiality and triviality, with protagonists who are closer to stereotypes than subtly nuanced, psychologically convincing characters. Taken together these aspects suggest that detective fiction is light, escapist reading – the "fiction of the sickroom and the railway carriage" (Ousby vii) – but nevertheless it can be argued that in the hands of its ablest practitioners at least, early detective fiction both arose from, and offered a critique of the intellectual and aesthetic currents of the day.

In this essay I will explore two such currents. The first is contemporary scientific thought, and I shall argue that although in his Sherlock Holmes stories Conan Doyle is advancing a secular and scientific worldview that owes its existence to the work of Charles Lyell (1797-1875) and Charles Darwin (1808-1882), he also offers some implicit criticisms of that view.

The second major aspect of Victorian thought to be explored is aesthetic and I shall argue that although detective fiction, like much Victorian fiction, is characterised by mimesis or the imitation of an "external reality" (Jackson 33) this dominant mimesis is invaded by elements of the fantastic, before going on to suggest some links with the late nineteenth-century Aesthetic Movement.

The main focus of this essay is Sherlock Holmes, not merely as he was the most popular Victorian detective (in fact J. E. Preston Muddock's Dick Donovan could compete for that claim in the 1890s at least) but as the most enduring of Victorian detectives. A secondary reason for the focus upon Holmes is that he was the detective that other writers responded to, either positively in emulation or negatively in creating detectives who were radically different from Holmes. Of these latter detectives, I shall use Father Brown, the creation of G. K. Chesterton, to contrast with Holmes.

In their simplest form detective stories have at their heart a crime, or what appears to be a crime, and their main business is with the processes by which the circumstances surrounding the crime are unravelled and the malefactor tracked down. This is the job of the detective, who may be professional or amateur, and either regularly involved in criminal cases or drawn to the role of detective on a single occasion only. Whatever his status, and regardless of the motives driving him, whether public good or private satisfaction, the detective will have made a conscious decision to solve the crime and bring the criminal to justice, and at the end of the case he usually shares his methodology, thoughts and actions with a partner, assistant or audience and thus indirectly with the reader.

However, the wide definition just offered embraces other works of popular fiction which share the characteristic features of detective fiction but are not normally considered as such. One such example is *The Strange Case of Dr. Jekyll and Mr. Hyde* by Robert Louis Stevenson, for despite its usual categorisation as Gothic, it has a crime (initially blackmail is suspected, but later murder is actually committed), a detective in the person of the lawyer, Mr. Utterson, and an ultimate explanation of the crime by means of Jekyll's final written confession which is read out by the lawyer.

This generic slippage from Gothic to detective fiction emphasises the latter's close relationship to sensation fiction, which secured its enormous popularity but simultaneously excluded it from the canon of serious literature. However, this inherent sensationalism also leads the genre itself to its most famous protagonist, Sherlock Holmes, who turns to cocaine and morphine when life fails to provide him with the intensity of sensation he requires. As he explains to Dr. Watson:

> My mind [. . .] rebels at stagnation. Give me problems, give me work, give me the most abstruse cryptogram, or the most intricate analysis and I am in my own proper atmosphere. I can dispense with artificial stimulants. But I abhor the dull routine of existence. I crave for mental exaltation. (*Sign of Four* 89-90)

Furthermore, and despite his criticism of Watson for having "degraded what should have been a course of lectures into a series of tales" by infusing each of his statements with "colour and life"

("Copper Beeches" 317), Holmes himself can rarely resist presenting his findings in the most dramatic way possible. Rather than simply returning a stolen document to a client, for example, Holmes conceals it under the cover of a dish on the breakfast table, which he then almost forces the client to lift, commenting afterwards that "Watson here will tell you that I never can resist a touch of the dramatic" ("Naval Treaty" 466).

A further example of Holmes' showmanship is in his return to Baker Street after his supposed death in the Falls of Reichenbach. Disguise is no doubt necessary for Holmes' safety, but to remove that disguise in the few seconds Watson's attention is distracted creates, in the detective's own words, an "unnecessarily dramatic re-appearance" ("Empty House" 486) which causes Watson to faint from shock.

The showman in Holmes is, however, eclipsed by the scientist, and here Conan Doyle is responding to the intellectual currents of the day in a number of ways. First, the interest in detection itself can be related to the general interest in science, the aim of which was to "provide a true description of the world" (Okasha 59), and, more specifically, to the rise of forensic science during the nineteenth century. Secondly, although many of the stories are unscientific in detail, with Holmes relying upon the outmoded Bertillion system and disregarding finger-printing which was coming to replace it, and apparently believing that starvation makes available to the brain "energy and nerve force" which otherwise would be used by the digestive system ("Norwood Builder" 505), Holmes himself is always presented as a scientist, a rigorous logician who is single-minded in pursuit of the criminal and a stranger to the emotions which have so large a role in the lives of most people.

For the most part, the presentation of Holmes as scientist is positive, since he uses his knowledge to benefit innocent people and for the good of society. However, there is sufficient ambivalence in the projection of the detective as scientist to suggest that Conan Doyle is offering a critique of the scientist and, by implication, of science itself. This sense of ambivalence is created largely by the emphasis on Holmes' emotional coldness which is depicted as a characteristic of the scientist, and it is this which deflects the reader's sympathetic identification away from the detective and onto his companion, Watson, whose main function is to mediate between the detective and the reader.

It should also be noted that the most ingenuous criminals are also men of science. Of Dr Grimesby Roylott, who has murdered one step-daughter and is about to murder another by means of a swamp adder, Holmes comments: "when a doctor goes wrong he is the first of criminals" ("Speckled Band" 270). Holmes' most dangerous opponent is yet another man of science,[1] Professor Moriarty, a "man of good birth and excellent education, endowed by nature with a phenomenal mathematical facility [. . .] a genius, a philosopher, an abstract thinker" ("Final Problem" 470-71). It is these very qualities which make him outstanding that also make him so dangerous when, because of a "criminal stain in his blood" (471) he turns to crime.

Although Stevenson's man of science, Dr. Henry Jekyll, is not actually a criminal, it is his actions which make the crimes possible, for wishing to pursue his "undignified" (Stevenson 65) pleasures without loss of public approbation, he takes a drug which will give an outward, physical body to the "lower elements of his soul"

---

[1] He is a mathematician and strictly speaking mathematics is not actually a science. It is, however, the language of science and its applications are scientific.

(62). The result is Edward Hyde, who is responsible for the crimes outlined in the tale.

This suggests that the role and powers of the scientist in the nineteenth century gave Stevenson some unease, as they did Conan Doyle, but in Stevenson's case they assume the specific form of recidivism, the fear of reverting to crime, thought to be related to a more primitive state of being. To some extent, then, this is the converse of evolution, for if mankind evolved from apes[2] through many pre-human stages to its sophisticated nineteenth-century form, then there is nothing intrinsically impossible in the degeneration back into the actions and outlook of an earlier, more bestial form.

Neither Stevenson nor Conan Doyle is in any sense opposed to science, but both writers raise concerns about the consequences of moral weakness in the individual scientist when this is fused with the powers that science confers, and this in turn raises questions of moral responsibility and the scientist's relationship to society – questions which have returned with renewed force in the twenty-first century.

Although the Holmes stories are, as I have suggested, unscientific in detail, at a more fundamental level they are deeply scientific in outlook and owe a large debt to the science of the day, particularly to the sciences of geology and palaeontology, which played a major part in the provision of a "true description of the world" (Okasha 59), both in its present form and as it had existed in previous aeons. The theories of Charles Lyell in *Principles of Geology* (1830-1833) and Charles Darwin in *On the Origin of*

[2] This is, of course, a crude rendering of the theories outlined by Darwin in *On the Origin of Species* (1859), but this was the popular notion of Darwin's teaching. It should also be remembered that in some versions of evolutionary theory, the starting point was the highest form of an organism with later developments being a degeneration of that original excellence.

*Species* (1859) and *Descent of Man* (1871) upheld a belief in uniformitarianism, in which the world is believed to have developed by fixed natural laws operating through time, rather than by the special intervention of a creator God, or even by a series of natural convulsions. Uniformitarianism thus opens up the way to a reconstruction of the past through the correct reading of the fragmentary evidence found in the present. For these scientists, the earth itself was a text or palimpsest which could be read by the expert who would learn from it what life was actually like in past ages which are no longer directly accessible.

To that extent, then, the science of detection itself is closely patterned on the methodology of scientists, for as one critic has argued: "Like the geologist or palaeontologist, the detective explains a fact or an event by placing it within a chronological series; he then imaginatively transforms it into a chain of natural causes and effects, reaching backward in time to some posited originating moment" (Frank 157).

Just as geologists "read" fragments of the earth, so Sherlock Holmes "reads" material objects which constitute the fragmentary evidence which is all that is left of a past state: from a watch handed to him by Watson, for example, Holmes reads the history of Watson's elder brother from prosperity to alcoholism (*Sign of Four* 92) and, incidentally, demonstrates in the process the emotional coldness already discussed.

Two things follow from this. First, the extraordinary importance of material objects, with even story titles reflecting this. Examples taken almost at random from J. E. Preston Muddock's Dick Donovan stories, which were published in the *Dundee Weekly News* in 1888, include "The Tuft of Red Hair," "The Pearl Necklace," "The Pearl Button" and "The Mystery of the Tin Box." Holmes, however, takes the scrutiny of material objects to new heights, not least because Conan Doyle often shows Watson's inept attempts at deduction from the same objects. Given the hat which is the starting point of "The Blue Carbuncle" Watson "can see nothing" while Holmes finds evidence relating to the owner's intelligence, his worsening financial situation, some "moral retrogression" probably linked to alcoholism, his marriage problems, sedentary lifestyle, the lack of gas in his house, and his lingering self-respect (246). As Holmes explains to Watson "you can see everything. You fail, however, to reason from what you see" (246). Holmes' proficiency as an expert is emphasised by this comparison, and an aura of superiority is the inevitable result.

The second thing to follow from the patterning of detection upon the methods of geology is the strong mimetic aesthetic underpinning the genre. Just as science depends upon the accurate observation and recording of data to provide a "true description of the world," so, too, does detection. This accounts for the frequent references Watson makes to his own notes made at the time of the investigation and to Holmes' encyclopaedic indexing system, both of which offer assurances of accuracy since they by-pass human memory which is notoriously unreliable.

The claim of the detective to unfold hidden events exactly as they happened imposes a particularly strict form of mimesis in which the detective writer is tied to the physical laws and conditions of the real world. Hard scientific fact is the overriding concern, making this a form of forensic mimesis which is closer to a case history written by a doctor than to a story written for its entertainment value, and it is, perhaps, no coincidence that this was both Watson's and Conan Doyle's profession.

The detective story's underlying mimesis of course links it to contemporary mainstream (or serious) literature and painting, both of which were predominantly realist in mode, in that they provided a representation (or "true description") of the world as it was experienced by the original readers and viewers. However, in both these art forms the dominant mimesis was modified by a strong vein of fantasy, and in detective fiction there is a similar invasion of realism by fantasy.

One way this is achieved is by presenting the detective as a magician or shaman possessing supernatural powers. In its mildest and least satisfactory form this becomes the hunch which ensures that the detective is uniquely positioned to gain the information he needs. In "The Lady in the Sealskin Coat," for example, Dick Donovan claims that some "vague, shadowy presentiment that something might turn up" (Preston Muddock 29) prompted him to linger at Glasgow docks long enough to spot the people he sought as they boarded the Dublin steam-packet just as she was about to sail – an identification which was crucial to the success of the investigation.

Without acting on mysterious hunches, Holmes is nevertheless often regarded by his inferiors in detection as a magician or wizard, but in his final exposition of the case he always shows that these magical effects are achieved through logical deduction based on accurate and minute observation of data: they simply appear magical because of the failure of others (including the readers) to see the significance he sees in the objects he finds during the course of an investigation. Disclaimers notwithstanding, however, a sense of the magical remains with the detective, and this mystique may be a reflection of that surrounding the scientist who also has knowledge which is hidden from the rest of society and is able to change things for better or worse by natural means not available to the general public.

A significant degree of authority is thus invested in scientist and detective alike, and on occasion this assumes disturbing aspects, for Holmes has a tendency to regard himself as apart from, or even above, the law. In "The Adventure of Charles Augustus Milverton" Holmes not only breaks into Milverton's house, an action which he regards as morally justifiable if technically criminal, but also watches as Milverton is murdered and refuses to do anything about it on the grounds that there are "certain crimes which the law cannot touch and which therefore [. . . ] justify private revenge" (582) while in "The Adventure of Abbey Grange" he allows the murderer to go free on the grounds that he acted under severe provocation.

In some instances an element of fantasy is created by a more direct suggestion of the supernatural. In *Jekyll and Hyde* what appears initially to be a case of the blackmail of a respectable by an unscrupulous man soon develops into the haunting of one man by his *Doppelgänger*, although in fact Hyde's malevolence is moral rather than supernatural and he owes his physical embodiment to a drug acting on the lower elements of Jekyll's soul – a far-fetched explanation, perhaps, but one which remains grounded within the realm of nature.

In *The Hound of the Baskervilles* Conan Doyle outlines the legend of the Baskerville family to suggest a curse upon the family, and the circumstances surrounding the death of Sir Charles Baskerville seem to support this idea, eventually convincing even the local doctor who has a logical and scientific mind. The aura of the supernatural is maintained until the very end of the story when it is revealed that the hell-hound who had been both glimpsed and heard by a number of people was in fact simply a huge mastiff daubed with phosphorous to make it glow in the dark, and was being used as part of a plot to kill the Baskerville heir, so that his cousin, living nearby but under a different name, might inherit the title and estate.

The supernatural is even more directly invoked in "The Adventure of the Devil's Foot," in which a woman, who seems to have died of fear, is found at a card table with two of her brothers who are clearly insane, while the third brother dies in a similar way the following day. The story is set in rural Cornwall, making it easier to suggest a supernatural agency directly at work, although Holmes correctly deduces that an obscure drug has been used.

In all these examples what seems at first to be supernatural is turned back on itself to emphasise the natural explanation and reinforce the mimetic mode of the fiction, and this is in opposition to the use of fantasy within mainstream fiction where fantasy is often used to qualify the predominant mimetic mode and offer a means of exploring unseen aspects of life, such as the emotional or the spiritual.

As already suggested, detective fiction is related to the intellectual, and particularly the scientific, context of the late Victorian period, and in its mimetic grounding it is related to the aesthetic currents of the day. More specifically, however, the Sherlock Holmes stories can be related to the Aesthetic Movement of the 1880s and 1890s. The most obvious point of comparison is in the person of Holmes himself, who can be seen as a Decadent hero attracted to the bizarre or even grotesque and dependent upon intense sensation for satisfaction, for as we have seen, dull routine causes Holmes to reach for cocaine and morphine.

It is clear, too, that although Holmes is a man of science, and his methodology is scientific, he nevertheless regards detection as an art, and is therefore highly selective in the cases he accepts. As Watson notes, "working [. . .] rather for the love of his art than the acquirement of wealth, he refused to associate himself with any investigation which did not tend towards the unusual, and even the fantastic" ("Speckled Band" 257). Holmes is not just a detective but also a connoisseur of crime, with connoisseurship (it scarcely mattered of what) being one of the badges of the Aesthetic Movement.

The importance of material objects which has been considered in relation to contemporary science results in detective fiction paying a "supreme attentiveness to the surface of life" (Ousby 154), which can also be linked to aestheticism's concern with superficiality: "All art" wrote Oscar Wilde, "is at once surface and symbol. Those who go beneath the surface do so at their peril. Those who read the symbol do so at their peril" (22). Only the surface does not deceive or disappoint.

In this context it is worth noting that Conan Doyle and Wilde were dining together with an American publisher who then commissioned each of them to write a story for *Lippencott's Monthly Magazine*. Wilde's contribution was *The Picture of Dorian Gray*, one of the most famous (or infamous) texts of the aesthetic movement, while Conan Doyle wrote *The Sign of Four*. While there is no suggestion of the direct influence of either of these texts upon the other, it does seem clear that *Lippencott's* saw Wilde and Conan Doyle as similar types of writers, the work of both of whom would appeal to their readership.

It would be unwise to press the comparison too far, however, for where Wilde suggested that an "ethical sympathy in an artist is an unpardonable mannerism of style" (21), Conan Doyle showed increasing concern for justice[3] and modified the character of Sherlock Holmes accordingly. Ian Ousby notes that in *A Study in Scarlet* (1887) and *The Sign of Four* (1890) Holmes is "not merely a less fully realised creation than he later becomes but is also more

[3] That this went deeper than his art is clear from Doyle's later championing of George Edalji in 1906, Oscar Slater in 1910 and Roger Casement, who in 1916 was hanged for treason having attempted to enlist German aid for an Irish Uprising.

inhumanly dedicated to the principles of science and more tinged with Decadence" but by the time the *Adventures of Sherlock Holmes* (1892) and the *Memoirs of Sherlock Holmes* (1894) were published Holmes himself was "more calculated to appeal to a middle-class readership than the earlier figure. He is moved as much by a passion for justice and a sense of *noblesse oblige* as by a love of scientific truth or artistic form" (151).

Frederick De Naples agrees that the earlier Holmes has much in common with the Aesthetic Movement for he argues that

> [i]t is not an accident that a figure like Holmes, with a knack for transforming sensation into ratiocinative exercise, gained the devotion of the 1890s readers. Each Holmes story [. . .] converts the presence of, or potential for, sensation into a rationally explained series of events, no longer threatening, or at least understood and, presumably, preventable. Holmes brings to each investigation a precise understanding not only of crime and criminals, but of the means of exposing them through logic and, importantly, science. Holmes not only explains away sensation, he also restores science to its role of aiding humans instead of threatening or betraying them. (216)

According to De Naples, then, the primacy of sensation, the need for logical thought and the importance of science, all of which have been discussed above, are fused in the person of Holmes himself, but in that fusion they are themselves disarmed. Holmes' need for sensation is converted into logical thought which benefits society by tracking down dangerous criminals, by means of a science which is rendered benevolent, rather than being a force which, through the work of Lyell and Darwin, banished the comforting "traditional notion of a young earth, ruled by human will within days of its origin" and replaced it with a universe of "incomprehensible immensity, with human habitation restricted to a millimicrosecond at the very end" (Gould 2).

This explains why despite Conan Doyle's promotion of a new secular worldview based on the uniformitarianism of Lyell and Darwin which was seen by many to be pernicious because of its denial of the working of a creator God, the overall effect of the Holmes stories was reassuring, for Holmes himself seemed able to control or negate the forces that were threatening the middle-class readership of the tales, and to defend their property and uphold their values.

However, the modification of Holmes' early, extreme scientism may also reflect Conan Doyle's uneasiness with some of the implications of the secular worldview, and increasingly Holmes seems to question life's meaninglessness, until at the end of "The Adventure of the Cardboard Box," he asks:

> What object is served by this circle of misery and violence and fear? It must tend to some end, or else our universe is ruled by chance, which is unthinkable. But what end? There is the great standing perennial problem to which human reason is as far from an answer as ever.
>
> (901)

This represents a significant retreat from the whole-hearted espousal of the secular and scientific worldview implied in the earlier stories and is a reflection of Conan Doyle's increasing interest in Spiritualism, which allows for the continued existence of individuals beyond the grave, and validates the spiritual dimension of life without strictly enforcing a belief in God or invalidating the work of Lyell and Darwin.

Although Conan Doyle continued to publish Holmes stories until 1927, these later works lack the bite of the earlier tales and are burdened with a nostalgia for the lost world of the 1890s metropolis and what Chesterton called the "poetry of modern life," the expression of which he sees as the "first essential value" of the detective story ("Defence" 4). It is no wonder, then, that the detectives created in the early decades of the twentieth century were often created in reaction against Holmes, even as they continued aspects of the Holmesian tradition, and never more obviously than in the case of Chesterton's own creation, Father Brown.

In many respects, Father Brown can be seen as the complete antithesis of Sherlock Holmes. Where Holmes is tall and lean, Father Brown is short and round; where Holmes maintains an aloof superiority from other people, Father Brown is fascinated by his fellow human beings, and where Holmes' occupation is that of consulting detective, Father Brown is a priest for whom detection is an incidental activity, a sometimes unwelcome distraction from his duties to his parish.

Most important of all, however, is that as a Roman Catholic apologist Chesterton was committed to a teleological view of life, in opposition to the secular view embraced by Conan Doyle, and this has several major consequences. In the first place, science cannot be seen as supreme: although it can be a secondary cause, it can never be the First Cause that the teleological view demands, and it follows from this that the detective's methodology is released from its scientific and, more specifically, its geological patterning.

One consequence of this release is that Chesterton can arrange his narratives in a completely different way, for where Conan Doyle usually begins with Holmes going to the scene of crime and interpreting events back through time to discover who committed the crime, gathering physical evidence as he goes, Chesterton often starts with Father Brown's involvement in a narrative which will later include a crime. In "The Secret Garden," for example, Father Brown is already at a dinner party during the course of which a murder will be committed.

A second consequence of the release of detection from its scientific basis is that objects are of less importance than they were in the Holmes tales, and what importance they retain differs in kind. For example, when in "The Wrong Shape" Father Brown finds an Oriental knife, and later that knife is used to kill someone he wastes no time "reading" its surface for its immediate history, details of who had held it, where it had been, or what else it had cut, as Holmes would have done. The point for Father Brown is that it is simply "the wrong shape in the abstract" (92). It is not that Father Brown gets no information from the objects he finds, but that they provide information of a different order from the information Holmes would extract.

These two factors taken together result in a different sort of tale altogether, for Conan Doyle creates a puzzle and through Holmes provides all the evidence by which it can be solved. It is this process which provides the reader with that particular kind of pleasure which detective stories alone provide. Chesterton's stories in comparison are much less ratiocinative, and in fact operate more as fairy tales, with a sense of mystery (as opposed to puzzle) and wonder, and this may explain the lack of interest in, or concern with, what happens to the criminal. "The Invisible Man," for example, ends with the other protagonists going back to their usual concerns while "Father Brown walked those snow-covered hills under the stars for many hours with a murderer, and what they said to each other will never be known" (77).

The bizarre in the Father Brown tales inclines much more to the fantastic than the grotesque. In "The Flying Stars," for example, a common diamond theft is transformed into a fairy tale by the uncommon thief who dresses as harlequin and accomplishes the theft as part of an impromptu amateur pantomime. The crime itself has become subordinate to the way it is committed.

In fact, Father Brown's whole methodology differs radically from that of most other detectives for he explains:

> I thought out exactly how a thing like that [the murder] could be done, and in what style or state of mind a man could really do it. And when I was quite sure that I felt exactly like the murderer myself, of course I knew who he was [. . .] I thought and thought about how a man might come to be like that, until I realized that I really *was* like that, in everything except actual, final consent to the action. ("Secret of Father Brown" 464)

Father Brown's lack of specialist knowledge or particular expertise leads him to be seen as an Everyman figure (and he therefore requires no Watson to mediate between him and the reader), but in "The Secret of Father Brown" the detective as Everyman is fused with the murderer as Everyman, lifting the stories onto a spiritual rather than a moral plane. While it is true that detective fiction in general can be seen as the most moral of all fiction, since its main business is the detection of crime, the punishment of the criminal and the protection of society, Chesterton takes this a step further and Father Brown is more concerned with sin than crime, and with repentance than punishment. Flambeau, the thief in "The Flying Stars," returns the diamonds, not because he is afraid of being caught or punished, but because Father Brown convicts him of his sin, causing him both to repent and to amend his life, so that in his later appearances in the Father Brown stories it is as a detective, not a criminal.

In this way Father Brown fulfils the requirements of both priest and detective, for he reclaims the sinner whose amended life makes punishment largely irrelevant but simultaneously he identifies the criminal and prevents further crime. This dual purpose is achieved by an act of imaginative sympathy with the criminal (using 'sympathy' in its original meaning of 'to feel with'), which in turn stresses the common humanity shared by priest/detective and sinner/criminal.

This stands in stark contrast to Holmes and, to a lesser extent perhaps, to Dick Donovan, both of whom can be seen as lonely quester figures, superior beings who, standing apart from humanity, identify criminals by an act of ratiocination, not imagination. Even where Holmes allows a criminal to go unpunished as he does in "The Adventure of Abbey Grange," as we have seen, this is due to extenuating circumstances, not because of the criminal's repentance which would constitute an essential inner change redirecting his life away from crime.

The difference between Conan Doyle and Chesterton at this point is so marked as to suggest that they are writing different kinds of detective stories, with their detectives standing at the head of quite distinct traditions. The Holmesian tradition emphasises the detective story as puzzle and his descendents include Dorothy L. Sayers' Lord Peter Wimsey (1923-1939), Edmund Crispin's Gervase Fen (1944-1977), and Ngaio Marsh's Roderick Alleyn (1934-1982). The Chestertonian detective tradition, on the other hand, emphasises the detective story as moral dilemma and includes Patricia Wentworth's Miss Silver (1928-1961) and Agatha Christie's Miss Marple (1930-1976), both of whom deny possessing extraordinary gifts, relying instead on their knowledge of people, their common sense and their common humanity to identify wrong-doers.

Although both traditions may justly claim to be moral, since both are concerned with the detection of criminals and the protection of society, it is the Chestertonian tradition which may lay claim to a deeper spiritual import, although this does not necessarily make for a better detective story, for as Colin Dexter has argued, when Father Brown "proclaims the great theological truths of his own (and later Chesterton's) Roman Catholic faith [. . .] the sermon is disproportionately long; tedious even" (11), and this must be accounted one of Chesterton's weaknesses as a storyteller. However, it is also this aspect of his work that ties his Father Brown tales closely to his work as a Christian apologist, for as Erik Routley notes:

> Only with Chesterton do we have a major contribution to detective literature which is doing the same thing as his other work is doing – using fantastic means instead of argumentative means to get the same thing said about something of primary importance, in this case his optimism about the common man's common sense. (114-15)

## Works Cited

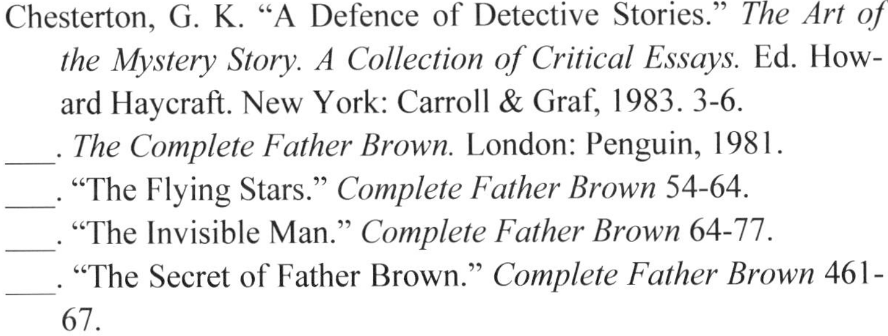

Chesterton, G. K. "A Defence of Detective Stories." *The Art of the Mystery Story. A Collection of Critical Essays.* Ed. Howard Haycraft. New York: Carroll & Graf, 1983. 3-6.

___. *The Complete Father Brown.* London: Penguin, 1981.

___. "The Flying Stars." *Complete Father Brown* 54-64.

___. "The Invisible Man." *Complete Father Brown* 64-77.

___. "The Secret of Father Brown." *Complete Father Brown* 461-67.

___. "The Secret Garden." *Complete Father Brown* 23-39.

___. "The Wrong Shape." *Complete Father Brown* 89-103.

De Naples, Frederick L. "Unearthing Holmes: 1890s Interpretations of the Great Detective." *Transforming Genres: New Approaches to British Fiction of the 1890s*. Ed. Nikki Lee Manos and Meri-Jane Rochelson. Houndsmill, Basingstoke, Hampshire: Macmillan, 1994. 215-35.

Dexter, Colin. Introduction. *The Father Brown Stories*. By G. K. Chesterton. Vol. 1. London: Folio Society, 1996.

Conan Doyle, Arthur. "The Adventure of Abbey Grange." *Penguin* 635-50.

___. "The Adventure of the Blue Carbuncle." *Penguin* 244-57.

___. "The Adventure of the Cardboard Box." *Penguin* 888-901.

___. "The Adventure of Charles Augustus Milverton." *Penguin* 572-82.

___. "The Adventure of the Copper Beeches." *Penguin* 316-32.

___. "The Adventure of the Devil's Foot." *Penguin* 954-70.

___. "The Adventure of the Empty House." *Penguin* 483-96.

___. "The Adventure of the Norwood Builder." *Penguin* 496-510.

___. "The Adventure of the Speckled Band." *Penguin* 257-73.

___. "The Final Problem." *Penguin* 469-80.

___. *The Hound of the Baskervilles*. *Penguin* 669-761.

___. "The Naval Treaty." *Penguin* 447-69.

___. *The Penguin Complete Sherlock Holmes*. Harmondsworth: Penguin, 1981.

___. *The Sign of Four*. *Penguin* 89-158.

Frank, Lawrence. *Victorian Detective Fiction and the Nature of Evidence: The Scientific Investigations of Poe, Dickens and Doyle*. Houndsmill, Basingstoke, Hampshire: Palgrave Macmillan, 2003.

Gould. Stephen Jay. *Time's Arrow, Time's Cycle: Myth and Metaphor in the Discovery of Geological Time*. Harmondsworth: Penguin, 1991.

Jackson, Rosemary. *Fantasy: The Literature of Subversion*. London and New York: Routledge, 1988.

Okasha, Samir. *Philosophy of Science: A Very Short Introduction*. Oxford: Oxford UP, 2002.

Ousby, Ian. *Bloodhounds of Heaven: The Detective in English Fiction from Godwin to Doyle*. Cambridge, MA: Harvard UP, 1976.

Preston Muddock, J. E. *Dick Donovan: The Glasgow Detective*. Ed. Bruce Durie. Edinburgh: Mercat, 2005.

___. "The Lady in the Sealskin Coat." *Dick Donovan* 16-34.

___. "The Mystery of a Tin Box." *Dick Donovan* 213-23.

___. "The Pearl Button." *Dick Donovan* 164-72.

___. "The Pearl Necklace." *Dick Donovan* 47-59.

___. "The Tuft of Red Hair." *Dick Donovan* 35-46.

Routley, Erik. *The Puritan Pleasures of the Detective Story: A Personal Monograph*. London: Gollancz, 1972.

Stevenson, Robert Louis. *The Strange Case of Dr. Jekyll and Mr. Hyde and Weir of Hermiston*. Ed. Emma Letley. Oxford: Oxford UP, 1987.

Wilde, Oscar. Preface. *The Picture of Dorian Gray*. Ed. Peter Ackroyd. London: Penguin, 1985.

# Interpreting the Work of Art and Reading Clues: Aesthetics and Detection in Wilkie Collins' *The Law and the Lady*

Elizabeth Anderman
University of Colorado, Boulder

**Abstract:** In his 1875 novel, *The Law and the Lady,* Wilkie Collins uses the aesthetic positions of John Ruskin and Walter Pater to articulate how best to read detective fiction. The reader must evaluate clues as if they were pieces of art which had the potential to reveal the truth or the mystery or the imaginative power of the criminal. Collins' juxtaposition of these two strategies suggests, however, that neither one is completely adequate. Instead it is imperative that the reader balance the two and maintain what Collins' argues is the key to any aesthetic judgment: common sense. The novel demonstrates the importance of reading clues as if they were aesthetic objects by having the mystery hinge on how a series of paintings are understood. The degree to which the reader is able to balance the pleasure of the paintings' wild imagination with the truth they reveal about their painter, is the degree to which the reader will succeed in solving the mystery before the novel reveals it.

In the middle of Wilkie Collins' detective novel, *The Law and the Lady* (1874-1875),[1] Miserrimus Dexter, a beautiful, legless, cross-dresser, announces that "Nature puts him out." Among the myriad of ideas this expression evokes, two stand out. First, it brings to mind the contemporary cultural debate about art and how best to represent nature. Second, it suggests that Dexter is marginalized

[1] David Skilton and Jenny Bourne Taylor have each done much to remove the novel from critical obscurity. Skilton locates the novel within feminist critical debate by arguing that the novel's female detective articulates a proto-feminist position which defies social and gender norms. By contrast, Bourne Taylor opens up discussion about the novel by exploring the way it, and detective fiction generally, illuminate the nineteenth-century fascination with "irrational states of mind" (xv).

by his society because he is legless. As Jenny Bourne Taylor argues, Dexter's misshapen body was understood to reflect the distorted nature of his mind. The two together represented the degeneration and decay of his family. Dexter, however, argues against the essentializing link between body and mind by choosing to address himself only to people who can see beyond his disability and perceive the power of his imagination. This is critical to the plot because the reader who reads Dexter's body as revealing the truth of his character will miss the fact that he is the mastermind of the novel's mystery. Dexter sets up the murder, manipulates the police, and sends the detective-narrator, Valeria Macallan, chasing a series of red herrings. His imagination controls the narrative and shapes detection. On the one hand, Dexter's use of aesthetic language in the inscription suggests that he is a living visual sign that cannot be interpreted from the dominant aesthetic position, which holds that good painting reveals the truth of nature. On the other hand, because he controls the novel's mystery, the aesthetic language suggests that there is a link between mystery and art – between reading visual signs and interpreting a detective story. Reading detective fiction, Dexter's inscription implies, is a balance between searching for truth – looking for Nature – and understanding the mental process of the villain – appreciating his or her imagination.

The inscription is evocative of John Ruskin's argument in *Modern Painters* (1843-1860) that works of art should attempt to represent nature without the strictures of specific aesthetic conventions. Instead, by elaborating the details, Ruskin argued, the work of art is able to represent all the levels of signification of what is being depicted, and hence its truth. In terms of detective fiction this implies that each detail or clue has the potential to represent the truth and must be valued as such. Collins mitigates this essentialist reading of the value of the detail by juxtaposing it with the ideas of Walter Pater. In a collection of essays entitled *Studies in the History of the Renaissance* (1873),[2] Pater argued, like Ruskin, that specific schools of art which codified success through specific formulae overlooked the value of many artists. Unlike Ruskin, however, Pater believed that the work of art had value, not if it was honest and represented the truth of nature, but if it provoked vivid sensations in its viewer. The trick was for the viewer to be open to "the power of being deeply moved by the presence of beautiful objects" (xxx). By being open to the emotional impact of the piece the viewer could have unmediated access to the imaginative power of the artist who created it. Nature was irrelevant in the exchange of sensation between viewer and art-work, art-work and artist because the painting's impact relied on imagination.

In the context of detective fiction, Collins' use of Pater's ideas implies that clues must be evaluated, not merely as natural and thus true, but as the outpouring of the imagination. The clue, like the work of art, has the potential to allow the detective (and the reader) access to the emotional state and imaginative power of whoever left that clue. The detective who is most open to the sensations the clue evokes will be best able to understand its significance in the plot. In other words, the clue is an open passage between the viewer and the artist – between the source of the clue and the person who finds it. The connection allows each clue to have multiple meanings depending on the perspective of the viewer and his or her ability to be open to new and provocative sensations.

---

[2] Although Pater's *Renaissance* was published just one year before *The Law and the Lady* was first serialized, parts of it had been previously published, including the celebrated conclusion which celebrated the power of art for art's sake (Phillips xii).

Collins' juxtaposition of Pater and Ruskin suggests that neither provides a completely adequate reading strategy. The reader, who reads as if everything were natural and true, overlooks the ambiguity of the clue and its potential to reveal the personality and motives of the person leaving it. On the other hand, the reader who looks merely for sensations and emotional impact will miss the potential significance of the clue in solving the mystery. By contrasting these two aesthetic ideas, Collins suggests that the pleasure of reading this novel and detective fiction in general comes from the constant play between sensations and the search for meaning. The trick is to keep the emotional and the intellectual in balance, even in a context where the sensational discovery and imaginative power of the clue obscures the truth. By using aesthetic language Collins also implies that visual signs are particularly provocative sites of meaning in detective fiction because they provoke emotional responses and can reveal truth. The paintings which follow the inscription are a perfect example of how a visual sign can provoke intense emotional responses and reveal truth. Ultimately, reading the paintings correctly is central to solving the mystery, suggesting that the aesthetic approach is central to all the clues, but particularly the visual ones which permeate the novel.

Despite the importance of the visual to *The Law and the Lady*, critical interest in the novel has tended to focus on how the first-person female detective, Valeria Macallan, disregards gender norms when, abandoned by her husband Eustace, she sets out to restore his good name. Both David Skilton and Jenny Bourne Taylor argue, however, that the novel fails to live up to its feminist potential because it ends with Valeria giving up her agency to bolster her husband's fragile masculinity.[3] Valeria's final reinscription in patriarchal culture points not only to the limitations of the novel's feminist position but also suggests that she is less important to the mystery than she at first appears. Although she is the detective, the entire narrative is guided by the imagination of Miserrimus Dexter (he is the source of the inscription and the paintings which follow it). Dexter invents the mystery by turning the first Mrs. Macallan's suicide into murder. He then manipulates all those who come into contact with it. He leads Valeria through a series of red herrings and doles out information as if it were sensual. Dexter creates the sensations of the novel and prolongs its mystery. When he finally reveals the truth of what happened he is silenced. Valeria simultaneously assumes the role of wife and mother, suggesting that she was only able to abandon her traditional gender roles while Dexter was in control of the mystery.

Dexter begins by concealing the suicide letter of the first Mrs. Macallan. He then points the police towards his "friend" Eustace Macallan as the "murderer" by using his disability to make it appear that he is an inept bungler who is trying to protect Eustace and his secrets. Dexter does all this because he loved the first Mrs. Macallan and believed that Eustace did not love his wife enough and was not worthy of her. At Eustace's trial, however, Dexter spectacularly rescues his friend from a guilty verdict by appearing in finery which highlights his disability and provokes the jury's pity. His deformity seems to allow him to speak truth, an idea Dexter relies upon when he upholds his friend's character but does not completely exonerate Eustace. His testimony leaves

[3] Skilton is critical of her final capitulation to the law of her husband and the duties of wife and mother because it ruins the proto-feminist promise of the novel. Furthermore, for Skilton it suggests that the female independent agency suggested by her detection is a kind of unleashing of the repressed which has to be re-repressed and controlled for the novel to end.

enough doubt in the mind of the jury for them to give Eustace a "Not Proven" verdict. Neither accused nor exonerated, Eustace lives under the shadow of guilt that he has killed his first wife. When he later marries Valeria he does so under an assumed name in order to protect her from his past. When she discovers it, Eustace has a breakdown and runs away. In order to restore her marriage, Valeria sets out to prove her husband's innocence. Dexter, however, manipulates her, playing on her jealousies of the women in her husband's past, in order to mislead her. Ultimately, her quest can be read as an attempt to understand him, since he is the source of the mystery. The trick is that he is a complex visual sign in his own right, one who exploits his ability to produce sensations in the people he meets.

Dexter is a legless dandy with a passion for feminine clothing and for performing Shakespeare, Nelson, and Napoleon. His deformity provokes a variety of emotional responses in those who come into contact with him, ranging from hate, to pity, from love, to anger. The forcefulness of those reactions obscures Dexter's intentions to most of them. Dexter, in fact, relies on the power of his disability to provoke sensations in order to manipulate the mystery. He uses it to make himself a living visual sign which has to be interpreted like his paintings through the lens of the inscription, in which he announces that he only addresses himself to people who do not look for mere Nature in the visual. In other words, he separates his body – the visual sign – from its potentially synecdochical relationship to his disability. It does not show truth, for to truly understand him means to acknowledge the power of his mind – of his imagination. At the same time, however, his paintings threaten to establish that he is insane because they are of horrible and violent scenes. The inscription attempts to forestall a purely Ruskinian reading which would see his abject body represented in the abject content of the paintings. Valeria's response, however, ends up being quite Paterian, despite her initial Ruskinian approach, because she is completely overwhelmed by the images in front of her. On the one hand, this implies that Dexter's imagination is powerful and worth considering. On the other, the intensity of her response to the sensations the paintings provokes keeps her from reading them as truth – from seeing them as representing what he has done. Collins maintains the ambiguity of the meaning of the paintings in order to keep the tension between imagination and truth at play in the novel because that is the pleasure of reading detective fiction and art.

Keeping imagination and nature in tension with each other as the basis of narrative is an expansion of Collins' thoughts on art, articulated in his non-fiction writings in the 1850s.[4] His 1851 review of the Great Exhibition published in the journal, *Bentley's Miscellany,* praises various painters for their "masterly adherence to the truth of Nature" ("Exhibition" 618) and for displaying a "touching truth to Nature, and a graphic eloquence of expression" (620). Both these references to the truth in nature seem direct nods to Ruskin's claim that the artist was like a poet who had to represent the essence and emotion of a scene without ignoring its de-

4 Much has already been made of the connection between Collins' writing and art. Critics such as Lillian Nayder, Dennis Dennisoff, Tim Dolin and Lucy Dougan have, arguing that his upbringing by a moderately well-known painter, William Collins, and his ongoing friendships with members of two important circles of mid-Victorian art, the pre-Raphaelite Brotherhood (particularly John Everett Millais and William Holman Hunt) and "the Clique" (a group of Royal Academy painters that included E. M. Ward, Augustus Egg, Richard Dadd, and Wiliam Frith), fundamentally influenced his writing practice. Nayder suggest that various levels of class conflict in his novels are Collins' response to his father's politically conservative artistic legacy. Denisoff argues that Collins used writing in order to erase the feminization of the term artist, and to position the artist as a middle-class, professional man. Dolin and Dougan argue that Collins takes up Ruskin's challenge to make the commonest trades honorable (15).

tails. Tim Dolin and Lucy Dougan argue that in *Basil*(1852) Collins shares Ruskin's "aesthetic aims – broadly, to develop an original for the representation of contemporary experience – which are responses to common social concerns [. . .]" (5). Even in his early writing, however, Collins was not uncritical of Ruskin or the pre-Raphaelite artists who seemed to take the idea of representing the truth of nature to an extreme. In the 1851 review he also argued that "the strict attention to detail [of the pre-Raphaelites present: C. Collins, Millais and Holman Hunt] precludes, at present, any attainment of harmony and singleness of effect. They must be admired bit by bit, as we have reviewed them, or not admired at all. Again, they appear to us to be wanting in one great desideratum of all art – judgment in selection" (624). As early as 1851 Collins perceived the distracting effect of representing the details of nature without a powerful imaginative frame to contain them. The danger of the detail is that it distracts from the whole. For the creator of a mystery the detail is useful because it can appear to be the critical clue and thus send the detective and the reader on a series of wild goose chases after various textual red herrings. By the same token it is dangerous because it threatens the breakdown of narrative coherence. As Derrida points out in *The Truth in Painting*, it is impossible to find truth when everything can be seen as a detail or frame of some other detail. The author of a mystery must fight to maintain meaning, to preserve the quest for truth, despite the excessive representation of details the form requires.

By 1856 in an anonymous article for Dickens' journal *Household Words*, entitled "To Think, or Be Thought For," Collins began to articulate a position which anticipates his use of Paterian aesthetics in *The Law and the Lady*. Although he does not directly argue for the power of the imagination, he disparages critical schools that blindly elevate certain artists and prescribe the ways to appreciate paintings. Instead Collins encourages readers to think for themselves and to value art on their own terms. He asserts:

> If anything I can say here on the subject of the Painter's Art will encourage intelligent people of any rank to turn a deaf ear to all that critics, connoisseurs, lecturers, and compilers of guide-books can tell them; to trust entirely to their own common sense when they are looking at pictures; and to express their opinions boldly, without the slightest reference to any precedents whatever – I shall have exactly achieved the object with which I now apply myself to the writing of this paper. (193)

Like Pater, Collins privileges the individual response to the work of art. Collins' call for "intelligent people" to value works of art based on their own common sense and without the constraints of guide-books can be read as laying the ground work for Pater's later claim that the true art critic should be open to "the power of being deeply moved by the presence of beautiful objects" (xxx). Unlike Pater's, however, Collins' theories are grounded in common sense. The practicality and rationality of this position reflects some of Ruskin's claims that true works of art are good because they represent a truth which everyone can apprehend without the need for critical intervention. *The Law and the Lady* reflects the tension in Collins' non-fiction writing between a proto-Paterian position and the practicality of Ruskin's. Although the inscription above Dexter's paintings makes a direct appeal to imagination, the simultaneous reference to Ruskin creates a kind of balance to the extremes of emotion that a strictly Paterian reading would engender. It reminds the reader that both are possible reading strategies but that common sense should prevail.

Valeria discovers Dexter's paintings, a series of images of the Passions and the life of the Wandering Jew, on her second visit to his house, which respectable friends and her mother-in-law have cautioned against because of the impropriety of visiting a man, particularly a mentally unstable man, alone. Valeria feels she can go, however, because Dexter is crippled – literally legless – and so does not represent the same dangers as other men. After a hair-raising trip, where Dexter's mentally handicapped hermaphroditic servant threatens to throw Valeria into the river because she is jealous of Dexter's attentions to Valeria, Valeria explores the lower level of the house while she waits for Dexter to receive her. Her solitary and unbidden penetration of the interior suggests that Valeria has a kind of independent sexual agency which makes her disregard propriety. "Indeed in the course of her investigations," Skilton remarks, "she runs real risks, which arise from a general assumption that a willingness to step beyond the social norms implies a readiness for illicit sexual adventure" (xii). By having Valeria behave in such an unladylike way, Collins implies that quests for the truth of nature are dangerous. The sexual overtones of the scene also imply, however, that there is a sensual pleasure in investigations that is inevitable.

Collins mitigates the sexual under-tones of the scene by setting up Valeria as a Ruskinian reader. The ekphrasis, or verbal description of a visual object, begins by Valeria attempting "to dismiss all ideas of Nature from [her] mind" (213). She is unsuccessful, however, for she reads the paintings as if they were taken straight from nature and represented "real" events. All she sees is the poor quality of the paintings: "Little as I knew critically of Art, I could see that Miserrimus Dexter knew still less of the rules of drawing, colour, and composition. His pictures were, in the strictest meaning of that expressive word – Daubs" (213). She frames the painting with her lack of knowledge about art. She immediately reinserts "nature" into the aesthetic experience, however, by claiming that the paintings do not represent the visual conventions of their day which privileged nature, color, and details. It is as if she cannot recognize that the paintings are works of art because they do not match her preconceived notions of what art is. She is one of those trapped, as Collins put it, "by all that critics, connoisseurs, lecturers, and compilers of guide-books can tell them" and cannot "trust entirely to their own common sense when they are looking at pictures" ("To Think" 193). Valeria cannot see the beauty of the paintings because she fails to understand, as Pater does, that "in the things of the imagination great strength always [bears] on what is singular or strange" (Pater 47). Instead, she remarks that "the diseased and riotous delight of the painter in representing Horrors, was (with certain exceptions to be hereafter mentioned) the one remarkable quality that I could discover in the series of his works" (213). Although Pater does not advocate representing horrors in art he does argue that "a certain strangeness, a something of the blossoming of the aloe, is indeed an element in all true works of art: that they shall excite or surprise us is indispensable. But that they shall give pleasure and exert a charm over us is indispensable too; and this strangeness must be sweet also – a lovely strangeness" (47). Pater opens up the possibility that beauty can be found even in the abject, as long as the scene provokes this lovely strangeness.

Valeria is sensitive to the power of this strangeness, despite her claims that the paintings represent the workings of a tortured and unstable imagination. Her ekphrasis of the paintings reveals a fascination with what she is representing. She lingers over the details of murder in the painting of revenge:

> The first of the Passion-pictures illustrated Revenge. A corpse, in fancy costume, lay on the bank of a foaming river, under the shade of a giant tree. An infuriated man, also in fancy costume, stood astride over the dead body, with his sword lifted to the lowering sky, and watched, with a horrid expression of delight, the blood of the man whom he had just killed, dripping slowly in a procession of big red drops down the broad blade of his weapon.
> (213-14)

Her language slows down in the last part of the sentence – each word dropping as slowly as the blood. She is clearly captivated even as she is repulsed by this abject scene. Julia Kristeva argues that the abject is inherently fascinating because it represents all that man most fears and most wants to see. It represents the tension between life and death, and hence is fascinating and disturbing. It is inherently sensual, however, and represents a sublimated sexual desire. In his ground-breaking work on ekphrasis, *Picture Theory*, W. J. T. Mitchell argues that while ekphrasis itself "typically expresses a desire for a visual object (whether to possess or praise), it is also typically an offering of this expression as a gift to the reader" (164). In this instance the abject is both what is desired and what is given in ekphrasis.

The sexuality of Valeria's ekphrasis is made explicit at the end of the passage when Dexter's whistle intrudes on her examination of the paintings. She is so deeply absorbed in the paintings that coming back to the real world makes her hysterical:

> For the moment, my nerves were so completely upset, that I started with a cry of alarm. I felt a momentary impulse to open the door, and run out. The idea of trusting myself alone with the man who had painted those fright-

> ful pictures, actually terrified me; I was obliged to sit down on one of the hall chairs. Some minutes passed before my mind recovered its balance. (215)

Her shattered nerves speak to the intensity of her response to the sensations provoked by the paintings. Her physical disorientation points to the sensual intimacy of her involvement with the pictures, making her a completely Paterian viewer. Furthermore, although she claims to be terrified of leaving herself alone with the man who painted the pictures, she immediately sits down and composes herself in order to be able to do so. Her desire to get at the truth is mingled with the physical desire created by the paintings. The two together compass a sensual residue from the interaction with the artwork that culminates in the following scene. When she sees Dexter, he tries to kiss her. The editors of *The Graphic*, where the novel was first serially published, were so outraged at the scene because of its sensuality and eroticism that they censored it.[5] The sexuality of that encounter suggests that the ekphrasis is so sexually charged that it constitutes narrative foreplay that provokes erotic responses.

Throughout the rest of the ekphrasis Valeria continues to give her readers the sexualized gift of the abject. Although she moves more quickly through her description of the images of cruelty she lingers over the most abject part of the painting of a tortured saint who is "hung up to a tree by his heels, had just been skinned, and

[5] Collins fought the censorship and had the scene reinserted in the novel. Though Collins strongly opposed the censorship and the allegation of sexual impropriety that went with it, it is clear that Dexter is also written as sexual. See Bourne Taylor's introduction to *The Law and the Lady* and Norman Page's *Wilkie Collins: The Critical Heritage* for further discussion of the original critical response to the novel and its censorship.

was not quite dead yet" (214).[6] It is a moment when life and death are completely entwined – when the human body is made perfectly abject because it is both alive and dead. What is remarkable is that she adds this element to her ekphrasis. A painting cannot show the most subtle markers of life, which indicate the transitional moment between life and death; the viewer must overlay this interpretation onto the image. Valeria insists on making the scene an abject moment when life and death are coexistent – suspending the last moment of life before a horrible death in a kind of infinite present. It is that intermediate state, according to Kristeva, which is the most abject because the body cannot be objectified but exists in an intermediate moment that represents life and death (11). Similarly, Pater recognizes the power of representing the body between life and death in his reflections on Botticelli's illustrations of Dante's *Inferno*. He argues that "there is an inventive force about the fire taking hold on the upturned soles of the feet [of those going down "quick to hell"], which proves that the design is no mere translation of Dante's words, but a true painter's vision" (34). Those upturned feet represent the moment when the individual and his destruction are coexistent. That abject moment is the one Pater privileges as the most imaginative of Botticelli's "grotesques," suggesting that he wanted to emphasize that it was not merely beauty which could provoke sensations in the viewer but the abject as well. The true art critic, like Valeria, must be open to the power of these sensations.

The reader of detective fiction, however, must be wary of the intensity of these emotions despite the pleasure of the sensations

---

[6] It is evocative of Titian's painting of *The Flaying of Marsyas* where flayed bodies hang on the edge of death. That painting is particularly disturbing because of the juxtaposition of the beautiful and the violent (a musician accompanies the scene and naked bodies sway to the sound, while two knives cut through the darkness surrounding the flayed bodies).

they provoke. Their very intensity must be balanced by nature so that the reader can see their narrative significance. In other words, as in Collins' own writing on art criticism, common sense dictates a balance between nature and emotion, so that the reader/viewer can apprehend his or her own personal response to the painting. The abject, however, resists the balance because it fundamentally seeks to "perturb an identity, a system, order. It is that which does not respect limits, places, rules. The in between, the ambiguous, the mixed" (Kristeva 12).[7] By insisting on the abject quality of the paintings, Valeria obscures their significance as a clue. Instead, they become an intermediary phenomenon that can be many things. They are a clue and a distraction. They might reveal "truth" and "nature" or only the workings of the imagination. They might signify Dexter's mental disturbance or his visual genius. Even more importantly, the abject suggests that the two can exist simultaneously – that the paintings represent the borderline between both interpretations. As such they can be read as either or as both. They represent the tension between the truth and the imaginary. They emblematize the power of every clue to be a red herring and a piece of useful information. The key for the reader is not to decide one way or the other, not to be led by Valeria or Dexter, the authors of guide-books to these paintings, or to one interpretation of the paintings. Instead, it is up to the reader to come up with his or her own common sense response to the meaning of the paintings – to think, not to be thought for.

Valeria, however, cannot maintain any ambiguity or tension about meaning in the scene because she must rely on Dexter to give her information about the death of the first Mrs. Macallan. Many reputable friends, from her mother-in-law to her father fig-

---

7 "Ce qui perturbe une identité, un système, un ordre. Ce qui ne respecte pas les limites, les places, les règles. L'entre deux, l'ambigu, le mixte."

ure, have insisted that she not trust Dexter because he is mentally unstable. To do so would mean that she could not turn to him for help and she perceives him as the only person who can help her figure out what happened. She uses the paintings to account for his emotional excesses and to convince her readers to do the same. In effect she insists on the abject quality of the paintings so that she can turn away from them: "Feeling no great desire, after these specimens, to look at any more of the illustrated Passions, I turned to the opposite wall to be instructed in the career of the Wandering Jew" (214). It is as if she uses the first paintings to acknowledge, even insist, on the dark quality of Dexter's mind. By making his paintings abject, however, she is allowed to turn away from them. Abridging the ekphrasis allows her to turn away, quite literally, from the outrageous parts of his personality. Instead, she turns to the other paintings and spends more time describing them in order to set Dexter up as a positive source of information. Her ekphrasis insists on the emotional power of the later paintings of the Wandering Jew and the Flying Dutchman to make Dexter look like a misunderstood outsider whose disability separates him from society. Like the Wandering Jew with his branded forehead or the half-dead Dutchman, Dexter's deformity marks him as other and misunderstood – and consequently, someone who will have an outsider's perspective on the events of everyday life. It is imperative for Valeria to set him up in this way if she is to rely on the information he gives her. It is impossible for her to read the first paintings of *Revenge* and *Cruelty* as summarizing Dexter's actions, which in fact they do, because to do so would mean that there would be no more mystery – nothing else for her to do but accept a passive female role, since the paintings point to Dexter's guilt and manipulation of the facts surrounding the first Mrs. Macallan's death.

Valeria's turn away from the Revenge and Cruelty paintings is also a turn away from acknowledging how her quest for truth is a kind of cruel revenge. Her desire to redeem her husband's name and find the truth is motivated, at least in part, by jealousy of the women in her husband's past. She assumes that Mrs. Beauly, her husband's special friend at the time of his first wife's death, must be the villain. Valeria almost cruelly looks for evidence of this woman's action in the death of the first Mrs. Macallan. When she finally discovers she is wrong, Valeria goes on to discover the truth about her predecessor in a way that maliciously reveals the first Mrs. Macallan's vanity and vindictiveness. Her actions also viscerally affect her husband, who continues to suffer from nervous trouble while Valeria pursues her detective work, thereby linking detection and quests for truth to the pain of exploratory surgery. The reader who reads the ekphrasis also participates in the cruelty of detection, because, as Mitchell describes it, ekphrasis itself suggests "the relationship of power/knowledge/desire – representation as something done to something, with something, by someone, for someone" (180). The reader is not given much time, however, to consider the meaning of the first two paintings, or his or her complicity in what they represent. Valeria immediately begins her description of the paintings on the other wall without a paragraph break or any structural pause. By truncating the ekphrasis of the *Passions* Valeria forces her readers to skim over the potential meanings of the first paintings and focus instead on the later ones.

The paintings of the Wandering Jew are painted as if he were the Flying Dutchman. Both characters are intermediary beings that represent a living death, since both are compelled to wander without cease as living ghosts. The paintings emphasize the abject by placing them in an almost carnivalesque setting:

> The next picture showed the Phantom Ship, moored (to the horror and astonishment of the helmsman) behind the earthly vessel in the harbour. The Jew had stepped on shore. His boat was on the beach. His crew – little men with stony white faces, dressed in funereal black – sat in silent rows on the seats of the boat, with their oars in their lean long hands. The Jew, also in black, stood with his eyes and hands raised imploringly to the thunderous heaven. The wild creatures of land and sea – the tiger, the rhinoceros, the crocodile; the sea-serpent, the shark, and the devil-fish – surrounded the accursed Wanderer in a mystic circle, daunted and fascinated by the sight of him [. . .]. A faint and lurid light lit the scene, falling downward from a torch, brandished by an avenging Spirit that hovered over the Jew on outspread vulture-wings. (214)

The image is slightly ridiculous. It is almost too much to conflate the Wandering Jew and the Flying Dutchman. It is almost too much to have the "little men with stony white faces," the "thunderous heavens," and "[t]he wild creatures of land and sea – the tiger, the rhinoceros, the crocodile; the sea-serpent, the shark, and the devil-fish," all united in one picture. The excess of representation is slightly disorienting. It is almost like a funhouse mirror room where no matter where you turn there is another horrible image in a kind of disorienting excess of the abject.

At this point, Valeria's attitude towards the paintings begins to shift. She sees the power of the imaginative act with greater appreciation. After the first of the Wandering Jew paintings she claims, "In this work, badly as it was painted, there were really signs of a powerful imagination, and even of a poetical feeling for the supernatural" (214). She sounds like a true Paterian viewer when she claims the second painting of the Wandering Jew had a "suggestive power in it which I confess strongly impressed me" (215). She is open to the sensations of the paintings and willing to feel the power of their undoubtedly strange loveliness. She forgets "nature" and is inspired by "imagination." Valeria is attracted to the later paintings of the Wandering Jew and the Flying Dutchman because they can be read as metaphors for Dexter and his disability which clearly position him on the fringes of society. Because he is wheelchair-bound he cannot find love; like fables of the Wandering Jew and the Flying Dutchman, his disability consigns him to search without ever having hope of success. Valeria is attracted to the pathos of Dexter's condition. She pities him and consequently believes he is telling the truth. She constructs his imagination as representing truth because it springs from his marginalized social position – as if the wheelchair-bound man can see and understand more because he is on the fringes of society. The ekphrasis of the later paintings overshadows the first ones, so that Valeria can prove that it was socially acceptable and intelligent to trust Dexter. Her emotional and sensual response to the paintings also distracts the viewer from the ways the ekphrasis positions him. Despite her claims that she doesn't want to be left alone with a man with such an imagination, the entire ekphrasis is working towards establishing him as someone that it is imperative for her to know. Valeria relies on the visual image to construct Dexter as a disabled figure, who is somewhat carnivalesque and over the top, yet harmless, like his own representations of the Wandering Jew and the Flying Dutchman. As Martha Stoddard Holmes remarks in her work on disability in nineteenth-century novels, disability is a melodramatic tool "for cranking open feelings, and everyone involved – disabled and nondisabled, viewers and actors – is somehow placed and defined by what floods out" (3). Valeria links the emotional power of the paintings to the melodrama of disability in order to establish her need to visit him and her own superiority as a detective. It is only right, she implies, for her to be the detective because she knows how to respond to Dexter, his disability, and the wildness of his imagination.

Valeria's ekphrasis begins with Ruskinian terms and shifts to Paterian ones in large part to convince her readers of the validity of her ideas. As someone who is looking for Nature she is able to question the artistic merit of the abject early paintings. Her conversion to a Paterian viewer blinds the reader, at least temporarily, because of the intensity of her response. The good reader, however, remembers the inscription which frames the ekphrasis and reinserts a hint of Nature into his or her consideration of the paintings. By claiming that he only addresses himself to people of imagination Dexter sets up the possibility of a "Natural reader," who will read him differently. He, like Valeria, works against the intrusion of such a reader by spectacularly performing his disability, in a variety of ways, all of which he relies on to keep the characters and the readers from evaluating his narrative clearly.[8] He implies that the only way to understand him is to treat him as a kind of living visual sign that must be evaluated for its sensational and emotional impact. Unlike his literary contemporaries, such as Jenny Wren in Dickens' *Our Mutual Friend*, he uses his disabled body as a negative visual sign which will provoke emotions in his "viewers" and thus allow him to manipulate them. Consequently, Dexter is able to distort the police investigation, the trial, and the narrator's quest for truth. As with the paintings, where the latter ones imaginatively overshadow the earlier ones, Dexter counts on

[8] Bourne Taylor argues his impersonations of Nelson, Napoleon, and Shakespeare are a "performance of a performance" (xxii), multiplying out the layers of performativity and the constructed nature of Dexter's character.

pity and the power of his physical difference to hide the impetus for his actions – revenge and cruelty. In order not to fall victim to Dexter's account, it is imperative for the reader to reinsert nature, or at least a hint of the rational, into any understanding of Dexter – to read against the grain of his spectacular performances – to read him as a living visual sign – part imagination, part truth..

In the scene in which Dexter appears to attempt to protect Eustace from police examination he is actively performing his disability. He moves his chair in order to pretend to hide an important clue. When he refuses to move the police officers physically move him: "I [one of the police officers] first opened the door; and then [. . .] gave the chair a good push behind with my stick, instead of my hand – and so sent It, and him, safely and swiftly from the room" (138). At first glance Dexter is the victim in this scene because the police so mercilessly take advantage of his disability – pushing him out of the room like so much rubbish. However, Dexter, as it turns out, is keenly aware of what he is doing. He purposely set out to make his friend look guilty by placing himself in a position that would call attention to what he was hiding. In other words, he used his wheelchair and his deformity to make sure that the police would notice the locked drawer in Eustace's bedside table which contained his diary – a diary that eloquently recorded Eustace's unhappy marriage, and attraction to Mrs. Beauly. Dexter performs his disability to manipulate the police and Eustace – the former into wondering what he could be hiding, and the latter into believing in his good, though inept, best wishes. Similarly, during Eustace's trial Dexter uses his body to influence the outcome of the case. He enters in a sudden calm that comes after the court has been called to order for laughing uproariously at his name. In this case his name, which seems to summarize the melodramatic power of disability – Miserrimus, or "the most miserable" – frames his physical entry into the courtroom, prejudicing the entire room's understanding of disability, making him pitiable because of his misery. The court room cannot perceive that he might be looking to seek revenge and cruelty in the entire mystery, because he is playing on their melodramatic response to his disability.

Dexter's body also frames how Valeria chooses to narrate his entrance into the courtroom. She uses her later impressions of Dexter to influence how she describes him in the trial, a time at which she had never seen him. "In mentioning his appearance as a witness at the Trial, I find I have borrowed (without meaning to do so) from my experience of him at this later time" (199). This supposed oversight colors Dexter's entire testimony for the reader because it places his physical disability spectacularly before the reader:

> A coverlid, which had been thrown over his chair, had fallen off during his progress through the throng. The loss of it exposed to the public curiosity the head, the arms, and the trunk of a living human being: absolutely deprived of the lower limbs. To make this deformity all the more striking and all the more terrible, the victim of it was – as to his face and his body – an unusually handsome, and an unusually well-made man [. . .]. Never had a magnificent head and body been more hopelessly ill-bestowed than in this instance! Never had Nature committed a more careless or a more cruel mistake than in the making of this man! (163)

Valeria returns to his beauty again and again, describing it with loving and thorough detail. The repetition of his beauty suggests her desire for Dexter, a desire which obscures her ability to read him, or to understand him for who and what he is. "Looking at him as a whole [. . .] I can only describe him as being an unusually handsome man. A painter would have reveled in him as a model for St John. And a young girl, ignorant of what the Oriental robe hid from view, would have said to herself the instant she looked at him, 'Here is the hero of my dreams!'" (200).[9] Her claim that ignorance of what the Oriental robe hides would make him more attractive, suggests, in an inversion of her heterosexual supposition, that knowing what is hidden under the robe of any man makes him unattractive. The young girl is not attracted, as Freud would later have it, to his phallus but to his potential lack of it – knowing what is hidden undermines the attraction.

Dexter is physically attracted to Valeria because she reminds him physically of the first Mrs. Macallan. He asks her to move a variety of items around the room and she is struck by how "his eyes were still strangely employed in what seemed to me to be the closest scrutiny of my dress. And stranger still, the result of this appeared to be, partly to interest and partly to distress him" (217). He puts her into motion so that he can have the pleasure of seeing her move – of treating her like a visual object. Dexter's desire is marked by how he pays attention. His attention is so fixed that it becomes transgressive. Aware of the impropriety of looking he asks if he has looked at Valeria "very attentively – too attentively, perhaps?" (218). He emphasizes the erotics of looking by remarking on how he was paying attention, which indicates that he is fo-

---

9 Aoife Leahy argues that this is a reference to Raphael's painting of *St Cecilia with Saints Paul, John Evangelist, Augustine and Mary Magdalene*, a painting in which St. John is represented as a beautiful man with many of the same features as Dexter. She goes on to suggest that Dexter's deformity is a kind of ironic physical manifestation of the painting. In the painting St. John's lower half is obscured by the two women in the foreground making him legless. Dexter's legless-ness is a kind of aesthetic pun.

cusing on her to the exclusion of other sensory input with such intensity that it is inappropriate. The correlation between looking and sensation is reminiscent, again, of Pater's description of the role of the art critic. In this instance, however, Collins suggests that being open to sensation provoked by visual objects is dangerous or potentially inappropriate, because it may un-man the viewer. At the same time Collins also seems to argue against a purely Ruskinian view of Dexter, which might see his body as a kind of visual truth – a distorted reflection of a distorted mind. Because of his role in creating the mystery Dexter is more than his disability. He is more than just a distorted body and consequently distorted brain. There is truth and power in his imagination that escapes the confines of a natural reading of his disability. His body metonymically stands in for his imaginative genius and his vengefulness. It is beautiful and abject. Like the paintings of the Wandering Jew he is attractive, even as he is grotesque, comical, and tragic. Dexter's body operates at the junction between the symbolic and the concrete, the sublime and the abject.

The significance of Dexter as an aesthetic object and an aesthete who is actively manipulating the narrative suggests that each visual clue in the novel must be considered in aesthetic terms. Even if at first glance they do not appear to be artistic, their status as visual objects marks them as important clues. Each of the visual devices Collins uses throughout the novel must be evaluated by the readers – their individual emotional response establishing the accuracy or truth of the clue. The reader who is open to the sensations they provoke will be able to place them accurately within the context of the mystery. The reader must be willing to go through incredible gyrations and absurd collections of facts and fancies – like all those beasts on the shore in the painting of the Wandering Jew – hoping to find the truth. The imagination is the basis of truth and consequently it is imperative neither to be a Paterian or Ruskinian reader but to enjoy the play between the two styles. Otherwise, as when Valeria finally compels Dexter to tell the truth of what he has done, the narrative becomes lifeless and formulaic. Without imagination guiding the mystery, the text, like Dexter, is left "nothing but a mute vacant face turned up to the ceiling, with eyes that looked blindly, with lips parted in a senseless, changeless grin" (322). Similarly, Valeria's quest for truth becomes stale and formulaic once Dexter stops guiding her. She gives up her agency and subordinates herself to her husband. Ultimately, she chooses to withdraw from the mystery and the story so that she can be a good wife and mother. Although her abdication of autonomy is generally read as a misogynistic foreclosure of female power it also demonstrates what happens when imagination and sensation no longer guide the story. Narrative itself thus becomes an imaginative act that can survive only if the teller and the reader are both committed to upholding the power of the imagination. The frame with which the paper begins, then, which invokes imagination over nature, is a call to writing and to understanding detective fiction generally – to be open to the sensations of the clues (particularly the visual signs) even while reading them for truth. Without both the mystery and the facts the pleasure of reading is impossible.

## Works Cited

Bachman, Maria K., and Don Richard Cox. *Reality's Dark Light: The Sensational Wilkie Collins*. Knoxville: U of Tennessee P, 2003.

Bourne Taylor, Jenny. Introduction. *The Law and the Lady*. By Wilkie Collins. New York: Oxford UP, 1992. vii-xxiv.

Collins, Wilkie. *Basil*. 1862. London: Chatto & Windus, 1889.

___. "The Exhibition of the Royal Academy." *Bentley's Miscellany* 29.174, June 1851: 617-27. *Wilkie Collins Pages*. Ed. Paul Lewis. 16 June 2006 <http://www.deadline.demon.co.uk/wilkie/etext/acadt.htm>.

___. *The Law and the Lady*. 1875. Ed. David Skilton. New York: Penguin, 1998.

___. "To Think or To Be Thought For." *Household Words* 14, 13 Sept. 1856: 193-98.

Dennisoff, Denis. "Framed and Hung: Collins and the Economic Beauty of the Manly Artist." Bachman and Cox 34-58.

Derrida, Jacques. *The Truth in Painting*. Trans. Geoff Bennington and Ian McLeod. Chicago: U of Chicago P, 1987.

Dickens, Charles. *Our Mutual Friend*. Ed. Adrian Poole. New York: Penguin, 1997.

Dolin, Tim, and Lucy Dougan. "Fatal Newness: *Basil*, Art and the Origins of Sensation Fiction." Bachman and Cox 1-33.

Holmes, Martha Stoddard. *Fictions of Affliction: Physical Disability in Victorian Culture*. Ann Arbor: U of Michigan P, 2004.

Kristeva, Julia. *Pouvoirs de l'horreur: Essai sur l'abjection*. Paris: Éditions du Seuil, 1980.

Leahy, Aoife. "The Evil of Raphaelesque Art: An Arc Throughout the Fiction of Wilkie Collins." Wilkie Collins Conference. University of Sheffield. 19 Mar. 2005.

Mitchell, W. J. Thomas. *Picture Theory: Essays on Verbal and Visual Representation*. Chicago: U of Chicago P, 1994.

Nayder, Lillian. *Unequal Partners: Charles Dickens, Wilkie Collins, and Victorian Authorship*. Ithaca: Cornell UP, 2002.

Page, Norman, ed. *Wilkie Collins: The Critical Heritage*. Boston: Routledge and Kegan Paul, 1974.

Pater, Walter. *The Renaissance: Studies in Art and Poetry*. Ed. Adam Phillips. Oxford: Oxford UP, 1986.

Rosenberg, John D., ed. *The Genius of John Ruskin: Selections from His Writings.* Charlottesville: U of Virginia P, 1998.

Ruskin, Walter. "Modern Painters." *The Genius of John Ruskin: Selections from His Writings*. Ed. John D. Rosenberg. Charlottesville: U of Virginia P, 1998. 17-120.

Skilton, David. Introduction. *The Law and the Lady*. By Wilkie Collins. New York: Penguin, 1998. vii-xxii.

## The Art of Murder and Fine Furniture: The Aesthetic Projects of Anna Katharine Green and Charles Rohlfs

Lucy Sussex
La Trobe University

**Abstract:** This paper will examine the detective aesthetics of writer Anna Katharine Green, in terms of her 1878 *The Leavenworth Case*, an important text in the development of the clue-puzzle, the dominant form of crime fiction's Golden Age. The mutual influence between Green and her husband, Arts and Crafts Movement designer Charles Rohlfs, will also be considered. It can be demonstrated that the couple had a shared aesthetic project in terms of Arts and Crafts ideals, and that the fine art of fictional murder can be paralleled with the creation of fine furniture.

In the year 1878 R. L. Stevenson published *The Suicide Club*. Other notable events of the year included the first incandescent light bulb, by Edison and Swan. But 1878 also marks a remarkable literary debut, by an author whose career would stretch into the twentieth century, until 1922. American Anna Katharine Green's detective novel *The Leavenworth Case: A Lawyer's Story* was hugely successful and praised – its fans would include Wilkie Collins, British Prime Minister Stanley Baldwin and Agatha Christie. It was her best-selling and most influential book; she would follow it with thirty-seven novels over the next forty years. *The Leavenworth Case* has been widely regarded as the first American detective novel, and the first by a woman, both erroneously – that distinction belongs to Metta Fuller Victor ("Seeley Regester") and her 1866 *The Dead Letter*. However, *The Leavenworth Case* would become the first detective fiction million-seller, with numerous international editions.

To put Green in context, in 1878 Poe had been dead some thirty years, and Emile Gaboriau, three; Conan Doyle was still only a medical student. Moreover, when *The Leavenworth Case* was published the label of detective fiction did not exist, not being used with reference to literary genre writing until 1886 (Stewart 27). Yet there was some awareness of crime writing as a generic category, with a variety of labels used, from "sensation" (as applied to Wilkie Collins' 1860 *The Woman in White*) to the "Romans Policiers" of Gaboriau.

Green's most obvious novelistic antecedents were not only Fuller Victor and Gaboriau, but the sensation genre, where frequently blood-spattered content would link with what we now recognize as the emergent mystery narrative form. Indeed, the major writers of sensation – Wilkie Collins, Mary Braddon, Ellen (Mrs Henry) Wood – would publish contemporaneously with Green. In 1875, Collins produced *The Law and the Lady*; and "Queen of sensation" Braddon published two fine crime novels in *Dead Men's Shoes* (1876) and *The Cloven Foot* (1879). Thus Green was not without competition from some of the best in the emerging crime business. Another instance, this time from the US – the same year as *The Leavenworth Case*, 1878, Fuller Victor published the serial "Guilty, or Not Guilty," in Street and Smith's *New York Weekly*.

Yet with the notable exception of Gaboriau, until Green there was no novelist to whom crime would represent, to quote Foucault's critique of the canon, "a certain unity of writing" nor a single "source of expression" (111). For Fuller Victor and the sensation writers crime was an intermittent if continuing preoccupation, amidst narratives of realism, romance, and social protest. Green differed, for her *œuvre* would be almost exclusively within crime fiction, one published play and a book of poems apart. Thus she is the first author to be defined primarily in terms of the new genre and its label, as a "detective novelist."

Academic writing about nineteenth-century crime fiction, has, to quote Anne Humpherys, excluded "the majority of such fiction (a good deal written by women) from critical attention in favor of an obsessive return of critical analysis to a handful of canonized texts" (259). She surveyed some 170 relevant publications published between 1980 and 1992, noting that the great majority – eighty – were on Sherlock Holmes. This focus has meant that most early crime fiction, thousands of books, to say nothing of the even larger quantities of work in periodicals, has been occluded.[1]

Among such writing is the work of Anna Katharine Green (1846-1935). She has, within crime fiction history circles, a certain historical status; she has also most recently attracted attention from feminists for her female sleuths. Yet, for the purposes of the academy, she is currently situated outside the canon of high literary detection. Certainly Green used a Victorian style that can seem over-ornate and melodramatic to modern crime buffs – in that she was typical of her time. But the importance of her texts is that they are not read for style, but primarily for their exquisitely sustained and structured mystery, complete with carefully sown clues and red herrings. Even after a century, the whodunit of her novels are not easily guessed. They ensnare the reader, keep them engaged to novel's end. In the detailed structural architecture of Green's novels can be determined a sophisticated aesthetic and intellectual project that cannot be underestimated.

Any consideration of Green's aesthetics cannot ignore the role of her husband, Charles Rohlfs (1853-1936), who established a

[1] Alan J. Hubin's *Crime Fiction IV: A Comprehensive Bibliography, 1749–2000* lists nearly 6000 books in English alone published between 1800-1900.

separate international reputation, as a member of and important spokesman for the American Arts and Crafts movement. Indeed, Green is most commonly pictured seated in an ornately carved chair, one of her husband's productions. After abandoning an acting career as a precondition of his marriage, he established a craft workshop, specialising in the design and manufacture of what he termed 'artistic furniture.' He has been popularly credited with originating the "Mission" style, and his work is held in numerous museums, including MOMA. His quoted philosophy of aesthetics parallels that of Ruskin.

Even during their lifetimes, the mutually fruitful pairing, which over half a century produced three children, many books and a body of highly collectable furniture, was regarded as unusual. A 1915 article commented: "The affinity of the carpenter's bench and the gum-shoe may not be apparent at once." It described Rohlfs as "a direct artistic descendant of William Morris" and Green as "the author of a particularly terrifying and puzzling brand of detective stories." The article cites the surprise created when the pair were linked: "'[W]hat's the novel-writer woman got to do with the furniture-designer chap?' 'Oh, nothing much, except that they are man and wife!'" ("Personal Glimpses" 1201).

When a couple are high achievers in widely different fields – as with economist John Maynard Keynes and his wife, ballerina Lydia Lopokova, to cite an extreme example – the disparity would appear not to admit of any mutual influence. That said, it is certainly possible to read Green's texts for possible mentions of Rohlfs' handiwork. Conversely, some of his furniture seems eminently suitable as props in crime fiction or movies, for example the ornate Gothic-style fall-front desk held in the Virginia Museum of Fine Arts, which with its multiple drawers could function very well as a hiding place for a missing will, or diamonds. Green could write in the Gothic, melodramatic mode, and often about purloined letters, wills and other valuables. But is it possible to go beyond such simple visual comparisons, to discover a mutually influential aesthetics between husband-woodworker and wife-writer?

Green and Rohlfs were a happy couple, living and working in intimacy. Green wrote at home; and for the first years of his furniture-making, Charles Rohlfs worked madly in the family attic. His craft surrounded her, as is evident from photographs of their Buffalo home reproduced in Michael James' 1994 biography of Rohlfs, *Drama in Design*. It is clearly a domestic environment created to both serve and express their needs, a fundamental tenet of the Arts and Crafts movement. Indeed, during the early years of Rohlfs' furniture-making, Green was credited as co-designer. Furthermore, the pair collaborated on the 1891 stage adaptation of *The Leavenworth Case*, in which Rohlfs appeared as the villain. He also gave dramatic recitals, including her verse, and each night took part in a mutual critiquing session of her writing work for the day, which he read aloud. They thus were very well aware of each other's avocation (James, *Drama in Design* 33, 23).

It is fruitful to investigate the possibilities of a shared aesthetic between Green and Rohlfs. Married couples are involved in aesthetics primarily in the domestic sphere they co-habit. Such mundane matters as, for example, the need for new curtains, and the consequent negotiating over what colours and styles are acceptable to both, force a couple to agree at a basic aesthetic level. But when both partners are creative, even in such different areas as writing and woodworking, it seems unlikely that that there is no mutual aesthetic influence, nor methodology.

Yet it is also worth noting that in terms of age, background, and education, they were very different. Rohlfs was the son of

German immigrants to the US, possibly a factor in the early important attention his furniture got in Germany and Austria. Unlike William Morris, cited as his artistic antecedent, he was genuinely a man of the people, being both a worker and a thinker. Rohlfs effectively had three careers, the first through financial necessity, the second from love, which he abandoned for the same reason, and the third, his true vocation, in which he won most renown. His earliest ambition was the stage, but when his father, a cabinetmaker, died when Charles was twelve, he became the family breadwinner in various low-skilled jobs.

Nonetheless Rohlfs maintained his education, via night classes at New York's Cooper Union, an institution which provided working men with further education. Rohlfs studied courses ranging from science to design, and was able to move into industrial design, working for cast-iron stove manufacturers. He was innovative, designing patented improvements, but the work, although creative, and sustaining him for twelve years, was not fully satisfying. Rohlfs still hankered for the stage, and from 1868 began to work in theatre, appearing with such notables as Edwin Booth. His favoured work was dramatic Shakespearean roles.

Anna Katharine Green's career path was completely different. She was born in 1846, in New York, the second daughter of Catharine Ann Whitney Green, and James Wilson Green, a criminal attorney. Both parents were middle-class, of early New England Presbyterian stock. Her father was politically active, indeed something of a force in New York politics, being an editor of the *American Republican*. Anna lost her mother at age three, but did not stint for female care, from her sixteen-year old sister Sarah, and later her stepmother Grace Hollister Wilson.

Green was among the most highly educated women of her generation, attending Ripley Female College in Poultney, Vermont, during the American Civil War. Ripley was one of the first institutions to offer university-level education to women, its students pioneers of female advancement. Yet her education gave her no way out of the conventional female life. After her graduation in 1866, she returned to her father's house, part of an extended family that included her brothers' wives and children. An escape, a future, was conventionally only acquired through marriage. Instead Green sought identity/employment via writing.

A description of her at this time survives from writer Mary Hatch, a friend, literary collaborator and relative via marriage, as a "tall, graceful girl, dressed in gray, with bright red berries on her hat" (a rare glimpse of frivolity with Green). Hatch recalls also Green's "calm belief of future success," surely the product of her education (159).

> In appearance she is rather striking than beautiful. Under a brow of almost masculine depth and power, her dark blue eyes express every emotion, while her mouth, which alone is beautiful, bespeaks sensitive delicacy and poetic feeling. Her form is elegant, being tall and willowy, but her crowning glory is her dark brown hair, which, unbound, sweeps just to the floor when she stands erect.
>
> (Hatch 159)

Green's success was not won without hard work. Like many literary young women of her era, she initially wanted to be a poet, something conventionally acceptable for the sex. Unconventionally, she also tried playwriting, without success, then crime fiction. For over six years she wrote and revised *The Leavenworth Case*, with only her stepmother Grace in the know and providing encouragement. At the end she had a manuscript of nearly 200,000 words. It was only when the work was finished to her satisfaction that she enlisted the confidence of James Wilson Green – and also his help, from his many New York contacts, which ranged from police to the literati.

Famously, Anna Katharine Green carried the manuscript in a shawl-strap to publisher George Putnam, who would later recall "the bright-eyed young lady" who arrived in his office "in the company of her gray-haired legal papa, with the manuscript (a very big manuscript) of the famous *Leavenworth Case*." Putnam found the novel to be "well constructed and ingenious" but requested "some addition to the title" to make it more "distinctive," and that the whole be cut. (letter of 1878).

*The Leavenworth Case* was bestselling, acclaimed, and even set as a Yale textbook to show "the fallacy of circumstantial evidence" (Hatch 161). Green was introduced to major literary figures, and attended a Presidential reception. Thus Green was already a celebrity author when she met Rohlfs. They both were professionally interested in the theatre; more importantly, they attended the same church. But Rohlfs' being eight years the junior, and an actor, caused parental disapproval from the patriarch James Wilson Green. He famously agreed to the marriage only if Rohlfs abandoned acting. He did, returning to industrial design. Anna was in her late thirties when the pair married, but she was also, thanks to her writing, financially independent.

If the mode of a marriage indicates a couple's joint aesthetics, then the Green-Rohlfs wedding showed an unostentatious practicality. They married in the South Congregational Church in Brooklyn, in November 1884. Within the context of the *New York Times'* wedding notices, with its brides clad in costly white silk and lace, Green was distinctive in getting married in a "travelling dress of fawn, trimmed with brown plush," a going-away outfit.[2] The date fell between two events of differing, though major significance to their respective professions: Oscar Wilde's 1882-1833 tour of the US, which introduced the nation to the Arts and Crafts Movement aesthetics; and Conan Doyle's first Sherlock Holmes story, *A Study in Scarlet*, in 1887. The latter was no doubt influenced by the English edition of *The Leavenworth Case*, published in 1884.

Green maintained her output of detective novels, generally yearly, despite giving birth to two children, born in 1885 and 1887. Probably to save money, they moved upstate, to Buffalo, where Green had lived as a girl. They bought land in 1890, and designed a Tudor-style residence for it. Homemaking kindled Rohlfs' interest in furniture design. He could find nothing he liked among the currently fashionable high Victoriana. His tastes ran to eighteenth-century furniture, which the couple could not afford. So he set to, designed and crafted what he wanted, one of the first pieces being a writing chair for Green, of oak, with "a wide, contoured right arm to accommodate her notebook" (Maida 28). His work attracted attention quickly, from friends who wanted similar pieces, then as an expanding business, with clients.

It is worth noting that in *The Leavenworth Case*, Green only sketches the High Society furnishings of the victim: "the extraordinary splendor of the room I was in; the glow of satin, glitter of bronze, and glimmer of marble meeting the eye at every turn" (9). Later her narrator Raymond comments wryly on this magnificence, "the mockery of *things*" (89). Green devotes far more space to a humbler upcountry home, of a plain-sewer, the widowed Mrs Belden:

---

[2] *New York Times* 26 Nov. 1884: 5.

> It was a pleasant apartment [. . .] square, sunny, and well furnished. On the floor was a crimson carpet, on the walls several pictures, at the windows, cheerful curtains of white, tastefully ornamented with ferns and autumn leaves; in one corner an old melodeon, and in the centre of the room a table draped with a bright cloth, on which were various little knick-knacks, which, without being rich or expensive, were both pretty and, to a certain extent, ornamental. (209)

Mrs Belden describes her tastes as "Loving what was beautiful, hating what was sordid, drawn by nature towards all that was romantic and uncommon [. . .]" (240). The room she inhabits, with its emphasis on tasteful simplicity, colour and utility, is Arts and Crafts aesthetics before the fact. It also seems prophetic of the Rohlfs' domestic interiors in Buffalo. Their living room was described as "cozy, cordial," with firelight flickering "fantastically over the originals of mission furniture" (qtd. in "Anna Katherine Green" 48).

Also notable in *The Leavenworth Case* is Green's cunning use of art, as when she introduces its heroines Mary and Eleanore Leavenworth via sentimental portraiture and classical sculpture. She notes

> [. . .] the force and eloquence of a certain picture which confronted me from the opposite wall. A sweet picture – sweet enough and poetic enough to have been conceived by the most idealistic of artists: simple, too – the vision of a young flaxen-haired, blue-eyed coquette, dressed in the costume of the First Empire, standing in a wood-path, looking back over her shoulder at some one following – yet with such a dash of something not altogether saint-

> like in the corners of her meek eyes and baby-like lips, that it impressed me with the individuality of life. (9-10)

Green mentions in the same scene "the clearer-cut and more noble features of the sculptured Psyche, shining in mellow beauty from the crimson-hung window [. . .]."

Mary Leavenworth is explicitly the counterpart of the enticing blonde in the painting, her cousin Eleanore is as pale, beautiful and "almost as immobile" as the Psyche (89), under which she sits.[3] Both are lovely; and it should be remembered that Green herself was not conventionally attractive, and therefore continually being judged as wanting in respect to the Victorian aesthetic ideal of the feminine. The Leavenworth women are suspected of the murder, something that torments Raymond, who finds it almost impossible to separate his conceptions of feminine beauty from the proper sex roles of well-bred young ladies. From the painting and the statue, he has predetermined that Mary is "not altogether saint-like" and Eleanore noble and above reproach. That they might be otherwise causes great angst, as with Eleanore: "[. . .] if that face of beauty was in truth only a mask [. . .] how could I bear to sit there and see the frightful serpent of deceit and sin evolve itself from the bosom of this white rose!" (54). Such prose is Victoriana at its stylistic worst, the counterpart of its overstuffed, over-ornamented furniture. Yet Green, as in the description of Mrs Belden's room shows, gives indication of a different aesthetic altogether.

We do not have a how-to book, a philosophy of creative writing/ woodworking from either of the Rohlfs. Indeed, Charles followed Ruskin's dictates in eschewing rules as applied to his work ("My Adventures" 99). However, they were public figures, acces-

---

[3] Curiously Green addressed Hatch in letters as "Lady Psyche."

sible to the press. From their separate interviews and articles a similarity of artistic values and intent can be discerned. Indeed, the pair mixed aesthetics and personal ethics in a manner entirely consistent with the ideals of Arts and Crafts.

The first notable feature is the importance of great literature, for enjoyment, and also for self-improvement. Both were lifelong devotees of Shakespeare, whose quotations introduce almost every chapter of *The Leavenworth Case*. Rohlfs recommended the study of literary classics, believing his reading of Browning, Shelley, Emerson (whom Green had met at Ripley), and chiefly Shakespeare "had forged his own creative spirit" (James, "Charles Rohlfs" 239). In his case Shakespeare was experienced both through study and personal performance. Green also was possessed of "great dramatic and elocutionary powers, can improvise and act with Corinne-like facility," wrote Hatch, though apparently only at amateur level (160). It is not known if she ever gave, as Dickens did, dramatised auctorial readings. In addition she emulated Shakespearean drama in her published and unpublished playwriting (James, "Charles Rohlfs" 233).

The second example of the commingling of ethics and aesthetics is a conception of the dignity of labour. For Rohlfs, his long hours in his workshop were almost sacred. James compares his beliefs to Ruskins' in *The Seven Lamps of Architecture*, "the essence of the arts and crafts movement" ("Charles Rohlfs" 239). Rohlfs saw labour, whether industrial or artistic (and he had experience of both) as a process that was inherently satisfying, even joyous. This joy was divinely inspired, a reflection of his and Green's profound Presbyterian beliefs. He furthermore stated that

> [t]he [arts and crafts] movement installs into the workingman a desire for artistic labor, that expresses his own

> individuality, and it prompts the public to look to the artistic in making their purchases. It is the leaven which keeps alive the artistic sense. (Rohlfs, "Address" 98)

Similarly Hatch records the young Green writing from nine to five, and even after decades of publications she worked every day. She described to Kathleen Woodward "the infinite labor, the planning, modelling, the sheer thought and attention to detail that went to the building of a mystery story" (Woodward 169). She also managed the family household largely by herself: only after the birth of a third child in 1892 did the Rohlfs employ a live-in housekeeper. Unlike conventional genteel ladies of the nineteenth century Green devised and tended her garden herself.[4] She also could make her own clothes, a creative act in which she could express her preference for what would now be termed the elegant vintage (Hatch 160; Maida 27).

From the above it can be seen that Green and Rohlfs neither separated the artistic from the artisan, nor from the domestic sphere. All labour was dignified. Rohlfs' first love was the theatre; Green had wanted fame as a poet. That they earned renown in other areas was personally unproblematic, for Rohlfs believed that each individual had an outstanding gift, that they could "do better than anything else" (James, "Charles Rohlfs" 230). Rohlfs' gift would win him international fame, and for decades Green was both the "Queen" of detective fiction, and the major American writer in the field. In 1913 Carolyn Wells cited her as exemplar in *The Technique of the Mystery Story*, in the same company as Poe, Conan Doyle, Gaboriau and Israel Zangwill.

---

[4] Green appears in her "lovely" garden, with trowel and in an eighteenth-century style gown, in a full-page photo in the *American Magazine* 87, Feb. 1919: 38.

Yet the couple's hard work was offset by a ready eclecticism regarding source material and a belief in inspiration. Rohlfs drew on medieval, folk, and exotic, even oriental influences in his furniture, and as various commentators have noted, was one of the few US Arts and Crafts designers to incorporate Art Nouveau elements, specifically the German version, *Jugendstil*. Green kept newspaper clippings of notable crimes, and had many readers send them to her ("Anna Katherine Green").

Rohlfs stated that he would draw upon the patterns within the grain of his preferred oak and ash for inspiration ("The Grain of Wood" 95). This use of the organic for determining and creating form could be whimsical, as when the curls of his pipe smoke suggested one of his carved embellishments (Clark 28). For Green, the "vivid, overpowering conception" was paramount, and something for which she was prepared to wait: "For years an incident would germinate in my mind. Then suddenly, perhaps in the night, I would wake with my story conceived from the first page to the last" (Woodward 169). To another interviewer she noted that a true crime narrative, told to her by a friend, took "three or four years" to germinate into her 1883 novel *Hand and Ring*. During that time she "had been revolving that plot subconsciously in my mind, and not in a mechanical way" ("Anna Katherine Green").

Both Green and Rohlfs abhorred the mechanical, the mass-produced. Rohlfs' workshop was a model of small-scale, meticulous craftsmanship, a minor Morris & Co. Unlike some of his Arts and Crafts contemporaries, he maintained an ideological purity by avoiding mass production and marketing. Woodward found Green a model of "high seriousness" regarding her craft. She ended up "blushing" for the slapdash "casual fecundity" with which modern writers like Edgar Wallace worked. Green regarded their mass-production as signalling the decline of the detective story, "the degeneration of Mystery to mere surprise." She worked for love of the work: "They, it seems, write only for dollars." As a consequence she read little modern crime and usually forebore to comment on it (Woodward 170, 169; "Detective Fiction"). Paradoxically, *The Leavenworth Case*, despite the care of its writerly craft, was a genuine mass-market phenomenon, with its millions of copies sold and multiple editions/translations. It was no doubt the income from this book and others by Green which helped give Rohlfs the freedom to work as an artistic craftsman, rather than as an industrial designer.

It is worth noting a dramatic subjectivity, an affect, which both partners in the marriage brought to their separate work. Rohlfs was almost a Method Actor in the intensity he brought to his designs. He believed in the concept of soul being put into a work, an emotional and spiritual identification, or transference: "If I make a chair, I am a chair" (qtd. in James, *Drama in Design* 35). Green told Woodward that writing *The Leavenworth Case* had "depleted her nervous energy" and left her physically never the same (Woodward 170). To another interviewer she described the writing of the climax to *The Forsaken Inn* (1890). In it a woman crawls through a passageway: "I knew what she was going to find there [a body], and when she was half-way through I was so frightened I could not take her any farther. I had to lay the manuscript away for a time." To avoid any spillover from her morbid plots, she gardened, chose cheerful company and even a cat called Fluffy, "pure white and of a most sane disposition" ("Anna Katherine Green").

The Rohlfs also followed William Morris in becoming involved with local and social issues, though stopping short of Morris' radical, even revolutionary politics. Both were actively part of their church, as Elder and committee-woman respectively. Rohlfs also gave time to "the social problems of his community," agitating for issues such as ballot reform. Green worked for auctorial copyright, and it was claimed she changed, via a personal cable, the mind of William Gladstone regarding the issue ("Personal Glimpses"; "Anna K. Green").

The importance of construction is evident in both the œuvres of Green and Rohlfs. This word recurs in descriptions of Green's work, and it is not a matter of mere semantics, for it describes her plotting. Rohlfs was well-known for his process of first designing an article of furniture on paper, then having one of his workmen make a miniature model, which would be refined via further models. Only when he was satisfied with his models would the full-scale version be built. This process is analogous with pre-plotting, a vital technique for crime fiction, with its need for clues to be artfully introduced or concealed, the mystery kept tantalising until the revelation at the end. Green always knew the endings of her books before she wrote them. As she herself stated: "I must have a central idea which appeals to my imagination; and an end of such point or interest that the reader will feel that it justifies the intricacies which are introduced to hold it back. In other words the heart of the labyrinth must be worth reaching" (qtd. in Wells ch. 24).

It is as a narrative constructor, an artificier, that Green can be most significantly placed as a significant crime fiction innovator. Wells described her as "one of the very best constructors of a detective story" (ch.13). She was a key developer, in novel length, of the clue-puzzle, "which invited and empowered the careful reader to solve the problem along with the detective" (Knight, *Form and Ideology* 107). Her most direct novelistic antecedent was Ellen Wood, most usually known for the crime melodrama of *East Lynne* (1860). However Green made the clue-puzzle her métier, and transmitted it to the new century, where it became the characteristic form of crime fiction's "Golden Age," the 1920s-50s. As the *New York Times* wrote, following Green's death:

> [. . .] with the possible exception of "The Moonstone" it was not until the publication in 1878, of the Brooklyn young woman's "Leavenworth Case", that the art of sending the reader on a false track regarding the guilty person, and, at the end, of taking him completely by surprise with a convincing solution which had never occurred to his imagination, was developed into a fine art. ("Detective Fiction")

Note those two last words. Green claimed to have started *The Leavenworth Case* with two notions, that the murderer should be the first to announce the crime, and that a conversation overheard should be misattributed ("Anna Katherine Green"). It is worth analysing the elaborate plot architecture she built on these premises. The book begins with Raymond, a junior lawyer and the narrator, being interrupted in his work by the news of murder. The firm's client, rich Mr Leavenworth, has been murdered in a locked room, his library. As an inquest is being held that day, the Misses Leavenworth (nieces and heirs) need a legal advisor present. Raymond is thus drawn into the drama, becoming an informal assistant to the New York detective, Mr Ebenezer Gryce.

Evidence is given at the inquest that no robbery was committed, and that the house was securely locked up on the night of the murder. Somebody within the household is guilty, but who? Hints of suspicion are dropped regarding the Misses Leavenworth – but also a servant girl, Hannah, is missing. The murder weapon, furthermore, has somehow ended up in Leavenworth's bedroom, reloaded. Raymond overhears a conversation between the two Miss

Leavenworths that suggests Eleanore has a guilty secret. It seems that Eleanore has both removed a letter from the library, and the key to its door.

Gryce, a man as mysterious in his intent as Sherlock Holmes – and Conan Doyle knew Green and her work (Maida 29) – directs Raymond to befriend a Mr Henry Clavering, a fine gentleman from London. Clavering knows the Leavenworth girls: he was also seen at the house on the night of the murder.

So far Green has nicely balanced Raymond's suspicions of both the Misses Leavenworths. Clavering becomes another suspect; and to complicate matters Leavenworth's secretary Harwell claims to have had a foreboding dream, implicating the Englishman. After some investigation, Raymond, a meticulous man, compiles a list of the evidence. He concludes the motive for the murder was a secret marriage, between Clavering and Eleanore, which would have caused an immediate disinheritance had Leavenworth known of it. Gryce merely remarks that he intends to prove Raymond wrong.

Gryce's assistant, known only as "Q," traces the missing Hannah to upstate New York, where she is hiding with Mrs Belden. But Hannah is found dead, from poison. She has left a suicide note, which Gryce shows to be faked. He sets up a scene in his office, in which he outlines a train of evidence against Mary Leavenworth, with two suspects summoned and within hearing distance. Upon his damning conclusion, the real murderer is provoked into a confession: Leavenworth's secretary Harwell, who loves Mary. He indeed, was the first to announce the murder. Hannah was a witness, who thus had to be eliminated. The words Raymond overheard, which led him to suspect Eleanore, were in fact spoken by Mary. Much of Eleanore's suspicious behaviour was, indeed, intended to protect Mary, whom she believed to be guilty.

Such is a rough outline, as the detailed analysis of Green's subtle introduction of clues or red herrings, her juggling of the suspects as one seems guilty, one innocent, would fill many pages. The novel comprises an almost architectural design of evidence, and even now a modern reader will not automatically suspect Harwell. As Green stated to Woodward: "She never wilfully, playfully or carelessly misled her readers; she only outwitted then with her nicer ingenuity, 'so that in the end they had to admit that had they but the eyes to see, the penetration to discover, there, from the start, was the solution of the mystery'" (169).

Various aspects of *The Leavenworth Case* – the locked room mystery, ballistics evidence, the series detective – had existed before Green, but she rediscovered and popularised them for a new generation of readers and writers. She also contributed innovations, including the body in the library, the butler (who didn't do it), and the reproduction of a torn but significant fragment of letter, which must be reconstructed. As Knight notes, "Many of the later 'whodunit' techniques are first found in a coherent sequence in Green" (*Crime Fiction* 53). In the hands of other writers, these features would become generic tics, ultimately formulaic in the manufactured texts she so abhorred. Knight again: "Green effectively shaped a model that 40 years later Agatha Christie and others would use and in some ways refine [. . . they] would not inherently or structurally vary the pattern Green established" (54).

It was the obvious intelligence of Green's design that helped legitimise the detective genre as more than blood-and-thunder voyeurism. She was also extremely logical and also realistic, avoiding the use of coincidence and incredible events. In this aspect she differs from her immediate predecessors, the sensation novelists.

Her high religiosity and seriousness additionally absolved her from charges of inciting crime, a persistent critique of crime fiction from the Newgate novel onwards. Furthermore, because Green was published in hardback, by a reputable publisher such as Putnam, she lifted the American mystery from the dime novel popular market to the middle-class audience.[5] By 1935, the year of her death, the *New York Times* was describing the reading of mystery narratives as "intellectual relaxation," the "habitual indulgence [. . .] even by individuals of serious minds," such as college professors. Thus Green helped create what the paper referred to, with a whiff of snobbishness, as "good" detective fiction ("Detective Fiction").

The critic Julian Hawthorne, in his discussion of Poe's "The Gold-Bug" describes the clue-puzzle, which he terms the "riddle story," in terms of a cleverly-constructed item of furniture, and as such his words could equally apply to the work of Green or Rohlfs:

> Look at the nice setting of the mortises; mark how the cover fits; how smooth is the working of that spring drawer. Observe that this bit of carving, which seemed mere ornament, is really a vital part of the mechanism. Note, moreover, how balanced and symmetrical the whole design is, with what economy and foresight every part is fashioned. It is not only an ingenious structure, it is a handsome bit of furniture, and will materially improve the looks of the empty chambers, or disorderly or ungainly chambers that you carry under your crown. Or if it

[5] Fuller Victor's detective novel *Too True* (1868) was also published by Putnam, but anonymously. Green differed in not being an isolated instance for the publisher, but rather a recognised, respectable "brand" name.

happen that these apartments are noble in decoration and proportions, then this captivating little object will find a suitable place in some spare nook or other, and will rest or entertain eyes too long focused on the severely sublime and beautiful.

**Works Cited**


"Anna K. Green Dies; Noted Author, 88." *New York Times* 12 Apr. 1935: 23.

"Anna Katherine Green Tells How She Manufactures her Plots." *Literary Digest* 13 July 1918: 48.

Clark, Robert Judson, ed. *The Arts and Crafts Movement in America, 1876–1916*. Princeton: Princeton UP, 1972.

"Detective Fiction." *New York Times* 14 Apr. 1935: 8.

Foucault, Michel. "What is an Author?" *The Foucault Reader*. Ed. Paul Rabinow. Middlesex: Penguin, 1984. 101-20.

Green, Anna Katherine. *The Forsaken Inn*. 1890. New York: Bonner, 1909.

___. *The Leavenworth Case: A Lawyer's Story*. 1878. New York: Dover, 1981.

Hatch, Mary R. P. "The Author of 'The Leavenworth Case.'" *Writer* 2 (1888): 159–62.

Hawthorne, Julian. "Riddle Stories." *The Lock and Key Library: the Most Interesting Stories of All Nations*. Ed. Julian Hawthorne. New York: Review of Reviews, 1912. 8 Sept. 2006 <http://www.gutenberg.org/dirs/etext00/sbmaa10.txt>.

Hubin, Alan J. *Crime Fiction IV: A Comprehensive Bibliography, 1749-2000*. Shelburne, Ontario: Battered Silicon, 2003.

Humpherys, Anne. "Who's Doing It? Fifteen Years of Work on Fuller Victorian Detective Fiction." *Dickens Studies Annual* 24 (1996): 259-74.

James, Michael L. "Charles Rohlfs and 'The Dignity of Labor.'" *The Substance of Style: Perspectives on the American Arts and Crafts Movement*. Ed. Bert Denker. Delaware: Henry Francis du Pont Winterarthur Museum, 1996. 229-41.

___. *Drama in Design: The Life and Craft of Charles Rohlfs*. Buffalo: Burchfield Arts Center, 1994.

Knight, Stephen. *Crime Fiction 1800-2000: Detection, Death, Diversity*. Houndmills: Palgrave Macmillan, 2004.

___. *Form and Ideology in Crime Fiction*. London: Macmillan, 1980.

Maida, Patricia D. *Mother of Detective Fiction: The Life and Works of Anna Katharine Green*. Bowling Green: Bowling Green State U Popular P, 1989.

___. "Personal Glimpses. A Little-Known Husband." *Literary Digest* 29 May 1915: 1201.

Putnam, George Haven. Letter to Anna Katharine Green. 19 July 1878. Harry Ransom Humanities Research Centre, U of Texas, Austin.

___. Letter to Anna Katharine Green. 16 Nov. 1925. Harry Ransom Humanities Research Centre, U of Texas, Austin.

Rohlfs, Charles. "Address to Arts and Crafts Conference." 1902. Rpt. in James, *Drama in Design* 97-98.

___. *Fall-Front Desk*. 1898-1900. Virginia Museum of Fine Arts, Richmond, Virginia.

___. "The Grain of Wood." 1901. Rpt. in James, *Drama in Design* 95.

___. "My Adventures in Wood-Carving." Rpt. in James, *Drama in Design* 99-100.

Ruskin, John. *The Seven Lamps of Architecture*. London: Smith, Elder, 1849.

Stewart, R. F. *...And Always a Detective: Chapters on the History of Detective Fiction*. Newton Abbott: David and Charles, 1980.

Wells, Carolyn. *The Technique of the Mystery Story*. Springfield, IL, 1913. *Gaslight*. 11 May 2000 <http://gaslight.mtroyal.ab.ca/>.

Woodward, Kathleen. "Anna Katherine Green." *Bookman* Oct. 1929: 169–70.

# Domesticating the Art of Detection: Ellen Wood's Johnny Ludlow Series

Alison Jaquet
The University of Western Australia

**Abstract**: This essay explores the Johnny Ludlow series of short stories by Ellen Wood and demonstrates how the art of detection in these texts is domesticated, tied inextricably to the private sphere, the family and the everyday world. I examine how the discourse of domestic detection is characterised by instability as various figures expose discursive structures while negotiating positions of power.

"You have heard of the skeleton in the closet, Johnny Ludlow. Few families are without one. I have mine" (Wood, "Roger Bevere" 313).[1] This confession marks the opening to the 1884 story "Roger Bevere," where, during a cosy breakfast in London, an acquaintance discloses his family's secret to the narrator, Johnny Ludlow. This scene aptly demonstrates the domestic underpinning of detection in Ellen (Mrs Henry) Wood's Johnny Ludlow series of short stories, which were published in the *Argosy* from 1868 to 1891. These fictional recollections of English rural life are a generic mix of detection, romance, mystery and crime, which, as Joanne Shattock asserts, form Wood's "best contributions to the magazine" (473).[2]

Ellen Wood (1814-1887) was a journalist, editor and writer of sensation fiction during the Victorian period. Wood's career as a writer began during the 1850s when she contributed short fiction and journalism to various British periodicals, including *Bentley's*

---

[1] I am grateful to Judith Johnston for reading and advising on drafts of this work.

[2] Bruce F. Murphy echoes these sentiments, describing the Johnny Ludlow stories as Wood's "best work" (535).

*Miscellany* and the *Leisure Hour*. She rose to fame with her bestseller *East Lynne* (1861), and became a major contributor to the proliferating genre of sensation fiction.[3] The 1860s saw increased debate over "sensation" novels with the serialisation of Wilkie Collins' *The Woman in White*, Wood's *East Lynne* and Mary Braddon's *Lady Audley's Secret* within 3 years of each other.[4] These novels disturbed and thrilled readers with their portrayal of the sensational and shocking possibilities underlying apparently respectable Victorian homes. As Anthea Trodd argues, the sensation novel intervened in the Victorian ideal of domesticity, destabilising notions of privacy, and complicating the ideal of the home as sanctuary (2). Wood's fiction, like most sensation fiction, functions to question categories of privacy and security by intruding into private, domestic spaces. Ellen Wood continued to publish sensation novels for several decades, often depicting domestic spaces compromised by murder, fraud, bigamy and other illicit secrets.

In 1867, Ellen Wood became editor of the *Argosy*. On its initial publication in 1865, the *Argosy* was intended to become a serious monthly magazine like the *Cornhill*. However, following the moral outcry over the serialisation of *Griffith Gaunt* by Charles Reade – a tale of bigamy – Ellen Wood was able to purchase the magazine cheaply and continue the trend of publishing sensation fiction

[3] Susan Balee insists that *East Lynne* was "*the* best-selling novel of nineteenth-century England" (143).

[4] The serialisation of Wilkie Collins' *The Woman in White* in *All the Year Round* from 1859-60, Wood's *East Lynne* in the *New Monthly Magazine* from 1860-1861 and Mary Braddon's *Lady Audley's Secret* in *Robin Goodfellow* and *Sixpenny Magazine* from 1861-1862 resulted in increased discussion and debate over "sensation" novels.

(Maunder 29).[5] Wood's particular brand of sensation was always a domesticated one, and the *Argosy* was targeted at a "respectable" readership. Jennifer Phegley indicates that the *Argosy* was a "family literary magazine" and she labels Wood's work as "domesticated sensationalism" (185). This domesticating tendency in Wood's writing continued in 1868 when the Johnny Ludlow short stories began appearing monthly in the *Argosy*. The stories are named after their narrator, who recalls his experiences as a young orphan living with a wealthy family in Worcestershire. Johnny Ludlow is enclosed within firm familial and domestic structures, and consequently, the mysteries he narrates (and participates in) depict and explore notions of home and the everyday. The stories revolve around incidents including theft, murder, mistaken identity and fraud, which implicate various family members, friends and servants. Even where the tales do not have an explicit crime at the heart of the narrative, there is always some type of inexplicable occurrence that requires solving. To situate mystery and crime within the home complicates the relationship between the private and the public, and the home becomes a place of threat from within and without. Hence, the Johnny Ludlow stories reveal the inherent contradictions of the discourses circulating around and within the Victorian domestic sphere. I will return to this point later, but I want to stress that these stories demonstrate a style that I will designate as 'domestic detection,' where the domestic is the operating aesthetic.[6]

This focus on the mysteries surrounding households and families points to the interrelation between sensation and detection.

---

[5] Here, Maunder estimates that under Wood's control, the magazine outsold Mary Braddon's *Belgravia* with a monthly circulation of 20,000.

[6] I have adapted this term from Catherine Ross Nickerson's discussions of the "domestic detective novel" (x).

This is explicated by Sally Mitchell, who labels the sensation novel as a "forerunner of the detective story" (vii) and Michael Cox makes a similar argument:

> It was within the uniquely Victorian matrix of sensation fiction that the detective story progressed towards maturity. In its key elements – episodic incident, the emphasis on plot rather than character, contemporary settings, the manipulation of actual events, murder, forgery and robbery, mistaken identity, and formulaic construction – sensation fiction provided the bridge between Poe and the true tale of detection as created by Conan Doyle. (xv)

Thus, Ellen Wood's Johnny Ludlow tales form part of this "bridge" between Poe and Conan Doyle. However, the art of detection in the Johnny Ludlow stories demonstrates clear differences in the processes of detection to the better-known Victorian detectives, Dupin and Holmes. As narrator, Johnny has what Cox describes as a necessary feature of the short story: "a credible and engaging narrative voice" (ix). However, Johnny blurs the roles in the discourse of detection because he simultaneously performs a narratorial function, like a Watson-figure, observing and assisting the detective process, but at other times, he becomes the overt detective. Frequently, Johnny Ludlow is simply an observer in the company of other detective figures and performs as an assistant, a messenger or merely a spectator. Johnny also occupies a liminal space in relation to social and cultural norms. As an orphaned teenaged boy, he is on the precipice of manhood and he is also an outsider figure, with only a temporary home in the Todhetley household. Johnny's guardian, Squire Todhetley, frequently makes private inquiries into various mysteries and (although often mistaken) is repeatedly appealed to publicly in his capacity as a local magistrate. Many of the stories involve Johnny and the Squire working in concert, and hence Johnny (and his style of detection) is often contrasted to the gruff masculinity of the Squire. This also demonstrates a divergence from the Dupin and Holmes models of detection as they live in homosocial anti-domestic structures while Johnny operates largely within the domestic sphere and demonstrates how the traditionally feminised category of the domestic can be masculinised. Johnny's narratives and his function of observer and narrator form part of the overarching pattern of domestic detection and this brief comparison to Holmes and Dupin serves as a useful jumping off point for my argument.

Alison Light gestures towards an aesthetic of detection when she likens the detective story to a jig-saw puzzle, as "a narrative whose break-up of linear development and continuities is only a temporary fragmentation, the pieces deliberately scattered for the express pleasure of putting them back together again" (91-92). What is particularly interesting about Light's choice of analogy is that a jigsaw puzzle is itself a form of domestic activity: a parlour game. However, the image of the puzzle points to a totality, which detection in the Johnny Ludlow series undermines. The dispersal of the detective function as it intersects with everyday, domestic concerns, complicates questions of authority in reconstructing the puzzle and representing the crime. I intend to show how the discourse of domestic detection and the continuum of the series, reveals a dispersal of, and a struggle for, power. While the stories focus on mundane domestic settings and the minutiae of everyday life, which might be interpreted as a conservative tendency, I consider the everyday to be fluid, contradictory and productive terrain. As Gardiner argues, the everyday can be theorised as not merely the "realm of the ordinary," but instead, "a domain that is potentially *extra*ordinary" (6). For the scope of this discussion I will examine the final run of 15 Ludlow stories, from 1878-1891, focussing in particular on: "Caromel's Farm" (1878), "The Story of Dorothy Grape" (1881), "A Mystery" (1882), "The Ebony Box" (1883), "Roger Bevere" (1884), "Caramel Cottage" (1885) and "Featherston's Story" (1889).[7]

Like the opening confession in "Roger Bevere," and elsewhere in the series, acts of storytelling are staged as specific "cases," puzzles or domestic mysteries that require detection and representation by various detective figures. At first glance, the short story form of the Johnny Ludlow series suggests limits and boundaries, and, like Poe's Dupin stories and Conan Doyle's Holmes cases, demonstrates how the short story form has shaped the art of detection. However, in the Johnny Ludlow stories, this frame of the short story intersects with the overarching series structure, to create a complex formal aesthetic. Like the Holmes series, and to a lesser extent, the Dupin stories, the Johnny Ludlow mysteries are implicated in a series impulse. In "Sherlock's Children: The Birth of the Series" Martin Priestman defines the series as "the form which repeats, theoretically ad infinitum, the same kind of action in roughly the same narrative space or time-slot, featuring at least one character continuously throughout" (50). While I am arguing that the "birth" of series detection proper predates the advent of the Holmes stories, Priestman provides an interesting counterpoint. He concludes his discussion with a comparison to modern television and argues that professionals such as "police detectives, doctors and nurses" are the ideal heroes of the series as their work

---

[7] The Johnny Ludlow series was subsequently republished in six volumes between 1874 and 1899. Here, the chronology of the original series was disrupted, and these later stories that I will survey were reprinted in the third to sixth volumes. I have chosen to use the pagination of the reprinted volumes as these are more readily available, however I will continue to refer to the dates of their original publication to elucidate their original relation to each other.

combines "the unique, personal interest drama of the individual episode and the reassuring repetition of the continuum" (57). This is important to my discussion, as the Johnny Ludlow series mirrors this episodic and repetitious form, but importantly, it refuses the heroism of the professional. Unlike the ideal professional that Priestman posits, Johnny is an amateur, who investigates mysteries that circulate within the everyday world and hence demonstrates how Wood's series domesticates detection. Importantly, the repetitive impulse is significant to the Johnny Ludlow series' focus upon everyday domestic spaces. Laurie Langbauer has theorised both the everyday and the series as foregrounding "repetition and ongoingness" (235). So, taken together, these definitions emphasise the episodic and continuous nature of series detection. In Wood's stories, this has important implications for the aesthetics of detective fiction.

The series structure of the Johnny Ludlow stories reflects how crime, mystery and detection continually repeat and circulate. Often, particular characters such as doctors and lawyers reappear to assist in the investigation of medical or legal aspects of the mysteries. For example, in "The Story of Dorothy Grape" (1881) the character of Dr Pitt, who was previously depicted in the story "Sandstone Torr" (1874) reappears unexpectedly in the narrative in which Johnny and the Squire uncover the truth about a spate of disappearances. But the Johnny Ludlow series resists vesting authority in these professional figures. Instead, the figure of the amateur detective is favoured, like the character of Captain Jack Tanerton who, in "Verena Fontaine's Rebellion" (1880) is accused of a murder, but becomes a detective figure in "A Mystery" (1882) to assist Johnny and the Squire in their investigations into a possible murder. Furthermore, while the settings of the stories shift from rural England, to London, and France, in all of these sites, the characters of the stories often derive from the same small Worcestershire towns. This permeation of characters into different locales suggests a continuum, as the characters will weave in and out of stories, often resurfacing years later. For example, if we return to "The Story of Dorothy Grape" (1881), the serendipitous discovery of the mysterious Dorothy Grape in London occurs when Johnny and the Squire are visiting Roger Bevere – a character who will not have his narrative told until three years later. Moreover, the reader is informed that Johnny Ludlow is already in the city, visiting a family friend – Miss Deveen.[8] Regular readers of the *Argosy* would have realised that this visit refers back to the events of the previous year's mystery, "Verena Fontaine's Rebellion" (1880) which also occurred in London. So there is a sense that the individual stories, which are framed as distinct narratives, actually intersect in chronological terms. This creates a world in which the everyday (and its attendant mysteries) are interlaced, where themes are repeated and characters circulate and recirculate.

So while particular crimes and mysteries might be resolved in an individual story, the criminals or other characters entangled in the mysteries will often resurface later. This emphasis on repetition and lack of resolution creates an effect, usefully described by Langbauer: "The paradox of the series is that, in seeming in its expansiveness to enclose *so* much, it exposes that totality as only an illusion. It highlights instead that there is simply more than we can ever enclose. Something must always be left out" (14).

The world created in a series ultimately exists in excess of its own parameters, and becomes only recovered fragments of an unrepresentable whole. Often in the stories, the reader can perceive

---

[8] Interestingly, Miss Deveen has previously featured as an amateur sleuth in "The Game Finished" (1869) to discover a jewel thief.

just whose voices are omitted in the discourse of detection. While each episode is contained in a short story, the reference to past (and sometimes future) events, characters and tales emphasises how the series impulse undermines this containment. This is ultimately expressed in the final story of the Johnny Ludlow series, "The Silent Chimes" (1891), which is a mystery that originates from the Squire's history. Detection is again thrown back into the past, the final mystery in the series circles back around and definitively refuses closure. The recurrence of characters throughout the series and constant shifts in time and place demonstrate how the series structure itself hints at an excess, an incompleteness, which can never be completely contained or represented. Returning to Light's analogy of the jigsaw, we can see how in Wood's stories, figures like Johnny might attempt to reconstruct a puzzle, but the form of the series reinforces that this is always a partial recovery of the fragmented whole. The completed jigsaw remains as an illusory fantasy, the mystery is always ongoing. While Johnny might attempt to discover the criminals in his cases and contain the "truth" in his narratives, their status as memories of the past undermines his attempts and again renders the puzzle incomplete

The narrator-function of Johnny Ludlow, and the series' presentation in a memoir form therefore has important implications for the art of detection. Like the narratives of Poe and Conan Doyle, which take a "case" or memoir form, Wood's stories are presented by the now older Johnny Ludlow, recalling the histories of his family, friends and various acquaintances. Dennis Porter points to this memoir form as a method used in detective fiction to create distance, contributing to a style of calm reasoning rather than thrilling action (86). However, I would suggest that this style of "calm reasoning" also gestures towards a domestication of detection, in opposition to detection as a professional and at times frenetic activity. Ludlow is recalling a past that is inexorably tied to the domestic realm, the homes and friends of his early life. Moreover, this memoir style emphasises that the detection narrative is overtly a construction, which foregrounds the role of storytelling and the power of the storyteller. To explain this further, Peter Thoms argues that nineteenth-century detective fiction is "an inherently self-reflexive form" and states: "narrative is not what *is* – an unproblematic mirroring of events – but what *is made*, and that process of construction becomes the very subject of these works" (1).[9] Hence in the Johnny Ludlow stories, as in other early detective fictions, detectives become authorial (but not necessarily authoritative) figures, and this is emphasised by the narrator who is recalling events from the unstable, subjective narrative of memory. This is overtly demonstrated in "A Mystery" (1882) when Ludlow addresses the reader with: "I scarcely know how to go on with this story so as to put its complications and discrepancies of evidence clearly before you" (39). Here and elsewhere, Ludlow is an uncertain narrator and detective, a far cry from the trademark egoism and control of Sherlock Holmes. Here, the work of storytelling is foregrounded and the process of reconstruction is neither transparent nor simple. Hence the notion of "solving" the mystery is itself destabilised, as Thoms puts it, "the resulting solution confronts us as an artifice" (1). It is clear that truth is produced by certain figures under certain circumstances and detection becomes a contested site.

For these reasons, domestic detection in these stories can be considered as a form of discourse. Sara Mills describes discourse

---

[9] Thoms clearly draws from earlier studies such as Albert D. Hutter's assertion that detectives are "inevitably concerned with the problem of knowledge" (194) and Peter Hühn's argument that the detective genre "thematizes narrativity itself as a problem, a procedure and an achievement" (451).

as a site of struggle to produce "truths" and always in dialogue and conflict with other positions (18-19). The discursive nature of detection opens it up to acts of reinterpretation and rescripting. This in turn assists to elucidate the circulating questions of truth and authority in the Johnny Ludlow stories. In these stories, the ability to read, know and articulate, represent or resolve mystery becomes paramount. While Ludlow is only one of many detective figures in the stories, he frequently performs this investigative role. As he states: "It is my habit always to try to account for things that seem unaccountable; to search out reasons and fathom them; and you would be surprised at the light that will sometimes crop up" ("Mystery" 29). Ludlow possesses a much-emphasised talent for detecting the truth about people: as we are told in "The Ebony Box" (1883) he "could read the riddles in a man's face and voice" (328). Furthermore, in an earlier story, Johnny is initially blamed for "making a mystery" out of his observations and he is often accused of having fancies and unreasonable suspicions which, of course, are revealed to be neither fanciful nor unreasonable ("Charlotte and Charlotte" 244). The operations of the discourse of detection reveal the domestic sphere to be a site of struggle and the role of the detective as an inherently unstable position.

As a domestic detective, Johnny often stumbles over mysteries in his everyday roles as a confidant to friends and by monitoring gossip. There is a pattern of references to the construction of narratives in the stories through the depiction of letters, statements and witness evidence. These become the building blocks of discourse. When Johnny narrates stories that are not from his own experience, or uses witness accounts, he will disclose the sources of the stories. This is illustrated in the story "Caramel Cottage" (1885), where Ludlow pauses in his narrative of the crimes to address the reader with "of course the reader fully understands that I am, so far, writing of what I knew nothing about until later" (84). Thoms describes this assemblage of the *real* as "an intelligible chain of narrative constructed from discovered information" (1). By this definition, the power of the detective figures is exposed by this staged construction of "truth." For example in "Featherston's Story" (1890), where a suspicious death occurs, we are told that the women at the centre of the story both kept diaries and the following: "But for that fact, and also that the diaries were preserved, Featherston could not have arrived at the details of the story so perfectly" (29). Several entries from the diaries are then recounted, but again the authority of these narratives is destabilised as we see, in one instance, an addendum between April 16th and May 1st when we are told that some "entries of little importance" have been omitted (29). The controlling hand of Dr Featherston, and ultimately the power of the narrator, Ludlow, work to frame the everyday experiences detailed in these women's narratives. However, this does not prevent an appeal to the "truth" value of these narratives later in the text:

> And now I come into the story – I, Johnny Ludlow. For what I have told of it hitherto has not been from any personal knowledge of mine, but from diaries, and from what Mary Carimon related to me, and from Featherston. It may be regarded as singular that I should have been, so to say, present at its ending, but that I *was* there is as true as anything I ever wrote. The story itself is true in all its chief facts; I have already said that; and it is true that I saw the close of it. (180)

The emphasis on truth here, borders on an anxiety. What is apparent though is that in this story, as in many of the Johnny Ludlow stories, the detective becomes a figurative writer or creator, constructing truths and producing knowledge. The use of everyday narratives such as letters, diary entries, newspapers, and witness testimony all have an effect of producing evidence, but also that of producing "reality." While as narrator (and sometimes detective), Johnny is a powerful figure in the struggle to produce truth in the discourse of detection, his is not the only voice.

In the Johnny Ludlow stories, power circulates through a dispersed system of detectives, as crime becomes a form of domestic politics. While crimes such as murder, bigamy, fraud and theft all motivate detection in the stories, they inevitably intersect with domestic issues such as inheritance, family secrets, marriage and the maintenance of respectability. In "The Story of Dorothy Grape" (1881) a young orphaned woman who is coerced into a hasty marriage is warned by her neighbour to "make inquiries in London" and "ask for proof" to verify the means and respectability of her suitor (331). Here, the art of domestic detection involves maintaining the privacy and respectability of the home and family. Later, in "Featherston's Story" (1890), the ability to read faces (and detect criminals), is situated in the characters of Lavinia Preen and Mary Carimon. Lavinia becomes a domestic detective when the suspicious Captain Fennel weds her sister and she immediately detects "a shifty look" in his otherwise attractive face (40). Lavinia's detection into the Captain's history is motivated by the potential threat to her family's reputation and position. Moreover, after Lavinia's suspicious death, a family confidant, Mary Carimon, begins to carefully watch Captain Fennel. We are told that the guilty Fennel dislikes Mary because "[h]e believed she read him pretty correctly" (156). Here, certain characters, notably females, are negotiating positions of power in the discourse of detection. This process of reading, observing and detecting also suggests that a dispersed system of surveillance is necessary to preserve the domestic sphere. These Victorian homes reflect what Mike Hepworth defines as "a kind of battleground: a place of constant struggle to maintain privacy, security and respectability in a dangerous world" (19). Certainly, the domestic spaces of Wood's short stories seem to necessitate a broad system of surveillance and detection. Often, servants and other local villagers also perform a detective function in the stories. In "Caromel's Farm" (1878), the blacksmith Dobbs spies on a property in which sightings of ghosts have lately occurred. When he is discovered covertly watching this neighbouring farm by Johnny Ludlow and the Squire, he says: "There's something uncanny in this place; some ugly mystery. I mean to find it out if I can, sirs, and this is the third night I've come here on the watch" (266). In this way, detection is a system to monitor potential threats to the village, and makes ironic the earlier claim that "people don't go prying into their neighbours' closets to look up their skeletons" (223). Domestic detection becomes a necessary and ongoing process in the protection of homes, families, ideology and the status quo. Hence, in the Johnny Ludlow series, there is no one detective with specialised knowledge. Instead, there are various figures negotiating positions for themselves in a system of domestic detection, with the outcomes organised by Johnny's narration.

Detection in these stories is staged in a way that reveals a pattern of distrust regarding the power to represent or narrate. Here, domestic detection is clearly linked to threats to privacy. For example, in an ambivalent depiction in "A Tragedy" (1886), the victim of a theft is investigating his own monetary loss and forthrightly asserts "I don't like detectives" (188). When the Squire and Johnny make private inquiries into his loss, it eventuates that the victim's own son perpetrated the deception – a fact that is suppressed. This investment in privacy that underpins domestic detection is reiterated in "The Ebony Box" (1883) when an amount of money disappears from a house and the owner informs the police. After an innocent man has been publicly tried for the crime and advertised as a criminal in the newspapers, the owner is warned, "he should have had it investigated privately" (316). Indeed, in several stories there is an outright fear of official detection, as family members are compelled to undertake roles as domestic detectives. In the Gothic story, "Caramel Cottage" (1885), a young woman, Katrine Barbary, suspects her father of killing her fiancé and becomes a domestic detective to discover the truth. Here, the family home becomes an oppressive site of fear and terror. However, Katrine ultimately fears others' detection of this potential murder more than her father. When she sees a shadowy figure observing her father digging a grave in the garden she speculates: "Was it an officer of the law, come to spy upon her father and denounce his crime?" (99). However Katrine is relieved as she suspects the figure's true identity is Johnny Ludlow, and gasps, "Oh, I pray that it may be! I think *he* would not betray him" (99). Clearly, there is a marked delineation between those entrusted with domestic detection and those who do not have legitimate positions in the discourse. Moreover, while privacy concerns ensure that official detectives become threatening figures, the detective function becomes dispersed among a circle of family members and concerned friends whose activity is as much directed at hiding the facts as it is to bring about disclosure.

This concern over the power to detect and to represent truths becomes an extra-textual concern, as the self-reflexivity of the Johnny Ludlow series extends the art of domestic detection to the implied readers of the stories. In the opening to "A Mystery" (1882) Johnny visits Dr Darbyshire, and tells us: "I had chanced to look in upon him one evening when he was taking rest in his chimney-corner, in the old red-cushioned chair, after his day's work was over, smoking his churchwarden pipe in his slippers and reading "The Story of Dorothy Grape" (1). By staging this cosy domesticity as a site for the reading of her stories, Wood overtly transforms the familiar into the uncanny.[10] This spectacle of the domestic complicates ideas of public and private, and reality and its representations. In this image, the domestic space of a potential reader is implicated in the represented domestic spaces of the stories. The readers of texts in the home mirror the domestic detectives in Wood's stories. Moreover, this figure of Dr Darbyshire as a consumer of the texts, locates a possible reader firmly within the middle-class. In this story, the doctor urges Johnny to embark on telling the current narrative because, as the doctor insists, "you seem good at telling of unaccountable disappearances" (1), implicit praise of the author herself. Johnny's role as a storyteller or author-figure is therefore explicitly staged, but the role is complicated as, at the conclusion of "A Mystery" the central murder remains unsolved. Instead, the reader is addressed with the challenge: "you must decide for yourselves, if you can, on which side the weight of evidence seems to lie" (60). This strategy implicates the reader of detective fiction by foregrounding how the problem of knowledge may need an extra-textual domestic detective.

Ellen Wood's Johnny Ludlow series emphasises how the art of detection is a domesticated discourse characterised by instability and circularity. The stories bring crime and other mysterious threats into close proximity with the domestic world of the nineteenth century to suggest that the site of the everyday is one that necessitates constant surveillance and detection from within.

[10] See Chase and Levinson.

However, it also demonstrates how the domestic is a complex and contradictory site, as the art of detection becomes a dispersed system, with multiple detective figures struggling to produce truths. The stories raise questions regarding acts of reading and signifying as they stage the construction of discourse. In the world of Johnny Ludlow knowledge may be recovered or represented, or conversely, may also be suppressed, depending either on the whim of the figurative storytellers or the narrator himself, or on the demands of domestic ideology. Detection, when it intersects with the aesthetic of the domestic in Wood's late-Victorian fiction, reveals a discursive complexity in stark contrast to the more straightforward masculine narratives of the pre-Edwardian era.

**Works Cited**

Balee, Susan. "Correcting the Historical Context: The Real Publication Dates of *East Lynne*." *Victorian Periodicals Review* 26.3 (1993): 143-45.

Chase, Karen, and Michael Levenson. *The Spectacle of Intimacy: A Public Life for the Victorian Family*. Princeton: Princeton UP, 2000.

Cox, Michael, ed. *Victorian Detective Stories*. Oxford: Oxford UP, 1992.

Gardiner, Michael. *Critiques of Everyday Life*. London: Routledge, 2000.

Hepworth, Mike. "Privacy, Security and Respectability: The Ideal Victorian Home." *Ideal Homes? Social Change and Domestic Life*. Ed. Tony Chapman and Jenny Hockey. London: Routledge, 1999. 17-29.

Hühn, Peter. "The Detective as Reader: Narrativity and Reading Concepts in Detective Fiction." *Modern Fiction Studies* 33.3 (Autumn 1987): 451-66.

Hutter, Albert D. "Dreams, Tranformations and Literature: The Implications of Detective Fiction." *Victorian Studies* 19.2 (Dec. 1975): 181-209.

Langbauer, Laurie. *Novels of Everyday Life: The Series in English Fiction, 1850-1930*. Ithaca: Cornell UP, 1999.

Light, Alison. *Forever England: Femininity, Literature and Conservatism Between the Wars*. London: Routledge, 1991.

Maunder, Andrew. "Ellen Wood was a Writer: Rediscovering Collins's Rival." *Wilkie Collins Society Journal* 3 (2000): 17-31.

Mills, Sara. *Discourse*. London: Routledge, 1997.

Mitchell, Sally. Introduction. *East Lynne*. 1861. By Mrs Henry Wood. New Brunswick: Rutgers UP, 1984.

Murphy, Bruce F. *The Encyclopaedia of Murder and Mystery*. New York: Palgrave, 1999.

Nickerson, Catherine Ross. *The Web of Iniquity: Early Detective Fiction by American Women*. Durham: Duke UP, 1998.

Phegley, Jennifer. "Domesticating the Sensation Novelist: Ellen Price Wood as the Author and Editor of the *Argosy Magazine*." *Victorian Periodicals Review* 38.2 (Summer 2005): 180-98.

Porter, Dennis. "The Language of Detection." *Popular Culture*. Ed. Tony Bennett. London: Routledge, 1990. 81-93.

Priestman, Martin. "Sherlock's Children: The Birth of the Series." *The Art of Detective Fiction*. Ed. Warren Chernaik, Martin Swales, and Robert Vilain. London: Macmillan, 2000. 50-59.

Shattock, Joanne. *The Oxford Guide to British Women Writers*. Oxford: Oxford UP, 1994.

Thoms, Peter. *Detection and its Designs: Narrative and Power in Nineteenth-Century Detective Fiction*. Athens: Ohio UP, 1998.

Trodd, Anthea. *Domestic Crime in the Victorian Novel*. London: Macmillan, 1989.

Wood, Ellen (Mrs Henry). "Caramel Cottage." 1885. *Johnny Ludlow: Sixth Series*. London: Macmillan, 1899. 54-125.

___. "Caromel's Farm." 1878. *Johnny Ludlow: Third Series*. London: Macmillan, 1899. 223-43.

___. "Charlotte and Charlotte." 1878. *Johnny Ludlow: Third Series*. London: Macmillan, 1899. 244-66.

___. "The Ebony Box." 1883. *Johnny Ludlow: Fifth Series*. London: Macmillan, 1899. 271-348.

___. "Featherston's Story." 1889. *Johnny Ludlow: Fifth Series*. London: Macmillan, 1899. 1-204.

___. "The Game Finished." 1869. *Johnny Ludlow: First Series*. London: Bentley, 1895. 238-55.

___. "A Mystery." 1882. *Johnny Ludlow: Fourth Series*. London: Macmillan, 1899. 1-60.

___. "Roger Bevere." 1884. *Johnny Ludlow: Fourth Series*. London: Macmillan, 1899. 313-67.

___. "Sandstone Torr." 1874. *Johnny Ludlow: Fourth Series*. London: Macmillan, 1899. 61-144.

___. "The Silent Chimes." 1891. *Johnny Ludlow: Sixth Series*. London: Macmillan, 1899. 257-398.

___. "The Story of Dorothy Grape." 1881. *Johnny Ludlow: Third Series*. London: Macmillan, 1899. 313-58.

___. "A Tragedy." 1886. *Johnny Ludlow: Sixth Series*. London: Macmillan, 1899. 126-229.

___. "Verena Fontaine's Rebellion." 1880. *Johnny Ludlow: Fourth Series*. London: Macmillan, 1899. 190-292.

# "The Accomplished Forms of Human Life": The Art and the Aesthetics of the Female Detective

Therie Hendrey-Seabrook
University of Sussex

**Abstract:** In this essay I suggest that the art and aesthetic function of late-Victorian and Edwardian fictional female detectives differs from those of their male counterparts, proposing that these women were subject to an intense, morally-charged scrutiny which scarcely touched their male contemporaries, and the resulting disparity in construction led to a gendered fissure in the aesthetics of detection.

In his preface to *The Renaissance: Studies in Art and Poetry* (1893)[1] Walter Pater suggests that the first goal of the aesthetic critic is to identify the particularity of the sensations that art produces in us. The critic's function is "to distinguish, to analyse, and separate from its adjuncts, the virtue [. . .] which [. . .] produces this special impression of beauty or pleasure, to indicate what the source of that impression is, and under what conditions it is experienced" (ix). Pater continues by insisting on a scientific analysis, likening the process to that of the chemist's reduction to basic elements, which then results in the ability to explain beauty in concrete rather than abstract terms. The whole enterprise of the aesthetic critic could, it seems, be equally true of the fictional detective who also, in the best scientific manner, sifts and separates clues, events and motives from their misleading circumstances, getting to the heart of the "special impression" – that is to say, to the fear and awful pleasure, or thrill, induced by the fictional representation of crime in general and murder in particular.

---

[1] Pater had published several versions of this text. The first version was published under the title of *Studies in the History of the Renaissance* in 1873.

The working of the analogy can perhaps be seen more clearly by practising an interpretative substitution of Pater's definition of the aesthetic critic's abilities with the terminologies of detection. Thus, in a later passage he proposes

> not that the critic [detective] should possess a correct abstract definition of beauty [crime] for the intellect, but a certain kind of temperament, the power of being deeply moved by the presence of beautiful objects [transgressive actions]. He will remember always that beauty [crime] exists in many forms. To him all periods, types, schools of taste, are in themselves equal. In all ages there have been some excellent workmen [fiendishly-clever criminals], and some excellent work done [fiendishly-clever crimes committed]. The question he asks is always: – In whom did the stir, the genius, the sentiment of the period find itself? where was the receptacle of its refinement, its elevation, its taste? [Who had the motivation? Where did the opportunity arise?] (x)[2]

That a "correct abstract definition" is not deemed necessary suggests analogously that a detective need not be professionally trained but must be motivated primarily by a temperamental abhorrence for crime and its consequences. Furthermore, the detective must not be swayed in his integrity by different types of crime but must always be alert to asking the right kind of questions which will lead to resolution. Thus the quality and kind of questions raised by aspects of art are similar to those articulated by a detective in his investigations and they inform the effect of the fictional detective on the reader.

---

[2] The square brackets contain my analogous interpretations of Pater's terms which precede them.

The possibility of art and detection having an analogical relationship had been mooted a generation earlier by Thomas De Quincey. In his 1854 essay "Postscript," which was an addendum to *On Murder As A Fine Art* (1827), he dramatised the infamous John Williams' murders of 1812, showing the potential of crime and criminality to be embraced as subjects fit for literature. De Quincey posited the sense of an aesthetic "thrill," that "frenzy of feelings which [. . .] mastered the popular heart" (83), which could be experienced in the effect the murderer's "art" had on the reader. To find art in the immoral was a transgressive aesthetic position, at odds with Immanuel Kant's rather different view on the relationship between art and ethics, for Kant had posited an intrinsic correspondence between beauty and morality as a fundamental condition of harmony.[3] However, Kant's notion of the sublime, that sense of terror which makes us aware of our moral position, could be accommodated within the new idea of aesthetic thrill and aspects of both Kant's and De Quincey's theorising would remain at the heart of aesthetic considerations of detective fiction.

Over the years, with the rise in perceived social chaos and the corresponding need for a figure to restore order and security, the aesthetic focus had necessarily turned from the criminal to the detective who would catch him. By the time Sherlock Holmes appeared in 1887, the figure of the male detective had long taken over the literary stage from the criminal and was becoming firmly established as the preferable aesthetic model.[4] However, the male

---

[3] See Kant's *Critique of Judgment* (1790).

[4] Throughout the essay I refer to Sherlock Holmes as the archetype of male detectives from whom so many other detectives sprang. Amongst these could be listed, for instance, Sexton Blake, who was the product of several authors and subject of many adventures; Joyce Muddock's pseudonymous hero, Dick Donovan; Herbert Jenkins'

detective remained heir to the trope of socially-marginalised loner and this gave his construction an edgy, criminal-like thrill of its own as he rubbed shoulders with those he tried to capture. Yet alongside this De Quinceyan thrill, the Kantian sense of the sublime could still be experienced in the awe induced in the reader by the super-intellectual qualities of Holmes and his like, while the coincidence of the thrill and the sublime together within the figure of the male detective were validated by Pater's aesthetic theorising and his discussion of the role of – male-led – art criticism. The aesthetic of the male detective, then, embodied a dual, but complementary, formulation.

So much for the male detective, but what of the female? Although one or two instances of fictional female detectives had appeared earlier in the nineteenth century, it was not until the 1890s that a veritable tide of these female versions, created by both male and female authors, surged into publication and it was only to be expected that the prevailing, male-constructed aesthetic would come under some pressure from this sudden onslaught.

Moreover, by the 1890s, Pater's ideas about aesthetics had been taken up by the Decadent Movement, embraced most famously by Oscar Wilde, who himself had something specific to say about crime and art.[5] In the popular consciousness, however, Pater's ideas became overlaid with and subsumed into a justification for a hedonistic lifestyle, for the experience of decadence, for the excuse to live life to the full and to avoid social responsibility. Certainly popular culture understood the aesthetic movement out

---

Malcolm Sage; Ernest Bramah's blind Max Carrados or E. W. Hornung's crime doctor, Dr. John Dollar. Whatever the variation, however, the Holmesian paradigm is well-enough known that I have deemed unnecessary here to give particulars in illustration of his or his brothers' aesthetic specificities.

[5] See, for instance, Oscar Wilde, "Pen, Pencil and Poison: A Study in Green."

of context and in simplistic fashion but, with detective fiction as part of that popular culture, this *mis*understanding had a bearing on the construction of detective figures. It was all very well for Sherlock Holmes to live a Bohemian lifestyle and to push the bounds of decadence because the sublimity of his detective work offset any perceived moral laxity, but even Irene Adler – *the* woman to inspire Holmes' admiration – could not support a Bohemian character without putting her reputation in England at risk.[6] So how could any women be accommodated in this updated and amended aesthetic and yet remain acceptable?

The Decadent Movement roughly coincided with the appearance of the figure of the New Woman, another construction of cultural anxiety. The New Woman was regarded as a challenge to the *status quo* as much as, but for different reasons to, the decadent male. She was the young woman who sought independence: financial, social and moral. She worked for women's rights, for the vote, for her living. She wanted an education and to be able to stand on her own two feet without incurring conventional restrictions on her movements and her choice of action. She was felt to challenge all the ties of family and community in her single-mindedness and, just like the male decadent figure epitomised by Wilde in *The Picture of Dorian Gray* (1891), so did the New Woman also become a subject of contemporary fiction. On first consideration it would seem intuitively apposite to equate the female detective with the New Woman and so to locate her within that aesthetic which seemed to offer a female equivalent of the male decadent. However, as Sally Ledger points out, it was "the perceived connection between the New Woman and decadence that meant that the fate of the New Woman was inextricably

[6] See Arthur Conan Doyle, *A Scandal In Bohemia* (1891).

linked to the public disgracing of Oscar Wilde" (94) which took place at his trial and subsequent sentencing in 1895. Ledger goes on to aver that "popular New Woman fiction dwindled dramatically after 1895" and, further, that the "fictional New Woman was almost certainly a victim of the moral rearguard action which followed the Wilde trials" (94). Yet it is immediately after this apparent excision of the New Woman from fiction that that positive flood of female detectives arrives to take her place. Clearly, the female detective of this period does not correspond straightforwardly with the figure of the New Woman after all, but perhaps she presents something even newer in aesthetic terms.

At this point it must be noted that the exception in this discussion might be C. L. Pirkis' detective protagonist, Loveday Brooke, who appeared in 1893, prior to the Wilde trial and prior to the disappearance of the fictional New Woman, and Loveday *is* different from the rest of her female colleagues in some respects. She goes into detection for different reasons to many of her contemporaries, needing and wishing only to earn a living for herself because of a "jerk of Fortune's wheel" which left her "penniless and all but friendless" (Pirkis, "Black Bag" 2), rather than for any more altruistic reasons of familial support or obligations of honour. Nor are there any men in her life at all except for those with whom she has dealings professionally. Loveday is truly independent and, in that capacity, resembles a New Woman much more than some of the female detectives to come, but even her construction – as detective – draws away from that New Woman motif, as will be considered in more detail later.

Apart from Loveday Brooke though, the majority of the British female detectives made their appearance in the very last years of the century. In 1897 George Sims created Dorcas Dene, a former actress who undertakes detection in order to support her blind artist-husband. 1898 introduced Clarence Rook's Nora Van Snoop, an American who comes to London and works to avenge her murdered fiancé; Grant Allen's Lois Cayley, who restores her fiancé's honour, while Fergus Hume's Hagar Stanley takes up work in a pawnshop to escape a forced betrothal and ultimately marries one of her clients. In 1899 Allen's second female detective, the nurse Hilda Wade, comes on the scene, marrying her admiring chronicler once she clears her dead father's name. In the same year, Florence Cusack, the collaborative issue of L. T. Meade and Robert Eustace, goes in for detection under the compulsion of an unexplained promise while in 1900 Matthias McDonnell Bodkin created Dora Myrl, a professional lady detective who eventually marries her male colleague. Of the Edwardian authors who added to this field, the most popular was Baroness Orczy who created the character of Lady Molly Robertson-Kirk in 1910. Lady Molly's reason for going in for detection has a similar moral impetus to that of many of her fictional sisters: it is revealed eventually that her goal has been to vindicate her wrongly-imprisoned husband.

As was the usual practice, several of these detectives appeared episodically in short stories published in magazines before being collected in volume form, so there is a sense in which their apparent ubiquity is owing to this speedy republication but, despite this, it is evident that the female detective was making a huge impact.[7] It should not be forgotten that while these were some of the main names to appear at the time, they were not the only female detectives at the *fin de siècle* by any means. They were joined by a variety of female one-offs – sometimes parodic, sometimes mere

[7] So, for example, Pirkis first published in *Ludgate Monthly*; both of Allen's creations appeared originally in *Strand* magazine, while Rook's, as well as Meade and Eustace's, detective fiction was first seen in *Harmsworth* magazine.

spoofs – appearing as magazine fodder which never made it to volume form, but which nevertheless played into the burgeoning interest around the female detective figure. Nor should it be forgotten that the configuration of the female detective which had appeared earlier in America continued to flourish across the Atlantic throughout this period, and very likely contributed to the British interest in terms of establishing and prolonging this increasingly familiar literary presence.[8]

Having noted the numbers in which these female detectives appeared after the demise of the fictional New Woman, it is interesting to observe that any alliance with that figure is also quite categorically denied, often in loud and clear protest, perhaps in order to distance the new aesthetic variant from its disturbing predecessor. For instance, Dorcas Dene's mother, Mrs Lester, is described as "looking contemptuously over the last number of the *Queen*, and wondering out loud what on earth young women were coming to with their tailor-mades and their bicycle costumes" (Sims 60). This derogation is followed immediately by a description of Dorcas herself lying on the sofa, her husband and pet dog close by, as far removed from New Womanry as it seems domestically possible. Nora Van Snoop's public entrance into the Café Royal without a chaperone is explained away by her nationality, rather than any gendered transgressiveness: "'American, you bet,' said one of the loungers. 'They'll go anywhere and do anything'"

---

8 For example, Anna Katharine Green, whose lasting fame has rested in particular on her first novel, *The Leavenworth Case* (1878), was regarded as *the* innovative contributor to American detective fiction. She created two very different female detectives: the nosy spinster, Amelia Butterworth (1897) and a younger sleuth, Violet Strange (1915). Neither are discussed here, but Green's impact on the genre should not be underestimated, her influence being acknowledged by, amongst others, no less a writer than Agatha Christie, whose own Miss Marple owes a debt to Amelia Butterworth.

(Rook 86). Hagar Stanley occupies a more overtly transgressive position, being an exotic Romany who was not "brought up under parental government" (Hume 50) and who now runs a pawnshop on her own, also without any chaperone. However, Hume goes on to reassure the reader that this will not take Hagar into New Woman territory. Having met the man she will eventually marry, Hagar reflects on her attraction for him. Within "her own social code, and that a strict one [. . .], she thought her mental attitude was unmaidenly and unworthy of an unmarried girl" (50). Hagar's idealised mental attitude is one of modesty and, while that does not preclude integrity and independence of spirit, neither does it encourage upsetting the social *status quo* any more than need be.

Of these post-1895 female detectives Lois Cayley seems a more likely reincarnation of the New Woman. A product of modern society, she is a graduate of Girton College but her modernity is featured primarily in her construction as an adventuress, while any configuration as a detective actually takes second place to her round-the-world travels and to her – unfeminine – bicycling and mountain climbing activities.[9] By contrast, Allen's second creation, Hilda Wade, who is trained and working as a nurse in St Nathaniel's Hospital, has a social life beyond her working life, one in which she continues to mix with people of her own class who still accept her as such. Thus Hilda remains unadulteratedly feminine without compromising her social status. In fact, it would seem that only Dora Myrl epitomises true New Womanhood, and this despite an explicit authorial denial that there is anything of the New Woman about her. Like Lois Cayley, she also is university-educated and indulges in bicycling and other modern pursuits, but Dora is independent to an almost unbelievable degree, being in

[9] The stories were collected under the descriptive title of *Miss Cayley's Adventures* in 1899.

business by choice as a professional detective, rather than performing as an amateur or by force of circumstance. Yet, ultimately, even Dora is rescued from the charge of unwomanly independence through her submission to love and marriage to her male counterpart and mentor, Paul Beck, and through her subsequent withdrawal from detection.

As Laura Marcus argues, in reference to the New Woman of the 1890s, the "concept of the 'new' suggests an evolutionary model of womanhood, in which women were seen as standing at the dawn of a new century" (vii). Perhaps it would be more accurate, then, to consider this flux of female detectives rather as true *fin-de-siècle* productions whose appearance just took timely advantage of the success of Conan Doyle's creation to provide a variant model of the detective figure and one which was calculated to form an effective and alluring contrast to the hatchet-faced supersleuth: in effect, a feminine imitation of the male detective aesthetic.

However, the imitation necessitated more than mere gender-substitution and, as Joseph Kestner points out, the "challenge for those aspiring to create 'Sherlock's sisters' was to differentiate their detectives, but not only from the masculine model" for "it then became necessary to distinguish one female detective from another" (29). Kestner suggests that this was mostly achieved through the different primary occupations of the women and the different motives that led them into detection. While this may be the case to a degree, it does not take into account the fact that these late Victorian female detectives and their Edwardian sisters undertook their detection with different skills and forms of knowledge to their male counterparts, whilst still managing to induce an aesthetic thrill from the very nature of their work: allaying the fears and anxieties engendered by crime and its propinquity through successful resolution and the restoration of order. Their different skill-base was, in fact, part of their appeal and has been acknowledged elsewhere, but little critical attention has been given to how those female skills and forms of knowledge responded to and enacted a complicated relationship with contemporary aesthetic concerns.[10]

All these women are accomplished in many ways, as befitted their class and status, but the typical accomplishments of a feminine woman of the period – singing, dancing, drawing, sewing, knowledge of a foreign language and so on – are not deemed to exist in the same category as Pater's "accomplished forms of human life." Womanly accomplishments are not art forms, not worthy of aesthetic acknowledgment, in this sense. However, it is not these kinds of accomplishments that the female detective draws upon in order to practise her detective art, but rather her attainments in "feminine intuition" combined with her powers of analytical reasoning. As Loveday Brooke experienced when she needed to make her way in life, of "[m]arketable accomplishments she found she had none" but she does have "so much common sense that it amounts to genius" (Pirkis, "Black Bag" 2, 3). This kind of ability makes the female detective's methods very similar to that of the male detective. So, for example, both Hilda Wade and Sherlock Holmes make deductions from the facts at their disposal and both detectives reach their conclusions silently and secretly, coming up with answers which they only deign to explain later. Hilda Wade is described as possessing "in so large a measure the deepest feminine gift – intuition" whilst her employer, the superintellectual Professor Sebastian, is said to represent "the oth-

[10] See, for example, Laura Marcus for a discussion of the attributes required in a female detective, such as a facility with disguises, nosiness or curiosity and an eye for detail.

er side of the same endowment in its masculine embodiment – instinct of diagnosis" (Allen, *Hilda Wade* ch. 1). Sebastian comments on Hilda's diagnostic abilities in reference to the effects of a new drug he is developing. Hilda has only divulged a partial explanation of her conclusions about dosage and Sebastian wonders how she "guessed it". The narrator, Dr Cumberledge, has a suggestion:

> 'Intuition,' I answered.
>
> He pouted his under lip above the upper one, with a dubious acquiescence. 'Inference, I call it,' he retorted. 'All woman's so-called intuition is, in fact, just rapid and half-unconscious inference.' (ch. 1)

Whether in Sherlock Holmes or in Professor Sebastian, the process of "diagnostic instinct" is regarded as almost superhuman and merits an intrinsic aesthetic value in its production of the sense of thrill in the marvelling reader, but in the women detectives the same process is seen as aesthetically serendipitous, something to be condescendingly admired, the feminine knowledge, or intuition, often being demoted by the male onlooker to merely having played a hunch. Female detectives are not allowed to share in this aspect at an aesthetic level. It must remain a purely masculine trait. Even the occurrence of intuition is not so much productive of thrill for itself as it is because it appears embodied in the woman, or lady, detective as they are so often termed.

Thus, for example, Florence Cusack's abilities are described hand-in-hand with her physical presence. As her admiring chronicler, Dr Lonsdale, expresses it: "As one glanced at this handsome girl with her slender figure, her eyes of darkest blue, her raven-black hair, and clear complexion, it was almost impossible to believe that she was a power in the police courts, and highly respected by every detective in Scotland Yard" (Meade and Eustace 93). Indeed, the insistence on the full physical description both distracts from and allows no room for belief in her intellectual capacities.

The female detective is put in a much more difficult aesthetic position than her male counterpart for the very notion of a female detective subverts the dominant cultural aesthetic which held that woman is the passive receptacle of beauty, whose function is to exist as muse, to be gazed at as the silent accoutrement of male achievement and power. A female detective turns this aesthetic on its head because she is an agent of the public – no matter whether in a private capacity or within the police institution – who has to enter places deemed unfit and unsuitable for women, who has to rub shoulders with and question criminals and suspects and who has no regard for the decencies of "proper" female conduct, allowing herself to see and to be seen. Unlike the male detective, then, she is deemed subversive and marginalised *a priori* because of her very gender. While he can revel in that edgy, criminal thrill which resonates in his detective function, she must somehow work to throw off her pre-supposed transgressiveness. While the male detective is the hero despite, or even because of, his criminal overtones, the female detective is the heroine whose embodied criminality also makes her as much a victim as those she seeks to champion. She is thus artist – producer of thrill; subject – the victim, *and* critic – the detective, and her position within the aesthetic thus carries that much more moral risk.

This position can be clarified by returning to contemporary aesthetic theory. Pater's essay had focused on the role of the art critic and Wilde's later summary of his own aesthetic opinions, given in the preface to *The Picture of Dorian Gray*, whilst obviously generated and adapted from Pater's work, focuses more on the actual problems to be encountered by the critic:

> All Art is at once surface and symbol.
> Those who go beneath the surface do so at their peril.
> Those who read the symbol do so at their peril.
> It is the spectator, and not life, that art really mirrors. (4)

The critic, or detective, especially if female, goes "beneath the surface" of the art or crime at their peril because they make themselves vulnerable to the transgressive influences of the criminal world. However, the spectator, or detective, is actually mirrored by the art or crime and, again, if female this means that the woman detective faces herself when she enters into detective activity. She must therefore face up to herself as a potentially criminalised reflection.

At this point, then, the position of the female detective becomes very interesting indeed, for she is not only the scrutineer of crime and the criminal, the seeker of clues, the spectator and observer, but she herself becomes a suspect, subject to scrutiny in a way that male detectives never experience. Patricia Craig and Mary Cadogan point out with regard to earlier nineteenth-century detective fiction that "the focus of interest shifted from the victim or intended victim to the disinterested onlooker who is also the investigator" (38). By the end of the century, however, the female investigator reintroduces the earlier interest in the victim, but now this is focused on her own person as she draws the gaze to herself, being simultaneously the subject and object of her literary conception. Thus, much as the male detective has a dual aesthetic formulation so does an aspect of duality assert itself around the figure of the female detective but, in her case, the duality is not so much complementary as indicative of double standards. For, no matter how closely they may be thought to have emulated or benefited from the paradigm of the liberated New Woman, all these female detectives incur both an objectified and a moral scrutiny which dismisses any presumptions of true aesthetic liberty.

To varying degrees they depart from the safety of the domestic environment and willingly take up the exposed position of active investigator. True, in the case of several of these women, we do not know until their stories come to a close that all along they have had ulterior motives as justification of their brazen claim to performance on behalf of the public – brazen even when they do so in the guise of *private* investigators. So for the most part detectives like Nora Van Snoop, Lois Cayley or Hilda Wade appear as marriageable yet unmarried young women, seemingly transgressing just for the sake of it, without any validating excuse. Superficially, then, because they are understood to have relinquished their modesty, they are set up as objects of the voyeuristic gaze, aesthetic commodities whose transgressive appearance on the public stage can be relished without guilt on the part of the male beholder. The female viewer or reader on the other hand is given a lesson to learn about women's ultimate return to domesticity because, once these women fulfil the moral compulsion behind their detective tasks, they return to the home, usually through marriage, and give up the career they never were allowed to pursue for its own sake. A double moral standard is evident here.

Dorcas Dene and Loveday Brooke are apparently exceptions to this commodified aspect of the aesthetic. Loveday, at the age of thirty, is beyond the stage of youthful attraction, being "nondescript" (Pirkis, "Black Bag" 3) and utterly respectable. It would appear from Pirkis' textual description that no sexual, or indeed emotional, frisson was intended to be attached to Loveday's character, but we have only to look at some of the illustrations which accompanied the Loveday stories to understand that this was not necessarily how the reader would perceive her. A strong selling feature of magazines at this time was the use of illustration. George Newnes had made it the policy of *Strand* magazine – in which Sherlock Holmes was published – to provide pictures on every spread and rival periodicals naturally followed suit. The subject of a female detective presented an ideal opportunity to exploit the visual aesthetics of the female form, regardless of how aptly the illustration might support the text. So, for example, in the story "The Redhill Sisterhood," the illustrator Bernard Higham depicts Loveday in a domestic interior in an illustration entitled "She Lighted the Gas" (43). The picture neither forwards nor adds depth to the plot; it seems to work purely as an excuse to show off Loveday's undeniably feminine and attractive figure, to reveal her first and foremost as "woman." In doing so, it also shows her as unaware of the scrutiny; her back is turned and the individuality that would be betrayed by seeing her face is denied the viewer.[11] She has been made the object of a merely visual aesthetic judgment and thus the spectator can conveniently ignore what, in his capacity as reader, he has actually been told about Loveday's lack of pulchritude.

Of Dorcas, it may be enough to say that, unusually for a female detective, she is married and is seen as a classically protective and nurturing mother figure, albeit in relation to her blind husband rather than to any children, but her partnership does desexualise her to a degree. Nevertheless, even Dorcas' exploits are narrated by a male admirer of this "brave but womanly woman" who character-

[11] Of course, Sherlock Holmes was the frequent subject of his original illustrator, Sidney Paget, in the *Strand* magazine but, as was in accordance with the Victorian public's understanding of physiognomical discourse, Holmes' facial features would be read for their intellectual capacities and thus they informed his detective function rather than his gender.

ises her as a "charming lady" (Sims 59, 60) and whose descriptions of Dorcas throughout the stories sing the praises of her personal attributes as well as of her detective talents. The effect of this is to reinstate her femininity, especially in that visual aspect, above the immunity afforded her by being married; the irony being, of course, that while she is gazed at by the reader through the eyes of the male narrator, her own husband cannot physically see her for himself, cannot protect her by enveloping her within his own proprietorial gaze.

The younger, unmarried women detectives are all described as handsome and attractive, but somewhat offbeat in their beauty. Nora Van Snoop is "not exactly pretty" but she is "beyond comparison with the commonplace" (Rook 86) and, in fact, none of them fit the stereotypical blonde-haired, blue-eyed model of angelic womanhood. Rather, like Florence Cusack, they are more likely to have dark, sparkling eyes, brown or black hair and clear complexions, all of which features arouse the vivid admiration of their narrators, their would-be lovers or their colleagues. Again, they may be made the subject of accompanying illustrations. The collected volume of Hilda Wade stories, for instance, was profusely illustrated with a total of ninety-eight pictures by Gordon Browne, many of which took the opportunity to show off Hilda's personal charms which had already been amply described by Dr Cumberledge. She had "a frank, open smile [. . .] looked about twenty-four, and had cheeks like a ripe nectarine, just as pink and just as softly downy [. . .] a row of semi-transparent teeth [. . .] certainly most attractive" (Allen, *Hilda Wade* ch. 3). The illustrations only serve to incite further aesthetic tension around the female detective's double embodiment of criminality and victim-status.

Here lies the crux of the aesthetic variation, the way it feeds into a moral dimension. For while the reader's mental *perception* of the male detective's transgressiveness forms part of the aesthetic thrill that surrounds him, the female detective is not only similarly perceived as, but also literally *seen* to be, transgressive and if she can be seen, then the moral impetus should be to catch her, like a criminal. Her moral being is in danger of being compromised by the very sexual *frisson* which accompanies that thrill of her appearance as detective and which, in turn, aestheticises her further as a sexual body to be gazed at. She is indeed caught – in a vicious cycle.

To counter this criminalisation, the construction of the female detective responds to the moral scrutiny, by and large, with various decisive and assertive strategies. So, for example, several of the women detectives are categorised in the story title or through the storyline as "lady detectives" – Loveday Brooke, Dora Myrl and Lady Molly being amongst these – and there is a validating, moral resonance wrapped up in the term "lady" which does not exist for the male detective. There is, after all, no corresponding nomenclature of "gentleman detective" being applied at the same period as it is not deemed necessary to make the statement in his case.[12] This morality is, of course, partially attached to the class implications and obligations of being a true lady and the majority of the women detectives tend to originate from the upper- to middle-class continuum. Those from the lower end of the social spectrum are much more scarce but a woman like Hagar, for instance, coming from a Romany tribe and thus not a lady by rank is, never-

[12] Of course E. W. Hornung created A. J. Raffles, the "Gentleman thief," in *The Amateur Cracksman* (1899) but maybe the contradiction in terms implicit in that title also has some consequences – whether they be tongue-in-cheek or otherwise – for the understanding and acceptance of "lady detective" as a self-validating description in its own right.

theless, endowed with natural, ladylike qualities. At the same time, however, the term also draws explicit attention to the femininity of these women and the problematics of their having unusual and unfeminine abilities, so it becomes all the more important that the denomination of "lady" should attempt to reclaim a measure of respect for that which is seen to be subversive.

Over and above the insistence that a personal virtue, inherent in being a lady, can combat some of the worse influences of aesthetic scrutiny, much store is also put in the actual practice of morality by these women. Catherine Ross Nickerson makes the point that "[o]ne of the functions of the detective in any style of detective fiction is the arbitration of morality" (9), going on to say in her particular discussion of Anna Katharine Green's Amelia Butterworth that "her strength as a detective lies in her ability to notice what is wrong and in her zeal for setting things right." Morality, then, has to work at two levels: the recognition of what is right or wrong and then the correction and restoration of balance. The necessity of this twofold operation reminds us of just how aptly Pater's original insistence on a "certain kind of temperament" in the aesthetic critic lends itself to that detectival recasting in which the detective has to present a temperamental abhorrence for both crime *and* its consequences. In addition to the acknowledged skills and attributes mentioned earlier, the female detective also has a personal energy or passion, which is balanced by the personal moral impetus behind her reason for actually becoming a detective, as well as being immersed in the moral processes and outcomes of detection itself. Whether she is Nora Van Snoop, Hilda Wade or Lady Molly, with a male relation – fiancé, father or husband respectively – to vindicate, all can be characterised in the same terms as those which sum up Hagar Stanley as a woman in full command of "her strict sense of duty, her upright nature, and her determination to act honestly, even when her own interests were at stake" (Hume 46). They are single-minded and unshakeable and they only rest from their self-imposed purpose once they have exhausted all possibilities and reached the just conclusion. Nora Van Snoop sinks into the "luxury of hysterics" (Rook 90) only once she has caught her fiancé's murderer. Hilda Wade – the woman with tenacity of purpose – is only free to marry her suitor once she has exposed the truth behind her father's death: "'I have vindicated and cleared my father's memory. And now, I can live'" (Allen, *Hilda Wade* ch. 12). Even Loveday Brooke, whose impetus to detection was primarily one of practical necessity rather than a moral wellspring, can only try to have a rest from her exertions when, in "The Ghost of Fountain Lane," "overtaxed in mind and body, [she] had fled for a brief respite from hard work" (72), only to find that respite denied her and her abilities still in demand.

While the unswerving integrity of purpose shared by all these women may not always be made manifest in the beginning in terms of making the reader aware of the catalyst which propelled them into detection, it unmistakeably underpins their whole attitude towards the detective process. This palpable womanly integrity is offered up in complete contrast to Sherlock Holmes, whose personal reasons remain largely unrevealed and neither inform his methods nor his code of honour. The contemporary reader has no interest in *why* the male detective goes into detection – there is no unnatural or unbecoming shock to undermine his position if a man becomes a detective. The question does not even have to be asked.

Yet also going unquestioned is the fact that the strict moral integrity we see in the women is actually compromised in the figure of Sherlock Holmes. He possesses a dual nature of vigorous energy on the one hand and extreme lethargy on the other and this duality is a reflection of his own moral nature. For Holmes can walk an ambiguous moral path when he chooses to serve his own vision of justice rather than the strict terms of the law itself, as when on certain occasions he takes the law into his own hands and either allows a perpetrator to go free or judges the criminal to have suffered enough.

The female detective cannot tolerate a similar ambiguity in her person, however, and the insistence on prioritising and valuing her unconventional physical beauty, which in Kantian terms symbolises the intrinsic goodness of her moral nature, indicates that she will never be that "disinterested onlooker" for she always has a driving moral purpose and must satisfy the good and the just. Moreover, she may not embody the law – that socially-constructed enactment of justice – as the male detective does. What works as a dual, but complementary, aesthetic for the male detective cannot cope with transference to "idealized but double-edged fantasy images of the female sex" (Craig and Cadogan 28) where the "double-edged fantasy" is exposed as the double standard society actually harbours about women at this period.

Yet that very double standard produced the fissure through which the aesthetic thrill developed along gendered lines. In the face of that moral rearguard action after the Wilde trial, the female detective's single-mindedness becomes less aligned with the New Womanly challenge to the ties of family and community. Rather it is understood as a necessary trait of her position as moral arbiter. Of course, as we have seen, she is set up not only as the subject but also as the object of moral arbitration, and so the thrill lies in watching how she deals with that intense moral scrutiny.

## Works Cited

Allen, Grant. *Miss Cayley's Adventures*. London, 1899.

___. *Hilda Wade: A Woman With Tenacity of Purpose*. London, 1899. *Project Gutenberg*. Produced by Don Lainson. June 2006. 6 June 2006 <http://www.gutenberg.org/files/4903/4903.txt>.

Bodkin, Matthias McDonnell. *Dora Myrl: The Lady Detective*. London, 1900.

Conan Doyle, Arthur. "A Scandal In Bohemia." 1891. *The Penguin Complete Sherlock Holmes*. Harmondsworth: Penguin, 1981. 161-75.

Craig, Patricia, and Mary Cadogan. *The Lady Investigates: Women Detectives and Spies in Fiction*. London: Victor Gollancz, 1981.

De Quincey, Thomas. Postscript. 1854. *On Murder As A Fine Art*. 1827. London: Philip Allan, 1925.

Green, Anna Katharine. *The Leavenworth Case*. New York: Putnam, 1878.

Hornung, Ernest William. *The Amateur Cracksman*. London: Methuen, 1899.

Hume, Fergus. "The First Customer and the Florentine Dante." 1897. *Twelve Women Detective Stories*. Ed Laura Marcus. Oxford; New York: Oxford UP, 1997. 46-62.

Kant, Immanuel. *Critique of Judgment*. 1790. Trans. Werner S. Pluhar. Indianapolis: Hackett, 1987.

Kestner, Joseph A. *Sherlock's Sisters: The British Female Detective, 1864–1913*. Aldershot; Burlington VT: Ashgate, 2003.

Ledger, Sally. *The New Woman: Fiction and Feminism at the* fin de siècle. Manchester; New York: Manchester UP, 1997.

Marcus, Laura. Introduction. *Twelve Women Detective Stories*. Oxford; New York: Oxford UP, 1997.

Meade, Lillie Thomasina, and Robert Eustace. "Mr Bovey's Unexpected Will." 1899. *Crime on Her Mind*. Ed. Michele Slung. Harmondsworth: Penguin, 1977. 91-108.

Nickerson, Catherine Ross. Introduction. *That Affair Next Door. Lost Man's Lane*. By Anna Katharine Green. 1897, 1898. Durham; London: Duke UP, 2003.

Orczy, Emmuska. *Lady Molly of Scotland Yard*. London: Cassell, 1910.

Pater, Walter Horatio. *The Renaissance: Studies in Art and Poetry*. 1893. London: Macmillan, 1910.

Pirkis, Catherine Louisa. "The Black Bag Left on a Door-step." 1894. *The Experiences of Loveday Brooke, Lady Detective*. Introd. Michele Slung. New York: Dover, 1986. 1-14.

___. "The Redhill Sisterhood." 1894. *The Experiences of Loveday Brooke, Lady Detective*. Introd. Michele Slung. New York: Dover, 1986. 31-45.

___. "The Ghost of Fountain Lane." 1894. *The Experiences of Loveday Brooke, Lady Detective*. Introd. Michele Slung. New York: Dover, 1986. 72-84.

Rook, Clarence. "The Stir outside the Café Royal: a Story of Miss Van Snoop, Detective." 1898. *Crime on Her Mind*. Ed. Michele Slung. Harmondsworth: Penguin, 1977. 83-90.

Sims, George R. "The Man with the Wild Eyes." 1897. *Crime on Her Mind*. Ed. Michele Slung. Harmondsworth: Penguin, 1977. 57-82.

Wilde, Oscar. "Pen, Pencil and Poison: A Study in Green." 1889. *Intentions*, London: Methuen, 1913.

___. *The Picture of Dorian Gray*. 1891. Ed. and introd. Peter Ackroyd. London: Penguin, 1985.

# *Trent's Last Case*: Murder, Modernism, Meaning

Linda Schlossberg
Harvard University

**Abstract:** The nineteenth-century detective novel, epitomized by Conan Doyle's Sherlock Holmes mysteries, relies on neat resolutions and a fixed narrative trajectory, in which the detective-reader analyzes the evidence, interprets it skillfully, and explicates it. In *Trent's Last Case* (1913), E. C. Bentley famously upends this narrative ethos by presenting his reader with a seemingly infallible detective whose over-reliance on the principles of logic and deduction results in an early solution to the crime that is fundamentally flawed. In drawing on the tenets of Victorian detective fiction, only to upend them and exploit them for his own purposes, Bentley introduces the reading public to a new and innovative genre: the modernist detective novel.

> [It] does not seem to have been generally noticed that *Trent's Last Case* is not so much a detective story as an exposure of detective stories.
> – E. C. Bentley, *Those Days* 254

> *Trent's Last Case* shook the little world of the mystery novel like a revolution, and nothing was ever quite the same again.
> – Dorothy Sayers, introduction x

During his St. Paul's schooldays with G. K. Chesterton, *Trent's Last Case* author E. C. Bentley invented the biographic-poetic form that would eventually take his middle name: the clerihew. In these miniature homages (beloved, as he would later suggest, by "connoisseurs of idiocy everywhere" [*Those Days* 151]) Bentley sends up the entire genre of the traditional biography, reducing the life story of great men to a scant four lines. Thomas Carlyle, for instance, who famously claimed that "the history of the world is but the biography of great men," is memorialized as follows:

Thomas Carlyle
Suffered with his bile.
He wrote *Sartor Resartus*;
But that shan't part us.

The clerihew's tiny form and basic rhyme scheme (a/a/b/b) suggest a playful disregard for Victorian ideals of "Heroes and Hero Worship" –and the massive nineteenth-century biographical tomes produced in its name. Bentley's clerihews, which depict many of their subjects in terms of dietary practice or gastronomical distress (Poe was "passionately fond of roe," and "Always chew some / When writing anything gruesome;" while "Tennyson / Wrote a virelai about venison"), render the great men of history recognizably, spectacularly, human. In this sense, they can be understood as an (extremely concise) intellectual precursor to one of the most influential texts of the modernist era, Lytton Strachey's *Eminent Victorians* (1918). Strachey famously sought to decenter the seemingly fixed, stable category of "greatness," and to question the tendency of nineteenth-century biographers to codify the lives of men in "two fat volumes" with their "ill-digested masses of material," "tone of tedious panegyric," and "lamentable lack of selection" (4). Ultimately collected in works titled *Biography for Beginners* (1905), *More Biography* (1929), and *Baseless Biography* (1939), the clerihews undoubtedly conform to Strachey's notion that the "first duty of the biographer" is to "preserve [. . .] a becoming brevity" (4).[79]

[79] *Those Days* (1940) devotes several pages to the composition of clerihews; Bentley sounds rather Strachey-like when he comments that "[o]ne must not [. . .] confine

Bentley's statement in his four-line "introductory remarks" to *Biography for Beginners* that "The Art of Biography / Is different from Geography. / Geography is about Maps / But Biography is about Chaps" suggests that he took a keen pleasure in mocking the Victorian desire for intellectual mastery and systemized knowledge – the peculiarly nineteenth-century drive to pin down the physical details of an increasingly complicated geo-political world and render it knowable in charts, graphs, and histories. It is this general suspicion regarding epistemic certainty that serves as the intellectual basis for *Trent's Last Case*. In this novel, which Chesterton later deemed "the best detective story of modern times" (61), we see Bentley once again using his genius for subtle parody to subvert an established literary genre as well as nineteenth-century ideals of individual heroism.

According to his memoir *Those Days* (1940), Bentley's decision to try his hand at mystery-writing was spurred by his dissatisfaction with the aesthetic and generic conventions of Victorian detective fiction – particularly the heroic, hyper-logical detective of ratiocination first seen in Poe's Auguste Dupin and ultimately perfected in Conan Doyle's Sherlock Holmes. Though Bentley professed himself delighted by the "originality" of Conan Doyle's writing and his "power of good-plain story-telling," he found fault with what he termed the "opulence" and "exaggerated unreality," of Holmes himself, the "educated Victorian who did not know that the earth revolved around the sun [and] had never heard of Thomas Carlyle" (250).[80] Bentley was equally "troubled" by the

oneself merely to what is historic, in the large sense, about the life that is in question. One has to depict the man as he was, not his achievement only" (155).

[80] Here, Bentley is referring to the famous observations Watson makes about Holmes in *A Study in Scarlet* (1887): "Upon my quoting Thomas Carlyle, he inquired in the naivest way who he might be and what he had done. My surprise reached a climax,

"seriousness" of Holmes, as well as the depiction of the many sleuths who attempted to follow in his fictional footsteps (251):

> Another thing that troubled me was the extreme seriousness of Holmes, and the equal seriousness of his imitators. It is true that they were within the limits of a period when lightness of touch in important persons was not generally tolerated – a period which I most sincerely respect and revere; which it chafes me to see held up to ridicule; but to which I do not and did not belong. Such phases of taste overlap: the one which included me was beginning to like to see great men whole, or as nearly whole as might be. (251)

In this passage, Bentley intentionally separates himself from the "limits" of the Victorian literary era and what he perceives as its too cautious deference to notions of individual greatness and moral seriousness. Bentley identifies his aesthetic sensibilities, his "tastes" in people and literature, with those of the modern era, an age more likely to dispense with Carlyle's notions of the "Great Man" in favor of a more variegated psychological and moral complexity.[81]

"Some time in the year 1910 it occurred to me that it would be a good idea to write a detective story of a new sort," Bentley writes, and this statement, though seemingly offhand, situates his endeavor in a very specific literary and cultural moment (*Those*

---

however, when I found incidentally that he was ignorant of the Copernican Theory and of the composition of the Solar System" (15). Owen Dudley Edwards notes that Doyle had great fun in "creating a Carlylean hero who was ignorant of Carlyle" (xxxv).

[81] Not to mention playfulness: "Even Mr. Gladstone," Bentley notes, "had manifested, at rare intervals, something that could only be described as a sense of humour" (251).

*Days* 249). As Virginia Woolf famously claimed in "Mr. Bennet and Mrs. Brown," "[o]n or about December 1910 human character changed." 1910 was the year E. M. Forster's *Howard's End*, with its dictum to "[o]nly connect" was published; it was also the year that Chesterton's first Father Brown mystery, "The Blue Cross," appeared to much acclaim in *The Storyteller*. A coincidence (certainly Dupin and Holmes would have dismissed it as such), but one that suggests that Bentley's impulse to create a "new sort" of mystery occurred amid a perfect storm of aesthetic and cultural influences.[82] *Trent's Last Case* gleefully disposes of the firmly established conventions of the detective novel, with its peculiarly Victorian faith in social classification and interpretive certainty, and borrows from the newly emergent aesthetics and ethics of modernism.

In *Trent's Last Case* (the title itself a modernist joke, since it's really Trent's *first* case[83]), Bentley set out to create a detective with recognizably human characteristics and emotions – as he put it, "not quite so much the 'heavy' sleuth'" (252). Philip Trent, who stumbles upon crime-solving almost by accident, is an accomplished painter with an impressive knowledge of Victorian poetry, and unlike Holmes, who is generally misanthropic and unlikeable, the good-natured Trent possesses what the narrator calls an "unconscious power of getting himself liked" (30). But Bentley's true innovation – the idea he found "most pleasing of all" – was his attempt to "show up the infallibility of the Holmesian method" (254). Trent is correct in his close readings of the case's more baffling minor details, but ultimately fails in his attempt to identify the criminal – and thereby reward the reader with inter-

[82] For more on 1910 and the years immediately following, see Stansky.

[83] Philip Trent will later appear in another novel, *Trent's Own Case* (1936), as well as *Trent Intervenes* (1938), a collection of stories.

pretive and moral closure. In making "the hero's hard-won and obviously correct solution of the mystery turn out to be completely wrong," Bentley directly critiqued the logic of epistemic certainty undergirding Holmes' method of intellectual inquiry (254).

As Chris Baldick points out, Bentley's desire to write a "new sort" of mystery did not preclude him from beginning "with several well-established clichés of the genre" (x). In *Those Days,* Bentley speaks of "cast[ing] about for a plot that had not been used before," but he also "drew up a list of the things absolutely necessary to an up-to-date detective story: a millionaire – murdered, of course; a police detective who fails where the gifted amateur succeeds; an apparently perfect alibi" and "a crew of regulation suspects, to include the victim's widow, his secretary, his wife's maid, a butler, and a person who had quarreled openly with him" (252-53). Bentley's innovation came in the creative use to which he put these stock characters: the logical detective falls helplessly in love with the murder victim's wife; the "triumphantly incriminated suspect prove[s] to be innocent after all, and a cleverer fellow than the hero" (254); and the solution to the mystery is revealed by the killer himself.

The plot is as follows: the millionaire Manderson's body is found; Trent, upon examining various clues (a set of false teeth; a pair of shoes stretched out by too-big feet), deduces that someone has impersonated the victim, and that the actual time of death was much earlier than originally conceived. Trent decides that Marlowe (the clever English secretary) and Mabel (the millionaire's beautiful wife) conspired to kill him. By this point, however, the detective has fallen in love with the widow; and out of a strange sense of gallantry and honor, leaves his solution for her in the form of a letter, leaving it up to her to decide if the "truth" should be revealed. We later learn that Trent's interpretation was incorrect: Manderson staged his own murder; his plan was to kill himself with the intent of implicating Marlowe, whom he suspected of having an affair with his wife (which it turns out, was untrue). Marlowe discovers the plot, but too late; Manderson is already dead. Marlowe decides to establish an alibi by impersonating Marlowe (the details too absurd to go into here). What is only revealed at the novel's end, however, is that Manderson never had a chance to actually commit suicide, but was instead shot by Trent's good friend (and Mabel's uncle), Cupples, who hated Manderson with a passion but claims to have acted in self-defense.

If all this sounds terribly confusing, it is; in no small measure because the novel systematically misleads both reader and detective, telling and retelling different versions of the crime. Peter Hühn argues that the detective's function is to narrate the definitive story of "whodunit," and that "[i]t is an essential premise of the classical [detective] formula that there ultimately exists such a determinate meaning" (455). In Bentley's novel, however, instead of hearing the mystery's solution from a single, authoritative Holmes-like source, we are treated in the last fifty pages of the novel to no fewer than three different narrative revisions of the crime. Trent must listen passively as first Mabel, then Marlowe, and finally Cupples present him with their version of the mystery's solution. Each of these narratives, though technically accurate, contain only elements of the "truth," as they all are limited by the speaker's individual perspective. (The final version, in which Cupples asserts that he shot Manderson in self-defense, provides little real closure, as we can't be sure if he's really speaking the truth.) These multiple revisions of the case force the reader to question the genre's dependence not only on scientifically verifiable "evidence" and "facts," but also on more ethically weighty concepts such as "guilt" and "complicity." In applying the aesthetic properties of modernism to what appears at first glance to be a conventional mystery, Bentley challenges his readers to accept the fallibility not merely of detection, but of the interpretive process more generally.

Although the novel's distrust of epistemic and ethical certainty is recognizable and familiar when we consider it within a *modernist* context, it is highly unusual within the annals of detective fiction. As Michael Holquist has argued, the 1920s and 30s witness the birth of two seemingly contradictory Anglo-American literary trends: high modernism (with its celebration of the inexplicable and the illogical) and the Golden Age detective novel (characterized by intricate puzzle plots, a faith in logic, and steadfast "rules" determined by writers such as S. S. Van Dine and Ronald A. Knox). Holquist notes that "[i]t was during the same period when the upper reaches of literature were dramatizing the limits of reason by experimenting with such irrational modes as myth and the subconscious, that the lower reaches of literature were dramatizing the power of reason in such figures as Inspector Poirot and Ellery Queen" (147). *Trent's Last Case* is often credited with inaugurating the genre's Golden Age, and is routinely "praised by critics and practitioners as a nearly perfect example of its type."[84] Yet the novel's ultimate rejection of what Poirot, with his "little grey cells," would call "order and method" make it an anomaly within the genre.

There was one potential problem with Bentley's attempt to take the conventional figure of the detective-hero and "make it new," as Pound would have it, and that, of course, was the risk of alienating his readers. "Detective-story fans," Bentley dryly noted, "do not want to be told that the detective hero has made an ass of him-

---

[84] See Grella 44.

self" (254). As critics like to argue, the detective can be understood as a figure for the "ideal reader," one who immediately makes sense of the myriad interpretive possibilities of a given set of clues. William W. Stowe argues that Holmes' "method is a practical semiotics: his goal is to consider data of all kinds as potential signifiers and to link them, however disparate and incoherent they seem, to a coherent set of signifiers, that is, to turn the into signs of he hidden *order* behind the manifest confusion, of the solution to the mystery, of the *truth*" (367-8). Only the detective has the ability to correctly perform this interpretive task; only the detective can effect meaning out of nonsense, order out of chaos, coherence out of confusion. Our readerly enjoyment comes not from figuring out the end (to do so, as every mystery reader knows, would spoil its pleasures); but in bearing witness to the detective's superlative interpretive/reading skills, the method first introduced in *A Study in Scarlet* as the "Science of Deduction and Analysis." In George Grella's words, "The reader cannot solve [the mystery] by the detective's means, and thus derives his chief pleasure not from duplicating but from observing the mastermind's work" (39). In *Trent's Last Case*, however, the real solution to the mystery is narrated by the killer himself, suggesting that the social and narrative "order" of the text is up for grabs. Indeed, the roles of criminal, detective, suspect, and victim are themselves in constant flux, calling into question seemingly stable or universal ideals of goodness, rationality, authority, morality, guilt, and complicity.

At first, however, the novel seduces us into believing that Trent will fulfill the detective's role as semiotician *par excellence*. In his recounting of Trent's "first" case (which happened some years before the current story takes place), the narrator explicitly analogizes Trent's interpretive methods to those of Poe's Dupin. Trent, though generally disinterested in crime, hears about an unusual murder, reads the "accounts given in several journals," and suddenly finds that his imagination "[begins] to work, in a manner strange to him, upon facts [. . .]" (31). He quickly writes a letter solving the crime, and dispatches it to the editor of a local newspaper:

> [H]e did very much what Poe had done in the case of the murder of Mary Rogers. With nothing but the newspapers to guide him, he drew attention to the significance of certain apparently negligible facts, and ranged the evidence in such a manner as to throw grave suspicion upon a man who had presented himself as a witness. [The newspaper editor] had printed this letter in leaded type. The same evening he was able to announce in the *Sun* the arrest and full confession of the incriminated man. (31)

Bentley's invocation of "The Mystery of Marie Roget" (1842) is highly suggestive; above all else, Poe's short story is an exercise in sustained close reading. ("Marie Roget" is perhaps the genre's best example of the detective-as reader analogy, as Dupin's superlative interpretive skills are literally trained upon written accounts of the crime.) It's also a sly echo of the beginning of *A Study in Scarlet*, in which Watson says to Holmes, "You remind me of Edgar Allan Poe's Dupin. I had no idea that such individuals did exist outside of stories" (21).[85] This reference to Holmes' first case firmly situates Trent in an established literary tradition, further

[85] Holmes, notably, refuses to see himself as part of a literary tradition, and professes disdain for both Dupin and Emile Gaboriau's Monsieur Lecoq: "Dupin was a very inferior fellow. [. . .] Lecoq was a miserable bungler" (21).

lulling the reader into believing that he will solve the crime in the concise, logical manner demanded by the genre's conventions.[86]

Trent himself seems to understand that his character is in part constructed by literary clichés and readerly expectations. At the beginning of the novel he speaks sardonically of his role as detective-hero, as if he is aware of Bentley's parodic intentions: "I have come down in the character of avenger of blood, to hunt down the guilty, and vindicate the honour of society. That is my line of business. Families waited on at their private residences" (20). A similarly playful tone informs his suggestion that the rules of the genre require him to suspect everybody in the Manderson household – particularly those individuals who comprise the servant class. Speaking to his friend Inspector Murch, Trent says, "Let us bend our spirits to a temper of general suspicion. Let us suspect everyone in the house to begin with. [. . .] By the way, what domestics are there? I have more than enough suspicion to go round, whatever the size of the establishment; but as a matter of curiosity I should like to know" (38). Trent mocks the detective's generic role as defender of social norms and the hierarchies of the British class system. In so doing, Bentley anticipates and satirizes a tenet of detective fiction criticism: that one of Holmes' crucial tasks is to unmask moral and social deviance and thereby reify the "naturalness" of the Victorian middle-class worldview – what Stephen

[86] The novel makes interesting use of the literary canon more generally. Trent frequently quotes nineteenth-century poets (including Emerson, Tennyson, Wordsworth, Shelley, and Keats) suggesting at first that he subscribes to conventional aesthetic and moral values. But, as Chris Baldick points out (xx), he often quotes them with a twist, confusing lines or intentionally mangling them to produce a humorous or sardonic effect. Trent's playfully irreverent attitude toward canonical poetry suggests that the conventions of nineteenth-century writing (with its dependence on moral certitude) may no longer be relevant to the changing social and aesthetic structures of the modernist era.

Knight refers to as the "central bourgeois values which operate through Holmes as the tools of maintaining order" (103).

The novel's biggest joke in this regard, however, is that it essentially condones the murder of Sigsbee Manderson, the American millionaire-plutocrat whose unwavering lust for money and power is depicted as being endemic to the racial character of the United States: "Forcible, cold, and unerring, in all [Manderson] did he ministered to the national lust for magnitude; and a grateful country surnamed him the Colosssus" (6-7).[87] Martin Priestman has argued that the first chapter of the mystery, which introduces us to Manderson's business dealings, "constitutes a detachable essay on the evils of American-style capitalism"(117); above all else, Manderson's evilness seems rooted in his callous disregard for the welfare of the laboring classes:

> Many a time when [Manderson] "took hold" to smash a strike, or to federate the ownership of some great field of labour, he sent ruin upon a multitude of tiny homes, and if the miners or steelworkers or cattlemen defied him and invoked disorder, he cold be more lawless and ruthless than they. But this was done in the pursuit of legitimate business ends. (6)

This is only one of several passages suggesting that Manderson's personality is the inevitable result of a capitalist economy that rationalizes greed and acquisitiveness at all costs. The British police and courts are content to lay the blame for Manderson's death on his many enemies; as one representative of the court says, "In the industrial world of America the discontent of labour often pro-

[87] The novel's discussion of class is somewhat complicated, as Manderson's immense wealth is a source of both anxiety and disdain for the novel's English middle-class characters. On this, see Kermode and Kestner.

ceeds to lengths of which we in England happily know nothing" (84). As it turns out, however, Manderson has not been killed by a group of violent American labor organizers, but rather by Trent's friend, the kindly old Cupples, a "retired banker" with "little imagination" who seems, at first glance, to be merely an exemplar of English bourgeois values (19). But Cupples is also a "highly regarded member of the London Positivist Society," who enjoys discussing "the economic constitution of society" over tea and toast (19; 24). As he says to Trent: "You know my views, I think, on [. . .] the proper relationship of the capitalist to the employee. [. . .] I regarded [Manderson], apart from all personal dislike, in the light of a criminal and a disgrace to society" (25). In a moment of supreme irony, the novel's murder victim is identified by his killer as a "criminal" and "a disgrace to society." This opinion is further endorsed by the narrative (Cupples is neither punished nor condemned for Manderson's death); suggesting that the changing socio-economic conditions of the industrialized world have rendered nineteenth-century social classifications such as "criminal" increasingly unstable and open to interpretation. The novel thus establishes empathetic points of identification and Forsterian "connections" across class differences, even as it blithely dismisses Manderson's violent end. (As Cupples says, "I am glad Manderson is dead. I believe him to have done nothing but harm in the world as an economic factor" [27]).

If the social world of the novel seems to be intriguingly "out of order," so too is the narrative itself. The classic detective novel is conventionally linear in form, in part to resolve the temporal chaos and confusion produced by the act of crime itself. The detective is charged with putting in logical order the various events that first present themselves as a muddle or jumble of unrelated, and hence un-narratable, individual facts. As Dennis Porter argues, "[The detective's] role is to reestablish sequence and causality. [. . .] A classic detective novel may be defined [. . .] as a work of prose narrative founded on the effort to close a logico-temporal gap" (29-30). The detective is supposed to function as our guide through this comforting process of temporal (and by extension, moral) resolution.

That Trent will fail at this crucial task is signaled by the fact that his solution to the crime, his attempt at narrative and interpretive closure, is presented far too early – approximately halfway through the text. As Hühn suggests, the solution *must* come at the end; or the mystery fails to possess meaning: "because the mystery was initially defined as the meaning of the text, no relevance remains when the meaning becomes extractable and the mystery is removed (the book then leaves nothing to be desired)" (458). It is precisely because Trent's solution is presented *out of temporal sequence* that we know that it must be incorrect; and it is at this point in the text that we begin to feel the novel's seemingly coherent narrative ground shifting underfoot.[88] We know that Trent's interpretive gesture is incorrect; the hundred or so pages yet to come tell us that quite clearly, and as a result we are left with the disconcerting, yet potentially thrilling, realization that our readerly ego-ideal has been shattered. What is ultimately produced therefore is a distinctly modern text – one in which our aesthetic and intellectual pleasure stems not from observing the intellectual machinations of an emotionless figure of hyper-rationalism, but from our identification with a complex, fallible reader experiencing complicated and disorderly emotions. Trent is no longer our objective, trustworthy guide through the hermeneutic process, but

[88] Certainly we are accustomed to seeing early, flawed interpretations of the crime, but they are presented by less talented readers (e.g., Doyle's Inspector Lestrade or Rex Stout's Inspector Cramer).

rather a well-intentioned yet fundamentally flawed, misreader of information. (In this regard he has more in common intellectually with Watson than Holmes, whose misguided attempts at figuring things out functions as an analogue for our own reading experience).

Ironically, however, Trent's misreading stems from the fact that he dismisses his subjective, intuitive feelings about people (Mabel and Marlowe) and instead adopts a resolutely scientific, Holmesian manner of reading the world. The most distinctive characteristic of Holmes' methodology is his ability to objectively read and decipher physical clues, whether in the form of trace evidence (footprints, fingerprints) or on the suspect's body itself. As Stephen Knight expresses it, "In terms of [Holmes'] epistemology we have a materialistic model, which can read off from physical data what has happened and what will happen" (74). It makes sense, therefore, that Bentley's parody of Holmes' "Science of Deduction and Analysis" reaches its height in chapter 9 ("A Hot Scent"), in which Trent displays his knowledge of fingerprint analysis in the highly specialized and scientific language characteristic of Holmes. Even the physical description of the usually calm and casual Trent ("He looked very pale, and his movements were nervous") recalls that of Conan Doyle's detective (85). Furthermore, the evidence he presents seems objective and irrefutable, at least according to the terms of both Victorian detective fiction and nineteenth-century forensic science. As Ronald R. Thomas suggests, the science of fingerprinting fit neatly into the Victorian obsession with criminal classification and surveillance, as it promised to make the morally or socially deviant body legible: "The fingerprint represents nineteenth-century criminology's ultimate achievement in transforming the body into a text" (203). The irony, however, is that Trent is explaining the science of fingerprinting to Cupples – who is ultimately revealed to be responsible for Manderson's death. Trent's gaze is focused on the minutiae of physical evidence, blinding him to the fact that the guilty party is seated right before his eyes.[89]

What fascinates us about Holmes (but ultimately alienates us from him) is his relentless objectivity, his ability to reduce people to scientific principles. W. H. Auden notes that Holmes' "attitude towards people and his technique of observation and deduction are those of the chemist or physicist;" one of Watson's friends describes Holmes, in *A Study in Scarlet*, as "a little too scientific for my tastes – It approaches to cold-bloodedness" (8). Bentley's detective, by contrast, is an artist; his idealization of the deductive process is constantly at war with his subjective feelings and more effete, artistic sensibilities.

Trent's faith in his own rational prowess is put to the test by his romantic feelings for Mabel Manderson. For no particular reason (other than, the reader assumes, his sexual attraction to her) Trent decides that she must be innocent, even though everything in his logical investigation seems to indict her. But when she in turn insists that she *knows* Marlowe is guiltless of any crime, Trent ascribes her interpretive certainty to a distinctly feminine "unreasonableness":

> Inwardly he was telling himself, somewhat feebly, that this was very right and proper; that it was quite feminine, and he liked her to be feminine. It was permitted to her – more than permitted – to set her loyal belief in the character of a friend [Marlowe] above the clearest demonstra-

[89] This is not the only time fingerprints will serve to distract Bentley's detective. In *Trent's Own Case* (1936), he mixes up his own fingerprints with those of the criminal.

> tions of the intellect. Nevertheless, it chafed him. He would have had her declaration of faith a little less positive in form. It was too irrational to say she 'knew.'[. . .] If to be unreasonable when reason led to the unpleasant was a specifically feminine trait, and if Mrs. Manderson had it, she was accustomed to wrap it up better than any woman he had known. (128)

The irony, as Mabel herself later points out to the shocked detective, is that Trent has used his subjective feelings for her as sufficient "evidence" of her innocence. As he tells her, "A man who, after seeing you and being in your atmosphere, could associate you with the particular kind of abomination I imagined, is a fool – the kind of fool who is afraid to trust his senses" (126). Trent's initial "sense" that Mabel must be innocent – despite all apparent evidence to the contrary – has everything in common with the epistemological method generally denigrated as "woman's intuition."

Ultimately, this mode of reasoning – deduction by emotion – is endorsed by the narrative and proved to be an accurate basis for uncovering the truth. From Trent's very first meeting with Marlowe, when the detective "note[s] with admiration the man's breadth of shoulder and lithe, strong figure," he finds himself "very much inclined to like young Mr. Marlowe" (33). As the narrative ultimately proves, Marlowe *is* admirable and likeable – not to mention innocent of the crime of which Trent accuses him. It is Trent's subjective feelings about the case that prove to be correct all along. The novel thus privileges the distinctively modernist and "feminine" ethos of feeling and subjectivity over the cooler, seemingly masculinist logic of traditional detection.

It is precisely this (ironically) happy realization that causes Trent to renounce not only his professional identity, but also the very principles on which his deductive abilities rest. As he says, "The Manderson affair shall be Philip Trent's last case. [. . .] I could have borne everything but that last revelation of the impotence of human reason" (177). In this final dismissal of the principles of reason and logic, the novel signals its disengagement with nineteenth-century ideals of intellectual and moral certainty – and perhaps, the mystery genre itself. Trent declares, "I am cured. I will never touch a crime-mystery again" (177). But Bentley makes it clear that Trent's failure, the apparent "impotence" of the supposedly masculinist logic of reason, is to be celebrated rather than mourned. The novel's decidedly cheerful ending tells us so; certainly both detective and reader are happier for this revelation.

## Works Cited

Auden, W. H. "The Guilty Vicarage: Notes on the Detective Story, by an Addict." *Harper's Magazine* May 1948. Rpt. in *The Complete Works of W. H. Auden*. Ed. Edward Mendelson. Princeton: Princeton UP, 2002. 261-70.

Bentley, E. C. *Trent's Last Case*. 1912. Ed. Chris Baldick. Oxford: Oxford UP, 1995.

___. *Those Days*. London: Constable, 1940.

Chesterton, G. K. *Autobiography*. London: Hutchinson, 1936.

Conan Doyle, Arthur. 1887. *A Study in Scarlet*. Oxford: Oxford UP, 1994.

Frank, Lawrence. *Victorian Detective Fiction and the Nature of Evidence: The Scientific Investigations of Poe, Dickens, and Doyle*. New York: Macmillan, 2003.

Grella, George. "Murder and Manners: The Formal Detective Novel." Ed. Larry N. Landrum, Pat Browne, and Ray B.

Browne. *Dimensions of Detective Fiction: The Figure on the Carpet*. New York: Popular Press, 1976. 37-57.

Holquist, Michael. "Whodunit and Other Questions: Metaphysical Detective Stories in Post-War Fiction." *New Literary History* 3.1 (1971): 135-56.

Hühn, Peter. "The Detective as Reader: Narrativity and Reading Concepts in Detective Fiction." *Modern Fiction Studies* 33.3 (1987): 451-66.

Kermode, Frank. "Novel and Narrative." Most and Stowe 175-196.

Kestner, Joseph A. *The Edwardian Detective, 1901-1915*. Aldershot: Ashgate, 2000.

Most, Glenn W., and William W. Stowe, eds. *The Poetics of Murder: Detective Fiction and Literary Theory*. New York: Harcourt Brace Jovanovich, 1983.

Knight, Stephen. *Form and Ideology in Crime Fiction*. London: Macmillan, 1980.

Porter, Dennis. *The Pursuit of Crime: Art and Ideology in Detective Fiction*. New Haven: Yale UP, 1981.

Priestman, Martin. *Detective Fiction and Literature*. London: Macmillan, 1990.

Sayers, Dorothy. Introduction. *Trent's Last Case*. By E. C. Bentley. New York: Harper, 1978. x-xiii.

Strachey, Lytton. *Eminent Victorians*. London: Chatto and Windus, 1918.

Stansky, Peter. *On or About December 1910: Early Bloomsbury and Its Intimate World*. Cambridge: Harvard UP, 1996.

William W. Stowe, "From Semiotics to Hermeneutics: Modes of Detection in Doyle and Chandler." Most and Stowe 367-83.

Thomas, Ronald R. *Detective Fiction and the Rise of Forensic Science*. Cambridge: Cambridge UP, 1999.

## Contributors

**Elizabeth Anderman** received her doctorate in 2006 from the University of Colorado, Boulder, where her dissertation was recognized as the best dissertation in the humanities that year. She is currently the associate director of and an instructor in the Farrand Residential Academic Program at CU. Her essays appear in various edited collections: "Hysterical Sensations: Bodies in Action in Wilkie Collins's The Woman in White" in *From Wollstonecraft to Stoker: Essays on Gothic and Victorian Sensation Fiction*. Her essay "No Reality Here: Sensation Novels and Photography" is forthcoming in *The Language of Images*. Her work currently focuses on the illustration of sensation novels in serial fiction. Her research and teaching interests include Victorian literature, visual culture, children's literature, and film and women's studies.

**Paul Fox** (Ph.D. University of Georgia) is an Associate Professor at East Georgia College. He has published articles upon fin-de-siècle aesthetics, Walter Pater, Oscar Wilde and J. M. Barrie and edited an earlier collection of essays in this series examining Decadent aesthetics and morality. He is currently completing a book-length study of Decadence and aesthetic time.

**Nick Freeman** is Senior Lecturer in English at Loughborough University. He has published widely on Victorian and later literature, and has also written on film, television and popular culture. His essay "Permissive Paradise: The Fiction of Swinging London" appeared in *Decadences: Morality and Aesthetics in British Literature*, an earlier volume in this series. His most recent book is *1895: Drama, Disaster and Disgrace in Late Victorian Britain* (2011).

**Rudolph Glitz** is Universitair Docent of English Literature and Interdisciplinary Studies at the University of Amsterdam. His monograph is titled *Writing the Victorians: The Early Twentieth-Century Family Chronicle* (2009) and he has written on various topics in the fields of literature, film, historiography, and computer game studies. In his current research, he investigates the age-group and generational politics of literary texts, ranging from Shakespeare to the present day.

**Therie Hendrey-Seabrook** is an Associate Tutor in the English Department at the University of Sussex. In addition to a specific interest in the development of detective fiction, her research embraces Victorian literature and print media more broadly, particularly in terms of their interaction with visual culture. She is currently working on a book about the influence of the humorous journal, *Punch*, on cultural concepts of the mid-nineteenth century.

**Alison Jaquet** is currently working as an Academic Skills Adviser at Queensland University of Technology. Dr Jaquet's research interests include pedagogy, popular culture and nineteenth-century literature.

**George M. Johnson** is Professor and Chair of English and Modern Languages at Thompson Rivers University in British Columbia. He has written entries on Algernon Blackwood and others for three volumes of the *Dictionary of Literary Biography* that he edited on *Late-Victorian and Edwardian British Novelists* and *British Novelists Between the Wars*. His books include *J. D. Beresford* (1998), *Dynamic Psychology in Modernist British Fiction* (2006), and a play, *Still Life With Nudes* (ArtAge 2013). Forthcoming works include *Mourning and Mysticism in First World War Fiction and Beyond: Grappling With Ghosts* (Palgrave, 2015) and a novel, *A Medium for Murder*, featuring a psychic detective based on Blackwood's John Silence.

**Aaron Parrett** is an Associate Professor of English at the University of Great Falls in Montana. In 2004 he won the Montana Historical Society's Friends' Choice Award for his essay "Montana's Worst Natural Disaster: the 1964 Flood on the Blackfeet Indian Reservation." He is currently working on a study of religion and gambling, tentatively titled *Chance and Faith in the Pursuit of the Divine.*

**Linda Schlossberg** is the Assistant Director of the Women, Gender, and Sexuality Studies Program at Harvard University, where she teaches courses in literature and creative writing. She is the author of the novel *Life in Miniature* (Kensington, 2010) and the co-editor, with Maria C. Sanchez, of *Passing: Identity and Interpretation in Sexuality, Race, and Religion* (New York University Press, 2001).

**Lucy Sussex** is a lecturer at La Trobe University, Australia. She has edited four anthologies, and her writing has been published internationally. Her novel *The Scarlet Rider* was published in the US in 1996. She is currently completing a study of the first women writers of crime and mystery fiction.

**Helen Sutherland** is a Tutor at the Centre for Open Studies at the University of Glasgow and editor of *The Journal of the Sylvia Townsend Warner Society*. Her research interests include Scottish literature, children's literature, and detective fiction, and she has published on British and American Gothic fiction, Charles Dickens, John Keats, Elinor M. Brent-Dyer (author of the Chalet School series of books for girls) and Sylvia Townsend Warner's fantasy tales.

## STUDIES IN ENGLISH LITERATURES

Edited by Koray Melikoğlu

ISSN 1614-4651

*1* *Özden Sözalan*
The Staged Encounter
Contemporary Feminism and Women's Drama
2nd, revised edition
ISBN 3-89821-367-6

*2* *Paul Fox (ed.)*
Decadences
Morality and Aesthetics in British Literature
2nd, revised and expanded edition
ISBN 3-89821-573-3

*3* *Daniel M. Shea*
James Joyce and the Mythology of Modernism
ISBN 3-89821-574-1

*4* *Paul Fox and Koray Melikoğlu (eds.)*
Formal Investigations
Aesthetic Style in Late-Victorian and Edwardian Detective Fiction
2nd, revised and expanded edition
ISBN 978-3-89821-593-0

*5* *David Ellis*
Writing Home
Black Writing in Britain Since the War
ISBN 978-3-89821-591-6

*6* *Wei H. Kao*
The Formation of an Irish Literary Canon in the Mid-Twentieth Century
ISBN 978-3-89821-545-9

*7* *Bianca Del Villano*
Ghostly Alterities
Spectrality and Contemporary Literatures in English
2nd, revised editon
ISBN 978-3-89821-714-9

*8* *Melanie Ann Hanson*
Decapitation and Disgorgement
The Female Body's Text in Early Modern English Drama and Poetry
ISBN 978-3-89821-605-5

*9* *Shafquat Towheed (ed.)*
New Readings in the Literature of British India, c.1780-1947
ISBN 978-3-89821-673-9

*10* *Paola Baseotto*
"Disdeining life, desiring leaue to die"
Spenser and the Psychology of Despair
ISBN 978-3-89821-567-1

11 *Annie Gagiano*
Dealing with Evils
Essays on Writing from Africa
ISBN 978-3-89821-867-2

12 *Thomas F. Halloran*
James Joyce: Developing Irish Identity
A Study of the Development of Postcolonial Irish Identity in the Novels of James Joyce
ISBN 978-3-89821-571-8

13 *Pablo Armellino*
Ob-scene Spaces in Australian Narrative
An Account of the Socio-topographic Construction of Space in Australian Literature
ISBN 978-3-89821-873-3

14 *Lance Weldy*
Seeking a Felicitous Space on the Frontier
The Progression of the Modern American Woman in O. E. Rölvaag, Laura Ingalls Wilder, and Willa Cather
ISBN 978-3-89821-535-0

15 *Rana Tekcan*
The Biographer and the Subject
A Study on Biographical Distance
ISBN 978-3-89821-995-2

16 *Paola Brusasco*
Writing Within/Without/About Sri Lanka
Discourses of Cartography, History and Translation in Selected Works by Michael Ondaatje and Carl Muller
ISBN 978-3-8382-0075-0

17 *Zeynep Z. Atayurt*
Excess and Embodiment in Contemporary Women's Writing
ISBN 978-3-89821-978-5

18 *Gianluca Delfino*
Time, History, and Philosophy in the Works of Wilson Harris
ISBN 978-3-8382-0265-5

## FORTHCOMING (MANUSCRIPT WORKING TITLES)

*Kevin Cole*
Levity's Rainbow
Menippean Poetics in Swift, Fielding, and Sterne
ISBN 3-89821-654-3

*Fatma Tuba Terci*
Postmodern Goddesses in Contemporary Chicana Feminist Novel
Peel my Love Like an Onion, Caramelo, or, Puro Cuento: A Novel and Face of an Angel
ISBN 978-3-8382-0023-1

*Geetha Ganga*
Historicizing Somalia through Literary Narrative
The Fiction of Nuruddin Farah
ISBN 978-3-8382-0083-5

*Busuyi Mekusi*
Negotiating Memory and Nation Building in New South African Drama
ISBN 978-3-8382-0232-7

***ibidem*-Verlag**
Melchiorstr. 15
D-70439 Stuttgart
info@ibidem-verlag.de

www.ibidem-verlag.de
www.ibidem.eu
www.edition-noema.de
www.autorenbetreuung.de